For my uncle, James Bell

Contents

Tables and Figures

FIGURES

Preface

Economists have long studied companies, but for decades nearly all of their energy was devoted to examining topics such as pricing behavior, antitrust policy, and industry-level comparisons. What went on inside of firms was of secondary interest to what came out of them such as profits, market share, and industry concentration. Starting in the 1960s, attention slowly began to turn to a better understanding of decision making within organizations. At first, this work took place in isolated pockets, appearing in separate journal articles and pieces of analysis disconnected from each other. Labor economists looked at incentives. Financial economists along with mathematical theorists looked at uncertainty, risk, and information. Political economists developed models and statistical studies related to legislative and bureaucratic organizations. Game theorists looked at strategic situations. Researchers in developing areas such as law and economics and newly forming areas of "organizational" economics considered corporate governance structures, contracts, transactions costs, and other topics. Over time, these separate pieces of organizational economics began to be integrated with each other so that books for studying organizations and management from economic perspectives started to emerge.

The same kinds of developments have occurred in the economic study of sports. From the 1950s through the 1970s, a few landmark studies cropped up such as Simon Rottemberg's examination of free agency and Gerald Scully's statistical investigation of value of Major League Baseball (MLB) players to their teams. During the 1980s and 1990s, the number of studies of sporting activities and leagues rose dramatically including topics such as racial discrimination, the NCAA, sports stadiums, and many others so that now the field supports specialized journals and textbooks.

This book is an outgrowth of these same kinds of developments and integration of concepts and interests on a personal level. My specializations during graduate training in economics in the early to mid 1980s focused primarily on the industry-level perspective of company behavior along with an adjoining emphasis on political economy and applied statistics. As my career developed, opportunities to apply some of these ideas to sports arose including a book about the NCAA that I authored with Trey Fleisher and Bob Tollison as well as a book making application of economics and statistics to sports topics that I edited with Bob Tollison. At the same time as my interests in sports economics grew, my background in the study of political organizations opened up into a broader interest in organizational decision making and structure. My involvement with the reemerging MBA program at my institution helped spur these interests. Soon, synergy built between my research and teaching interests in sports economics and the economics of organizations. I published some of these ideas in articles but began to envision a book that would permit a wider array of ideas to be considered and integrate more thoroughly the two than could be done in a few journal articles.

The volume that I have put together here differs from the existing studies of sports economics in its perspective. Rather than a study of the typical topics of interest for sports economists—pricing policies, stadium financing, antitrust problems, accounting issues, and the like—I have directed my attention toward managerial and organizational issues surrounding sports. As I discuss in Chapter 1, this is a book that is both about management and about sports and can be taken as one teaching management lessons with sports illustrations or sports lessons with management illustrations.

Readers that have an interested in exploring the background material for the concepts from organizational and managerial economics can turn to several helpful sources. These range from works that are relatively accessible to beginners to those that are probably best read as supplements to an MBA course to those that require extensive grounding in economics, finance, statistics, or mathematics. The more accessible books include *Executive Economics: Ten Essential Tools for Managers* by Shlomo Maital of the MIT Sloan School of Business, *Managerial Economics and Organization Architecture* by James Brickley, Clifford Smith, and Jerold Zimmerman of the Simon School of Business at the University of Rochester, and *Thinking Strategically* by Avinash Dixit and Barry Nalebuff from Yale's Business School. Books that require more of a background in economics include *The Economics of Strategy* by David Besanko, David Dranove, and Mark Shanley of Northwestern's Kellogg Business School and *Economics, Organizations, and Management* by Paul Milgrom and John Roberts of the

Stanford University Graduate School of Business. The two most comprehensive studies of the economics of sports are by Rodney Fort (*Sports Economics*) and Michael Leeds and Peter von Allmen (*The Economics of Sports*).

Many people have contributed to this book in a variety of ways. My editor at Praeger, Nick Philipson, has improved the final product in many ways with his suggestions. Countless conversations about sports-related issues with several colleagues at Western Kentucky University have broadened my knowledge and spurred my thinking over the years. I would especially thank Mel Borland, Richard Cantrell, Bill Davis, Roy Howsen, Bob Pulsinelli, Lou Turley, Reed Vesey, and Tom Wisely for these conversations as well as helping me on specific issues and for looking over outlines and ideas. Also, my lunchtime running partners over the years, Dean Jordan, Brent Baker, and Lawrence Kelly have augmented and endured my thinking. My mentor and coauthor on many projects, Bob Tollison, looked over early outlines of this project and has contributed helpful comments along the way. My former department head, John Wassom, and current department head, Bill Davis, along with the Dean of the Ford College of Business at Western Kentucky University, Bob Jefferson, have been supportive of this and other ventures on my part in a variety of ways. The MBA students who enrolled in my Sports & Managers course during the Spring of 2003 and suffered through using a rough draft of the manuscript deserve credit. Their comments and contributions in class filled in some of the gaps and helped me polish off some sections. Finally, the consistent love, stability, and encouragement of my wife and daughters have helped in ways that go beyond expression here.

1

Sports and Business: Is Sport Business or Is Business Sport?

The secret to winning is constant, consistent management.

—Tom Landry, former NFL Head Coach

[Red Auerbach] wasn't just talking basketball. He was talking about any enterprise where people are making products, where they have to compete, where they have to win.

—Lee Iacocca, former Chrysler CEO

Sports creates a diversion away from the other aspects of life. Whether playing a game or watching one, these events supply entertainment. Beyond the attention devoted to the playing of games and beyond the entertainment value of the games, sports permeates the culture in all kinds of ways. Children as well as adults engage in all kinds of competitive settings where objectives are identified, boundaries are set, order of play is identified, and so on. In many ways, these games of play mirror and are mirrored by competitive activities in nonsporting settings such as everyday business.

The lack of understanding of this visceral appeal of sports has led many to underestimate its influence and value. For instance, the famous sportscaster, Howard Cosell, derisively referred to sports as the "toy department" of life and sought to move beyond sports and into more serious broadcasting jobs his whole life. Sports grips American culture in a way that far exceeds the amount of money spent by fans attending games or by the dollars that advertisers pay for time during telecasts. Even when these dollars include merchandising revenues tied directly to professional sports teams or indirectly to colleges and universities because of their athletics programs, the monetary transactions related to sporting events fail to fully capture the scope and influence of sports in the United States. Every day, millions of office and break-time conversations center on the local team's most recent performance, an upcoming game, the impending draft, the current coach, or the future coach. Still, these conversations only begin to scratch the surface of the time devoted to sports-oriented topics. Daily, millions of people pour over televised, print, and online media sources to check out game outcomes, interviews, and opinions—not to mention the money and time spent on sports gambling or managing "fantasy" teams.

Just as other aspects of American culture, business is heavily influenced by sports. The vocabulary of sports and business share many terms in common such as competition, rival, teamwork, strategy, efficiency, production, and others that are just as easily used in one setting as the other. As Green Packer Hall of Famer, Jerry Kramer, noted in his reflections on his playing days, the legendary coach, Vince Lombardi, "compared the Packers to a large corporation, like GM, IBM, or Chrysler."[1] Lombardi's viewpoint concerning the overlap of sports and business management not only expressed his own opinion but that of many corporate leaders who shared his view of the intimate connection between coaching and managing a corporate enterprise. During the Green Bay Packers dynasty of the late 1950s and 1960s, Lombardi's popularity as speaker before top industry leaders soared. His presentations ventured well beyond the specifics of football strategy into general advice about leadership, motivation, personnel relations, and other matters related to managing a business.

Other coaches and sports figures preceded Lombardi and a truckload have followed him into the field of management consulting. For instance, John Wooden, who supervised the UCLA dominance of college basketball from the mid 1960s to the mid 1970s, made many speaking appearances before business groups but had to turn away many others because of time constraints. In more recent years, long-time football coach Lou Holtz's straight talk and one-liners have made him popular on the business speaking circuit.

In addition to speaking appearances, successful coaches, general managers, and players now routinely publish their wisdom concerning various aspects of management. For example, Holtz authored *Winning Every Day: The Game Plan for Success* as well as other similar titles. Joe Torre, the popular manager of the New York Yankees, authored *Joe Torre's Ground Rules for Winning: 12 Keys to Managing Team Players, Tough Bosses, Setbacks, and Success*. Duke University basketball coach Mike Krzyzewski offered the lessons of his experiences in *Leading with the Heart: Coach K's Successful Strategies for Basketball, Business, and Life*. Bill Russell, the legendary player for the Celtics who also served as a coach and general manager, offered *Russell Rules: Eleven Lessons on Leadership from the Twentieth Century's Greatest Winner.* His former coach, Red Auerbach, authored *MBA: Management by Auerbach: Management Tips from the Leader of One of America's Most Successful Organizations.* This list could go on and on.

In fact, the acceptance of coach-as-management-expert has become so widespread that the *Harvard Business Review* chose (then) retired NFL coach Bill Parcells to write the first article for a new department where coaches, religious leaders, or scientists could publish ideas pertinent for business executives. His article, "The Hard Work of Turning Around a Team," does not exactly equate football with business but finds many similarities. He says, "My guess is that the challenges I've faced are not all that different from the ones that executives deal with every day. I'm not saying that business is like football. I am saying that people are people, and that the keys to motivating them and getting them to perform to their full potential are pretty much the same whether they're playing on a football field or working in an office."[2]

The quotation from Bill Parcells runs parallel to the theme of this book. Whatever the title—chief executive officer, plant manager, district supervisor, coach, general manager, or other—the similarities between managing a sports team and managing any other business run wide and deep. The success of managers in most any endeavor depends on their ability to acquire and use resources, adjust to changing market conditions, gauge the actions and reactions of rivals, develop or imitate new methods of production, and hire, motivate, and empower people. At least so far as these common aspects are concerned, management is management whether the decisions are made in a corporate suite overlooking New York City, in a manufacturing plant in Bowling Green Kentucky, on a practice field at Redskins Park in Northern Virginia, on the court at Duke's Cameron Indoor Stadium, on the "frozen tundra" of Lambeau Field in Green Bay, or in front of the centerfield monuments of Yankee Stadium.

LEARNING THE RIGHT LESSONS

Casey Stengel, a longtime baseball manager known for great one-liners said, "Good pitching will always stop good hitting, and vice-versa." No doubt, the inconsistency in Stengel's proverb was there to obtain a laugh, but it happens to express a big question mark in the study of management whether in athletics or business. How can the lessons of successful management be determined whether the focus is on business in general or in sports managing and coaching?

For the coaches and managers who offer their advice in seminars and books, the primary method they use is simply to look back at their careers and attempt to sort out the most important influences behind their successes and failures. Ultimately, the composition of their lists depends on the seat-of-the-pants assessment of the person doing the writing. This is the way that Joe Torre finds his "12 keys" to successful management. Bill Parcells lists four or five major factors in accomplishing the task of turning around a team. John Wooden organized his ideas in a pyramid founded by five basic building blocks with four levels of blocks above that base. Vince Lombardi listed three essentials.

Not only do the number of "essential" or "key" factors differ, but sometimes the "lessons learned" and the advice given by successful people may even stand in direct conflict with each other. For example, Earl Weaver, one of the most successful baseball managers of all time with the Baltimore Orioles, made it a point to distance himself from his players to the point of rarely speaking with them. To put it in his own words, "A manager should stay as far away as possible from his players. I don't know if I said ten words to Frank Robinson while he played for me." In contrast, many other highly successful coaches such as baseball manager Joe Torre and basketball coach Mike Krzyzewski place open and clear communication with players as one of their most important keys to success. Some coaches, such as football's Bill Parcells and basketball's Bob Knight rely heavily on direct and even mean-spirited confrontation to try to pressure players into better performances, while others such as basketball's John Wooden consider such methods useless or even childish.

Sometimes, when such diversity is pointed out, the phrase "each coach must do what works best for them" crops up as the reply. If carried to it logical limit, such a conclusion would seemingly imply that nothing can really be learned about successful managing—it is totally personal in nature. While most students of management or leadership would agree that there are nontransferable attributes that likely enter into effective management, they do not make up the sum. Some lessons can be learned, but how?

The attempts by sports figures at ferreting out the main components of managerial success bear a strong resemblance to "behavioral" approaches or closely aligned "case study" approaches used to study management in many academic settings. In behavioral approaches, a business analyst might spend time in corporate suites observing the activities of the executives or might interview or survey executives regarding their decisions. The thrust of such research is to steer away from esoteric theories and opinions about managerial activities and get down to the brass tacks of what executives actually think and do.

Similarly, in MBA programs where case studies are the primary pedagogical vehicle, detailed accounts and histories are compiled on successful and unsuccessful companies and particular episodes for companies. Instructors and students use these cases as the basis for examining patterns and tendencies that led to success or failure. For instance, through the 1980s and 1990s, companies such as Microsoft, FedEx, Staples, MCI, Home Depot, and others showed tremendous growth in earnings, market share, employment, and other performance measures. As a result, students intensely studied them in management education cases. During the 1960s and 1970s, companies such as General Electric and IBM attracted enormous academic attention for the same reason. In essence, such case studies fit neatly under the "behavioral" approach heading in that they emphasize the concrete behavior of companies and managers as the basis for understanding management practice.

Behavioral methods for determining and outlining the basis of successful management practice are naturally appealing. They are realistic rather than hypothetical, concrete rather than abstract. They draw from experiences of real people and real companies and speak in the language of real-world practices. So, why not rely on the wisdom attained from people or companies such as Mike Krzyzewski, Lou Holtz, Microsoft, or Staples as templates to imitate? After all, "experience is the best teacher" as the proverb goes. Even further, management education is filled with this kind of learning-by-observing or learning-by-asking approach. Management advisors and analysts such as Peter Drucker and Tom Peters have gained worldwide reputations using these kinds of methods. Peters, in particular, has rejected the highly organized, "rational" study of management in his books *In Search of Excellence* and *Thriving on Chaos*. His basic tenet is to study what managers do and then adopt or adapt whatever works.[3] Among academics, Henry Mintzberg has been one of the most consistent and ardent advocates of this viewpoint.[4]

As appealing and seemingly straightforward as learning by simple observation or experiences of others may seem, it suffers from severe limitations. The difficulty in attempting to figure out meaningful lessons about successful management solely from experiences drawn from coaches, teams, executives, or companies rests in separating the truly general lessons that need to be learned from those that masquerade as general lessons but are not. How does a person really assess whether the critical factors to Joe Torre's success with the Yankees were really the "12 keys" that he identified? Possibly of these twelve, only half are genuinely important. Alternatively, maybe Torre overlooked two or three key ingredients that he used but did not fully appreciate. Sports sections of newspapers and magazines along with radio and TV talk shows are literally filled with analysis and commentary about why a particular coach or team was or was not successful. Looking for intersection of ideas across several successful coaches is not really a satisfying solution either. Vince Lombardi's "Trinity" of "repetition, confidence, and passion" do not readily fold into John Wooden's pyramid incorporating fifteen items.

These same kinds of difficulties arise when the unit of study is broadened beyond the philosophies of particular coaches. For example, the NFL currently serves as the en vogue model of sports league success. By contrast, Major League Baseball has been held up as the case study of bad management. After all, the NFL has been experiencing robust growth in revenues in recent years while MLB has been experiencing stagnant viewership and other problems. Critics and analysts of MLB's business problems frequently use the NFL as a guidepost. Just as with individual coaching philosophies, such lessons are enticing but are likely flawed. Possibly, the NFL's financial situation owes itself more to the sports consumer's appetite for their product than for the specifics of how the league has arranged interteam or player-team finances. "Common sense" observation of current NFL practices may end up highlighting the trivial and passing over the genuinely important points.

These points have been applied in a variety of ways ranging from Scottish philopher David Hume in the eighteenth century down to economist Robert Lucas and psychologist Daniel Kahneman, both Nobel Laureates, in more recent times. They apply equally as well to management. There is a lot of "stuff" going on within an organization as well as beyond its borders that has implications for the organization's success. In a country, millions of people interact with each other and with thousands of companies. In companies, hundreds or thousands of employers and managers interact with each other and serve hundreds, thousands or millions of customers. Picking out the right lessons by simply observing behavior or studying ten or twenty cases is next to impossible because of the overwhelming amount of information and the complex interdependence of factors. A team or business can be organized in a number of different ways. Many different people and players can be employed and then utilized in multiple combinations. Managers can usually pick from a wide array of strategies. They can set up a variety of compensation schemes and interact with employees in numerous ways—sometimes with obvious differences, sometimes with subtle differences. Sports teams and most businesses are just too much of a jumbled-up collection of facts to make accurate generalizations solely based on hunches and observations drawn from experience.

The flaw in an observation-alone or case study-alone approach to sifting out the key ingredients of managerial success has been illustrated time and time again. For instance, IBM became the object of intensive study at business schools during the 1970s because of its long-running success. Basing conclusions on IBM's practices, observers tended to emphasize the importance of hierarchical organizational structure and even formal attire among other keys to their success. At the time, few, if any, predicted or warned students and readers about the upcoming problems IBM would face in the 1980s and 1990s. Moreover, some of the very policies that had been vaunted as the keys to IBM's success, such as their organizational structure, now began to be seen as factors in their demise.[5] Every few years, the reigning management gurus turn over and a new set of ideas become the prevailing slogans. Even ideas that are sound become adopted and twisted into little more than buzzwords thrown around by hustlers of management advice. Over just the past few decades, "management-by-objective," "total quality management," "six sigma," "strategic management," "mission-oriented," "benchmarking," and many others have undergone these kinds of transformations.[6]

Such flip-flopping, though, is not uncommon when hunches drawn from experience and anecdote are the primary or sole bases used to try to determine successful management policies. Using coaches, their practices, and their advice has led to the same kinds of failures. Based on the success and popularity of coaches such as Vince Lombardi with the Packers or Bear Bryant with Alabama in the 1950s and 1960s, a generation of coaches imitated the tough-as-nails discipline of players. Lombardi himself helped to promote the focus on discipline because he viewed the discipline-intensive aspects as critical to his success. Yet, many coaches who emulated his intensive methods failed and sometimes failed miserably. In contrast, other coaches who ignored the Lombardi trends and developed a much less restrictive style, such as Oakland's John Madden, enjoyed tremendous success. Even today, many coaches still subscribe to the view that the extreme methods of Lombardi are the key to success even though many successful coaches have not used them and many unsuccessful coaches have.

The same thing is true when observing the practices of famous managers. People such as Alfred Sloan, legendary CEO of General Motors, and latter-day managerial whiz, Tom Peters, are at different ends of the spectrum in the kinds of advice they have drawn from their experiences. Sloan preached a highly rational, scientific approach to the analysis and practice of management. Peters promoted a looser, "management by walking around" philosophy. People such as Microsoft's Bill Gates and General Electric's Jack Welch fall somewhere in between these two extremes but tend to draw out principles that are unique to them or at least stated in somewhat unique terms.

Does this mean that experiences and anecdotes are useless in the study of management practice? No, it does not. The lesson is that observation and experience need to be kept in their proper place. Drawing from the experiences of managers and constructing case histories is a tremendous teaching tool. Cases offer illustrations that can open a listener's or reader's mind up to an important principle but they are not usually the best means of finding the right principles.

A second purpose for case histories and experience is that they serve as a means to initiate discussion and further study. The views of Joe Torre, Mike Krzyzewski, or some other sports figure, about their own success are not without merit. Whether listening to them or observing their practices, many interesting ideas can be gleaned. Further, rather than just taking the experiences of a single coach, it can be instructive to look for similarities in the methods used by different coaches, all of whom have experienced long term success. This provides an especially rich basis from which to speculate about the factors that are important. In this book, the cases and illustrations drawn from sports are put to both of these purposes.

If experience alone does not provide a basis for making reliable generalizations about sound management, coaching, or leadership practices, then what does? Unfortunately, for those looking for quick answers and single-page memos for success, the answer is a lot of hard work and clear thinking that includes careful simplification; meticulous logic along with extensive analysis of data.[7] This kind of work is not sexy. It does not make for light reading. It is not accomplished through merely carefree reflections and ruminations. It is not based on a "just-give-me-the-facts" mentality. In short, it is not the kind of work that tends to make for a lot of media attention or finds its way to bestseller lists. Instead, it requires long and tedious labor. It requires the ability to step back from some of the details of a problem or decision in order to partition the problem into digestible chunks. While different in its details, the methods necessary are not very different from those required to make advances in science and medicine. The ultimate goal is to distinguish the principles that are truly general in nature from those that may or may not be critical to success.

The difficulty involved in investigating the principles behind sound management in rigorous and sometimes abstract ways is one of the reasons why disciplines related to the analytical study of management—statistics, operations research, accounting, economics, and finance—are often not the most popular with students. Nonetheless, foundational principles built on clearly worked-out analytical principles provide a superstructure for understanding the world much in the same way that a foundation and frame provides the support and structure for a house. Over the last forty years or so, there has been a growing body of management principles that have been drawn from this kind of slow and rigorous process into a body of knowledge. This body of knowledge is incomplete and always in a state of flux. Nonetheless, it furnishes the backbone of this book.

THE LIMITS OF THE SPORTS-BUSINESS CONNECTION

While supplying a rich background in which to illustrate and consider managerial decisions, sporting environments have their limitations. For one, just as with any particular industry, leadership in sports contains idiosyncracies and trade-specific characteristics. Even among sports teams, not all managers face the same problems. College coaches, for instance, do not face the issue of how to fit players' salaries within limits imposed by owner or the league. College coaches deal with players who, by and large, are not as financially secure as most professional athletes. Because of this, they possess a degree of authority above their professional counterparts. Likewise, among professional coaches, with a roster of fifty players, an NFL coach can more easily release a player, even a good player, than can an NBA coach with a twelve-man roster.

Second, sports organizations are not large and complex. Even the largest sports teams pale in comparison to even medium-sized companies, much less national and multi-national firms. Players, coaches, front office personnel, and support staff for a football team would number under one hundred while the number of employees in a small to medium-sized company might number in the hundreds and few thousand. Large companies such as GM or GE employ over 100,000 people.

While this relative smallness supplies an advantage in that it allows sports teams to be studied in great detail, it also limits some of the issues that can be addressed. Beyond merely writing additional paychecks, additional problems are faced by managers as the size of the organization grows. Questions as to how to best organize a company into units and subunits become much more important and complex. A sports team might have to decide whether to roll the functions of GM and coach into a single person's hands or divide them between two individuals. Over time, the number of positional coaches and their responsibilities might change in football or similar organizational issues may arise in other sports. For a company with hundreds or thousands of employees located at several different locations and possibly producing a variety of goods or services to be sold in multiple markets, the structure of the company and the division of decision-making authority within the company becomes a critical matter.

Third, human relation issues often dominate sports organizations. People are important in practically in organization. One might even claim that people are the most important resource in any organization. Still, it is obvious that production in sports environments is highly labor intensive. Therefore, a large chunk of the critical decisions faced by sports managers revolve around personnel decisions—large even in comparison with many other organizations. Not surprisingly, the advice offered in nearly all of the coaches' books on managing and leadership steers heavily toward various aspects of dealing with people, such as how to motivate people. Without denying the importance of people to any organization's success, decisions regarding equipment, tools, structures, and other nonhuman capital are important in their own right. A sports-oriented approach will not go a long way in illustrating decisions in these areas.

Fourth, the culture surrounding sports teams in many ways differs markedly from the culture within most other organizations. The term "culture" here is used with regard to intangible sets of customs, rituals, expectations, and taboos present. Even the U.S. Supreme Court has recognized these cultural differences. In a case determining the definition and scope of sexual harassment, one Justice noted that the same action, such as a pat on the rear end, would be viewed quite differently depending on whether a coach delivered it to a player on the practice field versus if a manager delivered it to a secretary in an office whether the secretary were male or female.

Historically, sports teams, especially with regard to player–coach relationships, have exhibited a culture more like military and paramilitary organizations than like most business or political organizations. Coaches have held autocratic power more akin to that of a drill sergeant than a business manager. What the coach says goes, at least for the most part. Dissent is met with punishment or dismissal. The use of verbal intimidation has been rampant, and physical abuse occasionally occurs as well. This culture has slowly been evolving to look a bit more like the rest of the private sector. This is a subject considered more in Chapter 4. Still, attending a practice or a listening to a timeout huddle or halftime talk can quickly illustrate the fact that the sports culture in America differs considerably from most other organizational cultures.

Because of these differences, some of the tools and methods available to coaches are just not available to the same degree to all managers whether for the better or worse. Sometimes, in reading and listening to the coaches-turned-consultants, one is struck by the fact that many coaches do not appear to grasp these cultural differences, or if they do, they think they can be waived off. For instance, Bill Parcells advises, "The only way to change people is to tell them in the clearest possible terms what they're doing wrong. And if they don't want to listen, they don't belong on the team."[8] While there may be some truth in his view, not many managers have the ability to place an employee on waivers. Sole proprietors may have similar powers or a CEO may be able to determine the team of highest level executives, but few managers wield the hire/fire power of a sports coach or general manager.

A final obstacle in making use of management lessons from sports is that developing managerial skill is not merely a matter of digesting information or learning a particular set of strategies or tactics. Whether for the CEO of a large financial institution or the manager of a major league baseball team, the practice of management steers a course between art and science. Whether based on an analytical approach or some other approach, successful management cannot be totally reduced to a set of formulas and passed from one person to another. In this respect, consultants such as Tom Peters or academics such as Henry Mintzberg are on the mark. While they may carry the point too far, no amount of study of the brush strokes and use of color of Rembrandt will manufacture a painter equal to the Dutch master. Even painters of great skill who may imitate Rembrandt's methods cannot fully incorporate and imitate the creativity that made him a renowned painter. In the same way, becoming a skillful coach requires more than merely serving an apprenticeship under a highly successful coach. Developing into a successful CEO requires more than matriculating through a top-flight MBA program or reading the biography of a corporate magnate. The skillful use of "heuristics"—rules-of-thumb and other mental shortcuts—is valuable in solving all kinds of messy, complex problems. In fact, a small but growing field is emerging that considers such methods. The difficulty is using heuristics without overusing or abusing them.[9]

SPORT AS MANAGEMENT OR MANAGEMENT AS SPORT?

Is this a book about sports or a book about management? The answer is both. In its specifics, this volume is a sports book through and through. The following chapters are filled with examples drawn from sporting events and related episodes involving players, teams, coaches, executives, and leagues. Sports fans who are interested in evaluating the decisions made by players, coaches, and general managers of sports franchises should find the material of interest.

On the other hand, this volume is a management book. While it is certainly not a management textbook in the usual sense, every chapter in the book and every section within these chapters covers topics that transcend sports venues. At its core, the organization of the book centers around common issues and problems faced by managers regardless of setting. As a reader for current or aspiring managers or as a supplement to traditional textbooks, the following pages offer an opportunity for individuals who combine an interest in management with the fun of sports to explore important management lessons. Not every conceivable management topic is included. Some fit with the sports emphasis better than others. Still, the breadth of issues included is considerable.

Probably more analogies have been drawn between settings such as war to either sports or business than between business and sports. Coaches have long borrowed phrases with military overtones such as "it's time to go to war" or "you've got to take the fight to them." Even sports nicknames follow this trend on occasion. Long-time Indiana University basketball coach Bob Knight earned the title of "The General." Baseball manager Gene Mauch came to be known as "The Little General." Likewise, many managers and management educators have dipped into not only military terminology but into outright transfer of military concepts. The book, *The Art of War,* based its prescriptions on the writings of a Chinese general from antiquity. In spite of these common analogies, sports and everyday management bear a much closer relationship to each other than either does to warfare.

A case can be made, however, that the relationship between sports and business extends beyond mere analogy. Near the opening of this chapter, the point was made that rather than the "sport as a metaphor for life" idea, a more accurate rendering would be "sport is life." Sport, play, and the terms and phrases that go along with it pervade nearly all of society. Just as sports and everyday activities share much in common, sports competitions and everyday business settings share much in common in terms of the situations that the decision makers face—whether these decision makers are coaches, players, general managers, corporate executives, or laborers. These scaled-down versions of life exhibit highly observable versions of many of the same things that go on in business and life.[10] Yes, baseball may mimic life in some of its features, but other sports fill in many of the holes. For example, because football and basketball involve teamwork and strategy to a much greater extent than baseball, it provides more material from which to study these elements of managing and other elements such as new technologies.

LESSONS FROM ON AND OFF THE FIELD

The relationship between sports and managing can be described as ironic—maybe even schizophrenic. Established, successful coaches usually become national celebrities as recognizable to most people on the street as any national politician or Hollywood star. For instance, Vince Lombardi and Tom Landry would have likely been picked out by the man-on-the-street as readily as the President of the United States. As noted earlier in the chapter, the advice of these coaching celebrities may be sought out not only on sports-related matters but on varied aspects of management in general and many other matters as well. As their tenure lengthens, they sometimes evolve into the role of coach-statesman where even their philosophies on life in general became highly valued. In fact in a few instances such as Bear Bryant, the adulation rises to near worship, at least within the state of Alabama, so that whatever opinion the coach voiced, regardless of topic, becomes revered as holy writ to the devoted fan. Once a coach finds success and becomes established as a public figure, even diminished success is tolerated to a large degree. Fans and media may offer criticisms, but these remarks tend to be offered with respect, and at times, sympathy. Tom Landry's last couple of seasons in Dallas or Marty Schottenheimer's struggles in the first part of the season in Washington offer two cases in point.

On the other hand, "front office" personnel in sports—owners and to a lesser extent general managers—frequently typify the villain to reporters and fans. The names of Art Modell, Jerry Jones, Daniel Snyder, Jerry Krause, and many others are frequently accompanied by unflattering if not outright venomous remarks. The irony is that the same people who hang on each utterance of a successful coach roll their eyes at or snidely pass off statements and decisions made by owners, whether old-timers such as Art Modell or more recent entrants such as Jerry Jones. For many, these owner-executives are fat cats tainted with all that goes with the money side of sports—profits, contracts and salary negotiations, stadium deals, ticket prices, and luxury suites. To many fans and reporters, these aspects of sports are, at best, unavoidable annoyances and, at worst, miserable plagues.

These kinds of unflattering views of the upper management of sports franchises have reached their extremes when franchises have moved. The departure of the Dodgers from Brooklyn after the 1957 season for the warm breezes and deep pockets of Los Angeles stoked vitriolic feelings at the time and continue to do so over forty years after the move. The sense of betrayal by the generations of fans who grew up near Ebbets Field has been chronicled in numerous books, documentaries, and interviews. It frequently resonates more like the emotional outpouring of jilted lovers than of consumers of a branch of the entertainment industry.

Reactions involving only slightly less angst and anger litter the landscape of sports history involving the movements of other long-standing teams—the Browns from Cleveland to Baltimore, the Colts from Baltimore to Indianapolis, the Cardinals from St. Louis to Arizona, the Rams from Los Angeles to St. Louis, the Oilers from Houston to Tennessee, the Giants from New York to San Francisco. In some cases, the movements of particular players for financial reasons have also stirred similar emotions. When Canadian-born superstar Wayne Gretzky left the Edmonton Oilers of the NHL to join the Los Angeles Kings, fans in Edmonton mourned the loss much like the death of a family member. In a more recent case, pitcher Kevin Brown jumped ship from the Padres after a World Series season and traveled up Interstate 5 to join the hated Dodgers, sparking contempt not only for Brown and the Dodgers but for the whole free agency system that permits money to come into play. In other cases, the response may be a bit more measured but, nonetheless, negative toward the business side of players' and teams' decisions. The villain may be the team, player, or both depending on the circumstances. The movement of Roger Clemens from the Boston Red Sox to the Toronto Blue Jays brought derision toward the team. In the case of Alex Rodriguez, who shunned lucrative offers from his prior club, the Seattle Mariners, to sign a $250 million contract with the Texas Rangers, the Seattle fans and media directed their disgust at Rodriguez. Likewise, Rodriguez's insistence on a trade, resulting in his move to the Yankees, targeted him for the contempt of Rangers fans.

Not surprisingly, the owners and general managers responsible for financial matters in sports, the "money men," have often found themselves at the receiving end of fan and media contempt. While such views may be commonplace among media and fans, even coaches themselves often foster this outlook. NFL coach Bill Walsh of the San Francisco 49ers expressed the prevailing view toward the front office personnel when he generically referred to owners as someone who got "rich quick," the general manager as in the owner's pocket and receiving "a large salary for doing very little," and the player personnel man as "a frustrated former coach or player sending out scouts." In Walsh's view, the coaches would be working while the "owner, GM, and personnel director were having dinner, frustrated by the use of players." For these reasons, he thought that owners and general managers typically preferred coaches who showed little independence.

The irony and imbalance in these views is all the more striking given the popularity of coaches not just as coaches but as management consultants and advisors. Seemingly, coaches can understand management, but managers cannot understand coaching. Howard Cosell coined the term "jockacracy" to capture this kind of superior, "you haven't played the game" outlook. In spite of the unflattering views of sports owners and general managers and harsh words of coaches such as Bill Walsh, the similarities in the decisions of sports managers who toil "inside the lines" to those who work "outside the lines" are much greater than the differences. In fact, Bill Walsh is almost certainly very similar as a GM as he was as a coach. The decision-making processes likely imitated those he used as a coach on the field once he moved up into a general manager. The main difference is that as GM he, or any other person, faces a somewhat different set of incentives and constraints than does a coach.

Classified into its main roles, the on-the-field side of sports management (coaching) is akin to the operations or production side of a business while the off-the-field side (ownership, general managing) incorporates the financial, marketing, and strategic parts of the business. The owners and general managers in the "front office" usually center on performance measures such as revenues and profits whereas the operations side normally focuses on more narrow production goals such as wins and losses. Just as in other kinds of business, these differences in goals and constraints sometimes lead to hostility and confusion.

The production people—coaches, players—along with many fans and media do not readily see the similarities between the front office activities and those occurring "between the lines." Yet, just as the decisions between coaches and managers in other kinds of businesses share common features, coaches, front office managers, and owners also share common features once some of the facade is stripped away. In each of the settings, participants, regardless of title—president, CEO, owner, general manager, supervisor, coach—face decision-making problems. The success of managers inside and outside of sports or whether on the "business" side or the "on-the-field side of a sports franchise depends on key decisions regarding hiring, motivating, and empowering personnel. They must assess their resources at hand, weigh the likely consequences of their actions, make adjustments, gauge the actions and responses of rivals—all within the limits imposed by time, expenses, budgets, and information.

Depending on the particular business, the role of production decisions may be more or less critical and difficult than other elements of business decisions. Or, the role of production-side decision makers and financial-side decision makers may be more intertwined or even combine in the same office or person depending on the size or nature of a business. However, this is also true within sports itself. For example, the role of player selection, although important in any sport, is likely to be of even greater consequence in baseball relative to on-the-field strategy than in a sport such as football.

A LOOK AHEAD

The interconnection between sports and managing opens up a wide variety of topics for consideration throughout the following chapters. Chapter 2 provides an overview and introduction of basic concepts important to and common among effective managers in sports—the fundamentals. Many of these ideas crop up or are inherent in the discussion of the later chapters. The topics include recognition of hidden costs and tradeoffs, coordinating decisions, learning and adapting, and understanding the nature of uncertainty and risk. The term fundamentals is not intended to convey that these include all the important management concepts—just the building-block level ideas.

Chapter 3 covers the prerequisite for success in any kind of business, sports or otherwise—the relationship between the product or service offered and the consumers to whom it is offered. In the ongoing search and struggle for methods that yield productive teams, many a team and manager has lost sight of the fact that it is, ultimately, the value placed by consumers in the marketplace on the product or service that makes any of the other matters meaningful. Sports is ripe with examples, both good and bad, that help to illustrate several of the key matters regarding markets and management.

Chapter 4 goes into detail regarding the special issues and problems involved in the management of people. Because sports businesses have labor-intensive workplaces, they provide an especially illuminating look at decisions that managers frequently face regarding hiring practices, effective utilization of people, development and enhancement of skills, turnover, motivation, communication, and conflict.

Chapter 5 considers the role of information in managing sports teams and franchises. Emphasis is placed upon the quality and use of information and not just on the quantity of it in trying to deal with a complicated and competitive setting. Along with the analysis, examples are provided that provide warnings to those who would try to use information carelessly or as a substitute for critical thinking.

Chapter 6 examines tools for strategic and tactical decision making. Sports managers, just like business managers, face a variety of situations where their competitor's response cannot be taken as fixed. Instead, the best strategy depends vitally on expectations concerning the opponent's actions or reactions. Ironically, the name "game theory" has come to describe this kind of analysis.

Chapter 7 looks at innovation and adaptation by sports managers. The emphasis of the chapter is that, first, innovation or adaptation is critical to long-term success. Second, there are creative forces at work when innovations or adaptations are created or developed and these creative forces may not be easy to teach or foster. Yet, managers differ greatly in their ability and commitment to developing an environment where innovation is possible and obstacles are reduced. Also, the politics of innovation or adaptation must be considered in order to be successful.

Chapters 8 and 9 explore the role of managers within organizations and how they add (or subtract) value from the organization. Chapter 8 hones in on the question of how far the scope of any one manager's decision-making responsibility should extend. Also, the chapter tries to draw a critical distinction between effective management and unproductive over-managing. Chapter 9 considers managers more broadly defined.

REPLAY

1. Sports is fun but it also reflects and is reflected in life including business. While some of the specific knowledge needed differs, managers face common challenges across all kinds of settings. Managing the Yankees and managing lessons from on-the-field decisions share close relationships with off-the-field decisions inside and outside of sports.

2. Case studies of a particular coach or manager, whether Vince Lombardi or Mike Krzyzewski, can illustrate important facts about management and initiate useful discussion of management policy. Success and failure is too complex, however, for examination of single or multiple coaches or companies to provide a template for management.

3. Effective coaches and managers are part scientist, part artist. Clear reasoning and accurate data provide important tools to assist decision makers. They do not yield pat formulas that eliminate the value of discretion, experience, and personal interaction.

2

Managing Fundamentals: Benching a Hall of Fame Pitcher

It may be that you will need a great length of time to have it become automatic to you, and not be confused by the mechanics of the game.

—Branch Rickey, former baseball executive

Now the fundamentals have got to be more education. More information of knowledge, faster speed, more technology across the board.

—Jack Welch, former General Electric CEO

Most of the attention and adulation regarding sports flows toward the most visible participants—players and coaches. Few "executives" have extensive histories written about their exploits or philosophies. An exception to this rule is Branch Rickey, who helped to build the St. Louis Cardinals during the 1920s and 1930s, and later the Brooklyn Dodgers during the 1940s, into consistent winners as their general manager. Rickey has been called part entrepreneur, part scout, part philosopher, part preacher, and part snake-oil salesman for his wide-ranging activities and thoughts regarding baseball and business. These have been well-documented in anecdotes, biographies, and personal notes.

In both his basic outlook on players as well as within the organizational frameworks that he established for the Cardinals and Dodgers, Rickey stressed the importance of fundamentals. By fundamentals or synonymous terms, he was talking about the skills or characteristics from which the basic elements of performance could be built. Rather than just looking at a young player's hitting statistics, Rickey looked at the components of the young player's swing to see if he thought the mechanics present would lead to future success with development or whether the player, even with impressive statistics, might use unsound elements in their swing. He had made detailed notes on pitching, base running, and stealing along with coaching and drills.[1] He viewed the foundational principles of the game as so important that he institutionalized the instruction of them in the minor league systems of each team he supervised so that players coming up to the major league team would already be well-schooled in them. Because of Rickey's influence, the Cardinals and the Dodgers minor league systems became innovators in developing elemental skills such as situational hitting, base running, sliding, defense situations, and others. The stress on these fundamentals came to be so institutionalized that they came to be known as the "Dodger system."

Fundamentals are not just important for players. For managers inside and outside of sports, laying out and understanding the basic components of effective management are also important. Yet, because they are basic, many would-be managers and MBA students skirt right past them in their haste to get on to the sexier, contemporary topics. Just as a few players may ignore the basics and still excel because of innate abilities, the same holds true for managers. For the masses, though, skipping over the essential elements of decision making or playing a game because it seems obvious or boring invites a lot of hard knocks if not out and out disaster. Many of the biggest errors made by managers in sports and business grow out of their failure to fully appreciate the subtlety and scope of basic decision concepts. This chapter presents a few of the most basic but most important ideas behind successful management regardless of whether the manager is leading the Yankees or running an automobile dealership. In discussing "fundamentals," it should be stressed that these are elemental or building-block level components of sound decision making. Other ideas that utilize these will be developed in later chapters.

HUMAN MOTIVATION 101

During his tenure as head coach of the Packers, Vince Lombardi made a ritual of handing out five and ten dollar bills at weekly "award sessions" on Thursdays. Former Packer Gary Knofelc observed, "It was amazing how prideful you would become" in receiving these nominal sums of money.[2] Lombardi's policies fit in with what Green Bay assistant coach and Lombardi successor Phil Bengston noted as a key feature of Lombardi's understanding of player motivation "the player produces for himself and the team as an extension of himself . . . basic appeal to individual pride and performance."[3] He balanced the need for individuals to subjugate themselves to the needs of the team while continuing to recognize the importance of the individual.

The divergence between team goals and personal objectives is an example of what has been labeled as the principal-agent problem or just the agency problem—any situation where the principal's interests differ from the agent's interests. The agency problem may involve a divergence between ownership and management, between general management and divisional managers, between owners or managers and other employees, or between a player and his agent. The problem arises because the objectives of the two parties do not coincide perfectly or maybe very little. For instance, the owner is concerned about profits while the manager is concerned about his own compensation. General management may be concerned with overall company performance while a divisional manager may be interested primarily in the performance of his division. The agency problem is fundamental because it draws its source from the universal fact that people are different and pursue their own agendas. As a result, finding ways to solve or at least reduce the agency problem is one of the manager's most basic and critical functions.

One expression of the agency problem, whether in business or athletics, is the fact that the divergence in objectives within a team or organization can lead to problems of effort or of misdirected effort. Without some kind of monitoring or incentive system, many "agents" such as players or employees will not provide full effort. Some may back off only a bit while others may shirk to the fullest possible extent. Or, if they do work very hard, it may be directed in a way that generates greater personal statistics but not necessarily improving overall team performance. The basketball player who hogs the ball and shoots constantly is one example. One job of coaches and managers is to do things that make the interests of team members, and thereby their activities, more closely coincide with those beneficial to the team as a whole.

An intriguing point about Lombardi is not merely his recognition of the need for motivation but the depth of his understanding of the fundamental problems involved. Some coaches and business leaders hope to reduce the agency problem solely by preaching lofty platitudes about "team first" and through verbal harassment. Coaches invented and have long moralized with slogans such as "There's no 'I' in team" and "We not me." These kinds of attempts at instilling a sense of individual responsibility to the group have a place (as discussed later). It does supply a kind of incentive and may change preferences of individuals and their interests slightly, but really proficient managers understand that all of the slogans in the world do not change people into robots who think only of the greater good for the team. Groupthink babble will not make a player or employee who sees his own personal interest as standing far apart from the team's interest subjugate his own interest without some accompanying incentive.

People are people—not angels and not demons (for the most part). They are concerned primarily with their own personal goals and comforts and those of their closest family members. As longtime Princeton basketball coach, Pete Carill, put it, "Start with the premise that, in general, people would rather do something less difficult than something difficult . . . People resist giving that high level of effort. There is a tendency to settle for less and then have to overcome it." When it comes to subjugating their own goals and comforts to those of a group, a small percentage may wholly conform to some group-directed goals even without any special monitoring or motivations. A greater percentage will conform to some degree to group-directed goals while pursuing their own agendas to some extent. Finally, a small percentage will exploit any opportunity to pursue a personal objective to the fullest. Sloganeering may tweak these percentages a bit, but it will not change basic character dramatically.

For all of his loud preaching, Lombardi appeared to comprehend the need to attend to the needs of the individual, at least to some extent. In his view, if a coach failed to account for the personal goals, he would likely fall short of motivating people to their best performance. Although he used speeches, harassment, and intimidation extensively, he went far beyond these methods and explicitly factored in personal goals and satisfaction. An army of coaches and managers observed the louder aspects of Lombardi's style without sharing his depth of understanding of the balancing of personal and team objectives motivation.

At the University of Kentucky, Rick Pitino assembled highly-touted high school basketball stars, many of whom had professional basketball aspirations and skills. Pitino, like Lombardi and many coaches possessed plenty of ego and frequently used verbal assaults to try to root out lack of effort and other personal agendas. Yet, he did not rely solely on these methods. He understood that getting the players to merge their objectives with those of the team required some attention to their personal goals. So, he would encourage the team members to see their own personal rewards and attention as being increased if the team did well. By contrast, if the team performed poorly, much less attention would be directed toward them individually.

This is not to say that the "no 'I' in team" kind of talk has no place in motivating people. As noted above, the majority of employees want the team or company to succeed, but usually the team's success is secondary or at least only equal to the interest in their own personal welfare and that of their family. The sloganeering and preaching about the importance of the team's goals along with the fact that the players go through common experiences together may build a sense of comradery and brotherhood among team members. To some extent, the team may become an extension of the player's family. Most players who have been part of athletic teams, especially involving extensive teamwork and physical effort, do build emotional attachments to other players and sometimes coaches, leading the player to expend effort "for the team" that they likely would not without such emotional attachment.

Some coaches and managers go beyond just slogans and throwing the word "family" around to try spend an unusual amount of effort trying to build this sense of team or company as an extended family. George Allen coached the Washington Redskins during the 1970s and Joe Gibbs led them during the 1980s and early 1990s. Both of these coaches took the route of sticking by veteran players and tending to prefer veterans over young players. This kind of loyalty to players comes with a price—it may diminish the athleticism of players and slow the infusion of younger players. Yet, it also tends to build a much greater bond between these players and the team. Their attention to team-oriented goals and objectives are likely to be greater than on a team where the coach throws around the phrases like "we're a family" but treats veteran players like little more than nuts and bolts to be plucked off the assembly line.[4]

Yet, astute coaches and managers will realize that there is a limit to the team-as-family concept. For all of the rhetoric, teams and families are quite different. Even the most loyal coach is not going to treat the veteran player like his son or daughter who have lifetime membership in his family. By contrast, every player knows that some day, unless the player retires first, the playing relationship with the team is going to end. Young family members share the same loyalty from parents as old family members. Coaches who try to build bonds with veteran players frequently do so by treating younger players without the same loyalty or respect. Such a policy can have short-run benefits but entail long-run costs as younger players are not mixed well into the organization. Chapter 4 digs deeper into the discussion of motivating people and its ramifications for managing.

TRADEOFFS AND HIDDEN COSTS

From 1915 to 1919, Babe Ruth regularly pitched for the Boston Red Sox, throwing over 300 innings in both 1916 and 1917. Ruth not only pitched—he excelled at it as Table 2.1 indicates, leading the American League with the lowest Earned Run Average (1.75) and most shut outs (9) in 1916. His career Earned Run Average (2.28) would place him tenth and his career winning percentage (0.671) would place him fifth on the all-time list if he had pitched enough innings to qualify for the list. For further evaluation of his pitching prowess, his ERA falls just a shade behind legendary pitchers Christy Mathewson (2.13) and Walter Johnson (2.17). As is normal in baseball, a pitcher of such talents played sparingly at other positions, so Ruth played almost exclusively as a pitcher at least until 1918. Because of his hitting abilities, a new manager of the Red Sox, Ed Barrow, began to split Ruth's time between pitching and playing other positions. In 1918, his innings pitched dropped to 166 innings while he batted over 300 times, up from only about 100 times the year before. In his last year with the Red Sox, 1919, Ruth pitched only 133 innings—equivalent to a widely used reliever or an occasional starter in more recent times—while he batted over 400 times. Even with his part-time role as a hitter, Ruth led the league in home runs in 1918 and in home runs, runs, and runs batted in during the 1919 season.

After being traded to the New York Yankees for the 1920 season, Miller Huggins, his Yankee manager, took a much more drastic step. Ruth pitched only four innings during the 1920 season and merely thirty-one more innings the rest of his career, which ended in 1935. Of course, his hitting exploits over the rest of his career made him the most recognizable figure in American sports for decades to come. These figures are also provided in Table 2.1. He led the American League in homers twelve times, in slugging percentage thirteen times, in walks eleven times, in runs scored eight times, in runs batted in six times, and in batting average one time. He ranks first all-time in slugging percentage, home run percentage, and walks and second all-time in runs scored, runs batted in, and home runs—a record he held until Hank Aaron broke it in 1974. Had he spent his entire career playing in the field and hitting, he would have likely approached 800 career home runs.

Ruth's mammoth career hitting statistics made his switch from full time pitcher to full time position player part of baseball lore. It also makes the wisdom of the switch obvious. Yet, many managers outside of sports frequently choose to do what Ruth's Red Sox managers attempted—striking a balance in the utilization of a multi-skilled person. After all, even if Ruth led the league in homers in 1918 and 1919, the wisdom in removing a league-leading pitcher from the mound altogether only appears obvious with the advantage of hindsight in view of Ruth's enormous hitting exploits. In 1918 or 1920, the wisdom of such a move was not nearly so transparent.[5]

The decision faced by Ruth's managers in Boston and New York graphically illustrates a fundamental and critical aspect of managing in or out of sports and in business or personal affairs—a sound manager must be on the look-out for key tradeoffs, be able to gauge the costs and benefits embedded in these tradeoffs, and make correct decisions in view of them.

Table 2.1
Babe Ruth as a Hitter and Pitcher

Year	At-Bats	Home Runs	Runs	RBI	Innings Pitched	W-L	ERA	League ERA
1914	10	0	0	0	23	2-1	3.91	2.70
1915	92	4	16	21	217	18-8	2.44	2.90
1916	136	3	18	16	323	23-12	1.75	2.80
1917	123	2	14	12	326	24-13	2.01	2.70
1918	317	11	50	66	166	13-7	2.22	2.80
1919	432	29	103	104	133	9-5	2.97	3.20
1920-1930	475	44	131	139	2	-	-	-
Career Totals	8339	714	2174	2211	1221	94-46	2.28	
Career Rank		2nd	2nd	2nd	-	5th	10th	

Notes: Ruth did not pitch enough career innings to qualify for the official all-time list for W-L and ERA. These rankings reflect where he falls relative to the official list. *Source:* Rick Wolfe, ed., *The Baseball Encyclopedia* (New York: Macmillan, 1990).

These instructions may appear intuitive, even obvious, but observation of mangers reveals that the ability to grasp their full importance and the implications extending from them are far from obvious for many. Both sports and business managers frequently fail to grasp the importance of implicit tradeoffs where the costs or benefits may be enormous but hard to detect. They may only see the most obvious costs and benefits while overlooking those that are much larger but more subtle. In other settings, a seemingly successful status quo may freeze managers into complacent inaction, thinking that some success equals optimal management policy.

Possibly the most common mistake made by managers across all kinds of settings is fixating only on the most transparent consequences of decisions. Usually, the most obvious consequences attracting the attention of nearly any manager involve a direct outlay of cash. For instance, the decision to pay a free agent player such as Alex Rodriguez $20 million per year for seven years or financing a new plant worth $100 million will not be overlooked or taken lightly by most managers. The size of the expenditure coupled with its means of payment steers attention toward it. One can be sure that it will be carefully scrutinized by the media or by other decision makers in executive meetings or board meetings. In the end, disagreements may arise as to the wisdom of undertaking such large expenses, but they will not be decided without careful thought.

However, many decisions that make or break a team or company do not stand out so clearly in front of the decision makers. For instance, when viewed from a 1915 or 1918 perspective, the Babe Ruth story highlights the difficulty in accurately assessing the relevant tradeoffs. For Ruth's first two managers in Boston, Bill Carrigan and Ed Barry, the most obvious cost boiled down to reducing the time Ruth spent using his established pitching prowess. Later, Ed Barrow factored Ruth's hitting in more heavily and struck a balance between his pitching and hitting time. Viewed in 1918, Barrow's decision reflects a common managerial decision whether in or out of sports. It's easy to float through management life thinking that the idea of striking a balance in the use of a valuable person or other resource is prudent. A balanced approach holds the appeal as apparently avoiding extremes. The fallacy in this kind of thinking is that it ignores the "hidden costs" associated with striking a balance.

In Ruth's case, the hidden costs amounted to all the hits, homers, runs, and runs batted in that the Red Sox missed out on by having him split his time and that the Yankees would have missed out on by the hundreds if his Yankee manager had followed the course of his Red Sox managers. In retrospect, this likely added up to around 100 home runs and 300 to 400 runs and runs batted in over the four seasons that he either mostly pitched or split time. The problem for his early managers was that they could easily and fairly accurately estimate the costs associated with him pitching less because he already had a sizable track record in pitching. These costs were, in essence, the "cash outlay." In fact, the reluctance of the Red Sox to move him away from pitching stemmed from the fixation on this cost. Ed Barrow stated that fans would "string him up" if he quit using the best pitcher in baseball.

The more obvious and measurable costs frequently lure managers into the trap of placing more weight on them for the very fact that they are obvious and measurable. Sitting in 1916, his manager could only guess at the costs of Ruth missing batting opportunities. Writing down a firm figure for these costs—the home runs, runs, and runs batted in given up—for the next ten years would have been difficult. As a result, his manager that year and even later managers with some record of his hitting discounted the hidden costs of Ruth's future hitting and weighed heavily the more directly measurable cost of reducing his pitching time. Miller Huggins displayed genuine insight, decision making skill, and courage to remove Ruth from the pitching rotation altogether.

To correctly assess the relevant tradeoffs in using Babe Ruth, the critical comparison was his productivity as a hitter relative to his productivity as a pitcher. Ruth was, indeed, more productive than almost all major league players as either a pitcher or a hitter. Looking solely at this fact in isolation could easily lead a manager to switch him back and forth between the two positions. After all, moving Ruth exclusively to the outfield almost certainly meant that the pitcher replacing him would not be as effective as Ruth.

Yet, these facts were really irrelevant to sound decision making. The fact that as a pitcher he could outperform most others only muddled the picture. The relevant comparison was his hitting productivity relative to his pitching productivity. Ruth's value to his team as a hitter dwarfed even his impressive contributions to the team as a pitcher. He held a relative or comparative advantage versus other players in hitting as opposed to pitching. To use Ruth to his fullest advantage meant taking one of the best pitchers in the league off the mound for good. To do that took a manager with a keen grasp of comparative advantage and the subtle costs embedded in the pitch versus not pitch decision.

Another example of a coach grasping subtle aspects of tradeoffs is John Wooden. While many coaches scream about minimizing turnovers and yank players who commit them out of the game, Wooden's outlook differed by 180 degrees. He thought the team making the most mistakes (measured by turnovers) would win because that was the team that took the initiative and forced the action.[6] Obviously, Wooden did not encourage his team to maximize their turnovers. Instead, he recognized the tradeoff between cautious play that minimizes turnovers and aggressive play that yields more turnovers but also yields better scoring opportunities. Moreover, he not only recognized this tradeoff but openly attempted to manage his players in such a way so that they did not steer too far toward caution and lose out on many scoring opportunities. Many other coaches may have recognized the tradeoff to some extent, but very few showed the insight or courage to push their team to be more aggressive.

Effective managers share this ability with John Wooden to grasp the fact that there is an inherent optimal amount of just about everything—whether good or bad. Too great of an effort can be made to completely eliminate negative outcomes, such as a turnover in basketball or employee loafing, when the effort to eliminate these negative outcomes involve costs themselves. As one NFL coach put it when asked about contact in practice, he responded by saying his teams would have enough contact in practice but "not too much," they would run "but not too much," and so forth. His comments implied that he clearly understood these practice regimens to be useful but too much of them imposed too high of a cost. Many coaches, even at the NFL level, do not seem to understand that the NFL season is more like a marathon than a sprint. Physical and mental preparation is essential but the season does not end after the first game. The price of too much hitting and strenuous activity in August—injuries, dehydration, lack of mental sharpness—may reduce performance in November and December just as a marathon runner would experience a decline in performance by trying to run the first mile of the race at full tilt.

COORDINATED DECISIONS

During the late 1990s, the New York Yankees dominated Major League Baseball in a way that they had not been able to replicate since the 1950s and early 1960s, winning championships in 1996, 1998, 1999, and 2000 along with a narrow miss in the 2001 World Series. Based on regular season and post-season dominance as well as in the opinion of expert observers, their 1999 team ranked among the best baseball teams of all time. Some rival owners, as well as media writers, attributed the Yankees' success to the power of the dollar in the era of free agency in baseball. Indeed, the Yankees' revenue from their local market media rights considerably exceeds those obtained even by other large market teams such as the Dodgers and Mets and rise head and shoulders above the revenues of typical MLB teams.

Yet, the deep-pocket free agent explanation offers only a superficial analysis of reemergence of the Yankee dynasty and does not hold up to close scrutiny. The team enjoyed the same kind of financial advantage over the rest of MLB teams ever since the inception of free agency in the mid 1970s. Yet, after winning championships in 1977 and 1978, the Yankees did not win another one until 1996. Even more telling, they stunk over many of these years, at least relative to their own historical standards, appearing in the American League playoffs only twice between 1978 and 1996. In 1981, the Yankees reached the World Series but lost to the Los Angeles Dodgers by four games to two. In 1995 the Seattle Mariners eliminated them in the first round American League Divisional Series. For nearly twenty years, the financial advantage enjoyed by the Yankees translated into mediocrity in spite of ownership by a man, George Steinbrenner, who was obsessed with winning by all appearances and accounts.

What converted mediocrity into dominance for the Yankees over the mid to late 1990s? Their success came largely by the insight of their general managers in developing three young "position" players and two pitchers from within their minor league system. These three players became cornerstones of their team. The three young players assumed arguably the three most important positions on the field other than pitcher—Bernie Williams at centerfield, Derek Jeter at shortstop, and Jorge Posada at catcher. About the same time, the team developed two key pitchers within their minor league system—Andy Pettitte, a starting pitcher, and Mariano Rivera, a relief pitcher. Beyond these players, they used their financial leverage to add several good but not star-level complimentary players including Chuck Knoblauch (second base), Tino Martinez (first base), Scott Brosius (third base), Jeff Nelson (relief pitcher), and acquiring starting pitcher Orlando Hernandez as a unique free agent—a refugee from Cuba.

Another feature of their renaissance contradicts the usual winning-with-money story. They achieved their success without a bona fide superstar. In manager Joe Torre's own words, "Talentwise, there are no obvious superstars on the Yankees."[7] While the claim might be argued, none of the Yankees players over their late 1990s streak would qualify as the best at his position in the American League much less in MLB. Williams and Jeter were certainly very good, All-Star caliber players, but if either were playing in smaller media markets, their statistics would not be attention grabbing to average fans in other cities. The Yankees' only high profile, expensive additions over this time frame were pitchers David Cone and Roger Clemens—both of whom were attained via trade. Although both players contributed, neither could be viewed as the keys to the success of the Yankees at least through the 2000 season. Cone never attained superstar performances with the Yankees and faded badly during the 2000 season. Clemens pitched with only modest success in 1999 and half of 2000, improving markedly late in the 2000 season but regaining superstar form only during the 2001 regular season. Neither keyed the Yankees' postseason heroics in any of the years.

The lack of "the best" individual talents also stands out relative to the past Yankee dynasties. Their great teams of the 1920s and 1930s boasted legends such as Babe Ruth and Lou Gehrig. During the 1940s, Joe DiMaggio and Yogi Berra led the way. By the 1950s, Mickey Mantle replaced DiMaggio as the team's marquee player along with pitcher Whitey Ford. All of these players were not only the best at their positions during their playing eras but stand out with the best players across any era. Among these all-time greats were peppered highly skilled players of the caliber of Williams, Jeter, and Posada.

What lesson does the Yankees success during the late 1990s illustrate? No doubt, luck accounts for a part of their success. Coaches, along with many successful entrepreneurs, disdain references to luck, somehow thinking it diminishes appreciation of hard work and sound decisions. Coachspeak notwithstanding, at the very least the development of young players from teenage draftee to major league contributor can be a shot in the dark even with good scouting and minor league coaching. For every major hit from the draft, a big bust can usually be found. The Yankees' early picks in the 1991 and 1992 amateur drafts showcase this fact. They selected Derek Jeter as the sixth overall pick in 1992, and he has developed into one of the game's leading shortstops. In 1991, they picked Brien Taylor, who never developed into a major leaguer. In fact, out of the yearly top ten picks for all of MLB between 1975 and 1989, more than one-fifth never rose above the minor leagues.

Beyond luck, the Yankee story epitomizes a basic canon of sound management, that is, decisions are interrelated and not independent of each other. For twenty years the Yankees attempted to regain their form largely by using their financial clout to woo one highly publicized free agent superstar after another. This list includes high profile hitters such as Dave Winfield, Rickey Henderson, Jack Clark, Danny Tartabull, Jesse Barfield, and Wade Boggs along with "name brand" pitchers such as Jimmy Key, Andy Hawkins, Tim Leary, Jim Abbott, and Steve Howe. Some of these players, such as Winfield and Henderson, performed well. Others, such as Barfield, Clark, and Tartabull, struggled. Overall, these decision lacked cohesion. When the Yankees started making sound decisions that dovetailed with each other, their fortunes improved dramatically.

In their book *Managerial Economics and Organizational Architecture*, a set of Rochester University business school professors describe management decisions as three legs of a stool.[8] For them, these three legs are the allocation of decision responsibilities within the firm, the evaluation of individual and unit performance, and the set of incentives provided to hire, retain, and motivate managers and other workers. While various academics, business people, or coaches might disagree as to how many legs support the stool, the analogy makes an important fundamental point. Making adjustments to one leg of the stool alters the support provided by the other two legs. The idea closely parallels the age-old proverb, "a chain is only as strong as its weakest link."

From the late 1970s through the early 1990s, Yankee management made decisions that not only did not fit together but negatively effected the organization in other ways. Like most businesses, the Yankees' faced key decisions about using their funds in selecting and attracting members of their workforce as well as keeping their workforce motivated, making appropriate evaluations of people within their organization, and making adjustments to the environment dictated by the enforcement of rules like strike zones and rivals' capabilities and strategies.

Then, during the 1990s, the Yankees began making decisions that were not only sound individually but well-coordinated with each other. Much of the credit goes to their General Managers—Gene Michael and Bob Watson. Rather than blowing huge amounts of money on the biggest-name free agents, the team built their nucleus around relatively young players. This had a number of benefits beyond providing them solid players at key positions. The youth of these players meant that they came with relatively small price tags for several years. The Yankees then used the money left over to plug in the holes with a very good set of complementary players. To the whole mix, they ultimately added a manager, Joe Torre, who excelled in effectively integrating the full set of players into the team's overall effort. In particular, he not only mentored younger players, integrated veterans, and made solid use of his pitching assets, but he excelled in recognizing the difference in personal statistics of players versus evaluating how well players contributed to the ultimate goal of winning. Additionally, he related well to his players, and by most reports, they enjoyed playing for him.

As a principle on paper, the idea of managing so that decisions are not only sound in isolation from each other but coordinate well together seems simple enough. In reality, recognizing and effectively juggling interconnections of decisions presents one of the toughest problems faced by managers. By its very nature, handling these interconnections involves complex interactions not always easy to see or predict. Whether in MLB or other management settings, too many managers read a book, gain a few years of experience, or observe a role model or a rival that convinces them that successful management is all about one or two things in isolation from nearly everything else. The manager then pursues this myopic view of the world, possibly even experiencing some success that only reinforces their narrow and piecemeal view of managing. Sooner or later, though, the imbalanced stool becomes unsteady and crashes to the floor.

Were the opportunities to make similar decisions open only to teams with the big bucks like the Yankees? Obviously, in sports leagues not everyone can excel simultaneously. One team's success must come at the expense of one or more other teams. Nevertheless, most of the moves made by the Yankees were open to others even though their pocketbooks may not have been as deep.

Over part of the same time frame, the Seattle Mariners exhibited the same kind of grasp of the interconnectedness of decisions. Furthermore, Seattle performed well without the extra money of a mega-TV market like the Yankees. Even more enlightening, they even accomplished the feat while losing three future Hall-of-Fame-caliber players—pitching ace Randy Johnson, centerfielder Ken Griffey, Jr., and shortstop Alex Rodriguez. The magnitude of these losses is hard to overstate. Each of these three players were or were very close to being the best player at his position in all of MLB. Moreover, their positions, along with catcher, are typically viewed as the most important positions on any team. *Wall Street Journal* columnist, Allen Barra, likened their exodus to one team losing Hall-of-Fame legendary players Willie Mays, Mike Schmidt, and Steve Carlton in the course of two seasons. In the case of Rodriguez, a free agent, the Mariners received no players in exchange. They did receive players for Johnson, but because he would become a free agent at the end of the year, his trade value drastically diminished. In Griffey's case, they obtained players who would be important to their future success, but players not nearly as heralded as Griffey. In addition to these losses, injuries sidelined one of their most accomplished remaining sluggers, Jay Buhner. In spite of these obstacles and without the New York media revenues, the Mariners advanced to the playoffs in 2000. In 2001 they tied the major league record for the most wins in a regular season (116).

How did the Mariners cope with these losses without the money-to-burn of the Yankees? In short, they employed the same kind of managerial skill as the Yankees—making sound decisions that were exceptionally well connected with each other. Seattle did not panic and attempt to sign the highest priced players available as replicas of the players they had lost. They did not set up a plan to fix everything within a month, then stop that plan when it failed and start another. Instead, the Mariners front office made a sequence of reasonable acquisitions of less heralded, less expensive players but valuable players who fit together to fill the voids they experienced. These players included obtaining starting pitcher Aaron Sele and reliever Jeff Nelson via free agency, neither of whom came with the price tags of the exiting players. They also used innovative approaches by signing two premier Japanese players without prior MLB experience and by obtaining a young and developing centerfielder in exchange for Griffey.[9]

As with the Yankees, an element of luck surfaced in how quickly the team responded from losing its key stars. Likely, even the Mariners themselves did not expect to reach the performance levels they obtained during the 2001 season. Still, their story fits right in with the Yankees story—making sound and well-coordinated decisions on developing young talent, taking the plunge on foreign players, prudent use of dollars to bring in players needed to plug holes, and staying the course without hitting any panic buttons. Without getting as much attention, the Houston Astros accomplished the same kind of feat over the late 1990s, continuing to excel, at least in the regular season, while suffering the departure of several successful pitchers.

One of the most interesting sports cases illustrating the importance of coordinated decisions is one that turned out well in the end but nearly got sidetracked along the way. It is the case of the Los Angeles Lakers in recent years. It is an especially interesting case because it involves one of the most highly acclaimed general managers in all of sports, Jerry West—known in particular for his ability to judge talent.

Although the Lakers had experienced some moderate success during the 1990s based on West's drafting of unrecognized players such as Nick Van Exel, Eddie Jones, and Eldon Campbell, they did not appear to be very close to reaching the championship level. West made the decision to go after Shaquille O'Neal, a player with tremendous physical skills but whose basketball skills and savvy were still doubted by many. In addition to O'Neal, West shocked the basketball world by drafting a six-foot six-inch high schooler named Kobe Bryant. Up to this point, the few high school players drafted had tended to be those much closer to seven feet tall.

After making these monumental decisions about the players on whom he would try to bring another championship to L.A., West then set out to fill in the complimentary pieces—a journey that nearly proved to be the undoing of West as GM. West traded Van Exel, whose considerable talents were sometimes overshadowed by his temperament. Then, West sent Jones and Campbell packing to Charlotte for Glenn Rice with the intention of securing better perimeter shooting to go with the inside play of O'Neil and the slashing of Bryant. However, in trading Jones, West took a considerable risk. Jones and Bryant were of similar size, yet Jones was noted as a much better defender and team player than the still developing Bryant. For two seasons, the team appeared stuck—possessing tremendous talent but bowing out in the playoffs to teams of seeming lesser talent. Finally, West added the piece that balanced the legs of the stool when he attracted Phil Jackson to be the coach. Jackson's forté during his six championships as coach of the Bulls had been finding the right team chemistry.

In contrast to these examples of sports managers who have grasped the importance of coordinated decisions, many other sports franchises illustrate just how costly making disconnected decisions can be. The Texas Rangers present a premier example of disconnected decision making over roughly the same time frame as the Yankees and Mariners built their success. The Rangers, who moved to Arlington from Washington, DC at the end of the 1971 season, experienced some good, some bad, and many mediocre seasons during their Texas tenure but had never visited the playoffs until 1996. With relatively young talent developed within their minor league system, including American League MVP Juan Gonzalez and All-Star catcher Ivan Rodriguez, the team began to improve under the ownership of Tom Hicks. After making the playoffs in 1996, they returned again in 1998 and 1999. Their team emphasized slugging with only average pitching and defensive abilities. However, in each of these playoff appearances, the Yankees humbled them with the Rangers winning only a single game over the three years. These disappointments set in motion a sequence of decisions by Ranger management reminiscent of the futile efforts of the Yankees during the 1980s and early 1990s. More than any single errant decision, the sequence illustrated poorly connected decisions.

First, the Rangers seemed to pursue a path of trying to imitate the Yankees since it had been the Yankees who had demolished them. At the end of the 1999 season, the Rangers' Yankee-aping started by adding left-handed pitching and better defense—two features associated with the Yankees success in the 1990s. They traded their most marketable player, two time American League MVP Juan Gonzalez, to Detroit for three untested position players, a young left-handed starting pitcher who was experiencing arm problems, and a minor league relief pitcher. In separate deals, the club added two other veteran left-handed pitchers.

Even with the young left-handed pitcher obtained from Detroit still injured, the 2000 season started out all right for the Rangers. They entered June with a winning record and near the top of their division. Then, their prized young centerfielder, Ruben Mateo, broke his leg and the team's fortunes began to slide as their hitting fell off. Later in the summer, their perennial All-Star catcher, Ivan Rodriguez, was also lost for the remainder of the season to injury. After these two key players were lost, the remainder of the season flopped. The team's pitching rated dead last in the league.

Rather than stay on course, attribute some of the losses to injury, and try to obtain improved pitching or more hitting depth, the Rangers appeared to scrap completely their original plan to remake themselves in the Yankees image. During the 2000–2001 off season, they went after and caught the biggest fish in the free agent market—former Seattle Mariner shortstop Alex Rodriguez for a record $250 million, ten-year contract. The size of the contract drew much criticism from the baseball press not only for its magnitude but also for the fact that it diminished the Rangers' ability to go after and sign pitching, which was universally recognized as their biggest weakness. Owner Hicks and General Manager Doug Melvin felt that the opportunity to obtain a player at such a key position at shortstop who had demonstrated outlandish hitting feats for a shortstop was too good to pass.

However, instead of using Rodriguez as the basis for a new long term plan for success by plugging in young players in the field and acquiring better pitching with whatever dollars were left, the team made an effort to jump from last to best in one season. The dollars that could have gone for pitching help went toward signing several late-thirty-something players in the free agent market—third baseman Ken Caminiti, second baseman Randy Velarde, and designated hitter Andres Galaraga. All of these had been very successful players over their careers, but Caminiti and Galaraga had both begun to show decline in their output. As a result of the influx of veteran sluggers, when wonderkid Mateo returned from his injury, he was pushed down low in the batting order.

By mid-May of the 2001 season, the push from worst to first became a disastrous slide from bad to even worse. In view of the abysmal start to the season, the "win now" philosophy became moot, and the Rangers implemented a two or three year plan for long-term improvement. They released Caminiti and traded Galaraga as well as Mateo, who had struggled to regain his form after the injury and his relegation to platoon player rather than superstar in waiting. In the end, through all of this, the Rangers had traded two of their three most marketable players, Gonzalez and Mateo, without improving their woeful pitching and by sliding from a divisional winner to being out of the pennant race by June. But this is exactly what managers and general managers in sports or other business should expect when decisions over time reflect a hodgepodge of benchmarking, shifting of strategies, and short-term focus.

Before the 2002 season began, owner Tom Hicks replaced Doug Melvin with John Hart as General Manager. Hart had built highly successful teams with the Cleveland Indians during the 1990s. From the outset, the clear intent in bringing in Hart was an emphasis on the "win now" philosophy. Hart signed free agent Chan Ho Park who had fallen out of favor in Los Angeles, resigned Juan Gonzalez as a free agent, added veteran players with recent problems Carl Everett and John Rocker, and added a few additional veterans. Several injuries and mediocre performances by the acquired players sent the Rangers into a "building for the future" mode that should have started with the signing of Rodriguez two years prior. By this time, Rodriguez had tired of the losing and pushed for a trade but only to World Series contenders such as the Red Sox or Yankees. The Rangers made a deal with the Yankees before the 2004 season. The Rangers received a budding hitter in Alfonso Soriano in return but had to pay all but about $5 million of Rodriguez's salary to make the deal. Ironically, the deal finally put them squarely on the path of relying on their talented young players, who responded with an unexpectedly strong 2004 season.

The complexity of managing means that few if any managers in any kind of operation will make all of the right decisions. Mistakes will be made. Luck—both good and bad—plays a role. Over the long haul, though, those managers who key in on the important decisions and link them together will stand the best opportunities for success. The ones who manage only from problem to problem, day to day, with no sense of how things work together must hope that good luck overwhelms their managerial weaknesses.

ELEMENTS OF UNCERTAINTY AND RISK

When the NCAA adopted the 3-point shot in 1987, the most obvious effect was to benefit teams with excellent outside shooters or those who developed good shooters. In bare statistical terms, these teams stood to increase their point production relative to other teams. By comparison, a team with only average outside shooting would likely stay at about the same place they started. No doubt, the success enjoyed by several teams mentioned in the preceding section with the advent of the three-point shot came about because of this effect.

However, several coaches such as Paul Westhead at Loyola Marymount and Rick Pitino at Providence displayed a more subtle understanding of the effect of the rule change. The rule change permitted teams the option of not only changing their average outcome but also changing the range or variability of their outcomes. This option arose because the rule change allowed teams to adopt a riskier strategy—taking a large number of three point shots. Because these shots had a lower probability of going in the basket than closer shots, teams choosing to shoot a large number of them risked the possibility of enduring woeful nights with terrible offensive performances. On the other hand, the increased risk also raised the specter of nights where many of the shots went in and the teams were able to challenge seemingly more talented opposing teams. In fact, Westhead openly remarked that his team's style of play opened up the possibility for big upsets but that fans had to realize that it also meant that some nights the results would look disastrous.

Figure 2.1 strips the logic of the strategy down to its bare statistical essence. Here, the range of likely point outcomes for a team with a lower average scoring ability (Team 1) is compared with the range of likely outcomes for a team with a higher scoring ability (Team 2). The likelihood of the underdog team beating the favorite is equal to the area of overlap of the two ranges. By adopting the strategy of shooting a lot of three-point shots, the underdog (Team 1) can "stretch out" its range of likely outcomes. In other words, the variability of its point outcomes increases. This implies that some nights the team will score fewer points than if it stuck to a more conventional shooting strategy but some nights they will score more points, increasing the area of overlap between their point distribution and the favorites, meaning a higher chance of winning.

To Westhead, the ultimate object was trying to win more games rather than concern about point differential, and this higher risk strategy raised the chances of winning. Teams such as Loyola or Providence could have played a traditional style of basketball, likely only to lose against taller teams more talented at playing those styles. By going to the unconventional, more frenetic style, these teams not only tried to influence the average outcome, but played on the greater variability of outcome such a style generated. In essence, they intentionally adopted a riskier style. They might lose by bigger margins some nights, but would also give themselves a chance to win on other nights. Playing a more traditional, "safer" style would reduce the sizes of some losses but would also likely eliminate a chance to win against some very talented teams. It should be noted that the increased chance of winning arises even if the underdog does not improve its average point level.

Many coaches and successful business managers disdain the mention of

Figure 2.1
Increasing Likelihood of Winning by Using Riskier Strategy

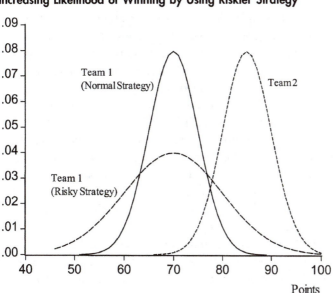

luck—either good or bad. To them, references to bad luck seem to be a way of providing illegitimate excuses for bad outcomes while references to good luck seem to be a way of diminishing the importance of hard work and smart decisions. In spite of such contempt for these ideas, citing good or bad luck only gives expression to a basic fact of decision making—that is, decisions are constantly made without knowing the exact state of events in the future. Practically all real-world events play out in ways that cannot be fully anticipated. The same shot taken by the same player under nearly identical circumstances sometimes falls in the bucket and sometimes rims out. The ball that flies out of the park for a game winning home run one night is caught on the warning track another night because the wind is blowing in or because the field has larger outfield fence dimensions. No one knows the future with complete predictability, yet decisions must be forward looking because decisions ultimately relate to events and consequences ahead rather than behind. This places every decision maker, whether in personal or management settings, at risk that things will not play out as expected.

A critical part of successfully managing tradeoffs is the ability to recognize and use risk to one's advantage or minimize the disadvantage. Of course, the idea of managing risk is not novel to this book. In recent years "risk management" has become an industry in itself. Such usage of the term, however, usually refers only to part of what is at issue in this chapter—diminishing the financial risks to a company of potential future hazards such as fire, theft, lawsuits, injuries, health care and so on. More broadly considered, risk management involves the ability to evaluate and make sound decisions that involve risks. The subject has become course material for economists, business professors, psychologists, and statisticians at many leading universities such as Chicago, Harvard, Duke, and UC Berkeley.[10] For example, widely acclaimed economist Richard Thaler, from the University of Chicago, has students evaluate critical decisions from sports settings such as the World Series in class.

While no one can grasp the future with certainty, all future states of the world are not equally likely and current decisions usually will have an influence on these future states. Whenever possible, establishing the boundaries and detailing some of the characteristics of what these potential outcomes can be can pare the uncertainty down into chunks that can be analyzed and managed. For example, one characteristic that can often be determined is where the typical outcomes are centered or bunched. What are "average" outcomes? Through past experiences on his own team or other teams, a coach might be able to get a handle on the likely point differential if they play a particular strategy against this team or the average rate of success that a batter is likely to have against a particular pitcher. Likewise, almost any manager can benefit from gaining a perspective on average outcomes whether they be about the number of sick days, health care claims, productivity, interest rates, or other items of interest.

Determining the most likely outcomes is a first step toward dealing with uncertainty and risk, but it is only a first step. In many circumstances, the greatest risks are faced because of atypical outcomes. To really get a handle on what is typical or atypical, a manager must collect data or get a feel for the full variety of possible outcomes and, at a minimum, establish a general idea of their likelihood as well as the consequences if they come about. This is the very heart of dealing with risk. Westhead and Pitino might not have ever used graphs such as those in the figures above that depict "probability distributions," but they did realize that using a strategy that increased the variability of outcomes provided their undermanned Loyola and Providence teams a chance to win that pursuing a strategy that narrowed the possible outcomes would not. They put a bridle on risk and used it to their advantage rather than just seeing risk as something to be minimized.[11]

One difficulty in correctly assessing risks is that the same decision can imply a different tradeoff and cost depending on the situation. For instance, if a team is favored using a less risky strategy, then increasing the variance by taking on a riskier style would be detrimental to the team. On the contrary, a style that reduced risk would provide benefits. In addition, the manager must give attention to the effects of the style not only on the variance of outcomes but the average outcome. The up-tempo, three-point shooting style of play was not only an innovation that increased risk and volatility of outcomes but also increased average performance for their teams, at least for a time.

Baseball also illustrates how decisions regarding risk can change depending on the specific situation under consideration. Managers and their assistants determining whether to position players closer to the third and first base foul lines exemplifies this principle. For typical hitters during the course of a game, the first and third basemen play several steps away from the foul lines. However, when leading late in games, baseball managers often choose to position players much closer to the foul lines to reduce the likelihood of a batter hitting a double or triple. The wisdom of this approach, even when leading late in a game, depends on the score. Although sometimes used, the strategy does not make sense when a team leads only by a single run. The logic is this: if playing the third and first basemen in their normal positions limits opponents to the fewest runs, on average, when tied or behind, then it will continue to be the best run-limiting defensive strategy when leading only by one run. However, if the team leads by two or more runs late in the game, then "guarding the line" may be optimal because using this technique may in fact reduce the likelihood of multiple run innings even though it increases the likelihood of giving up a single run.

Golf also provides fertile ground for the examination of risk management. Whether high-handicap amateur or highly-skilled professional golfer, all golfers frequently find themselves asking questions such as "Can I carry that water hazard? Should I hit my driver or another club off the tee? Should I aim away from trouble or toward the center of the green?" Couched within each of these questions is a risk–reward tradeoff. Unlike settings where the uncertainties are so great as to make decision making solely guesswork or impulse, the nature of the uncertainties involved in golf permit genuine "analysis" of the risks. For one thing, the decisions come in discrete bites with plenty of time for thinking and planning. Also, each decision involves a combination of certain known features of the course, playing ability, and position along with uncertain aspects such as the specifics of the way the ball will be struck and the influence of external influences such as wind.

One common risk management setting facing golfers of all abilities involves recovering from trouble. All golfers from Tiger Woods to "Joe Duffer" sooner or later find themselves behind a tree, in long grass, on unstable footing, or facing other hindrances. The decision at hand usually involves how best to recover from the trouble—"how much should I try to get back with this shot?" The ability to deal with these situations is one of the main characteristics separating golfers on the PGA Tour from those who may be relatively good golfers on their home course. Professional golfers are uncanny in their ability to turn seeming bogeys into pars or double-bogeys into bogeys, although even they make some widely-publicized mistakes, especially when facing the extra pressure of a "major" tournament. The key to the decision is recognizing that an optimal amount of risk exists to endure—going for enough but not too much. Many amateur golfers swing between the extremes. On one shot, the amateur will go for a "circus shot" that might be successful in 1 out of 100 attempts. After attempting such a shot a time or two and seeing the dire consequences, the player is apt to take a complete risk minimization approach and just punch out. Unless the shot takes place near the very end of a tournament, professional golfers are much more likely to stay away from these extremes. Tiger Woods will play a shot that has a high likelihood of success but involves some risk. Inherent in this successful management of risk in this situation by a Tiger Woods, or Jack Nicklaus in the prior generation, is honest assessment of one's own abilities.

Another common problem facing people making decisions with risk is illustrated by what happened when the American League adopted the Designated Hitter rule in 1972. With this new rule in place, the American League pitchers no longer faced the direct consequences of throwing at hitters from the opposing team. As a result, the number of batters hit by American League pitchers went up relative to their National League counterparts.[12] In economics and insurance this is called a "moral hazard" problem—the circumstance where decision makers do not bear the full risks associated with their decisions and, as a result, take on more risk and expose others to additional risk. Insurance settings provide fertile ground because individual policy holders pay premiums based on the average risk of their group. This drives a wedge between their individual risk based on their decisions and the consequences of their actions. Individual policy holders end up engaging in riskier behavior, driving up claims and premiums for the group as a whole.

The problem is not limited to insurance settings. Any kind of business setting where an employee or manager does not bear the full consequence of risky activity poses the same dilemma. For example, the compensation for a CEO or CFO, although linked to changes in firm's net worth, may not be perfectly linked. In some cases, the CEO or CFO may not bear the full consequences of risky decisions. Especially in situations where company earnings are declining and the corporate officers begin to seek means to boost them in order to maintain their own employment, they may engage in activities that expose the company's shareholders to risks that they may not face themselves. Just as in the insurance case, a tradeoff exists between the benefits from limiting the exposure of policyholders or corporate executives to risk and the increase in the potential for moral hazard problems. Pooling risk in the form of insurance groups helps individuals to lower the likelihood of the inability of meeting large but infrequent expenses. All changes in stock value are not due to decisions of corporate officers. Providing some compensation to these executives that does not go up and down with the stock price is a way of the company reducing some of the risk of employment with the executives just as firms do with other employees. However, these policies also create the potential for the moral hazard outcomes.

Usually mentioned in the same context as moral hazard is the problem of adverse selection. When people or projects must be chosen with limited information, it is possible that the process of sorting through the alternatives tends to weed out the most desirable ones and leave in the least desirable ones. The essence of the problem is that the people making the selection decisions have less information than the people applying. For example, the work environment for assistant coaches is sometimes barely above indentured servitude. Assistant coaches often work extremely long hours and are compensated very little, at least in lower-level positions. While such a setting may weed out individuals who have little passion for coaching, it also tends to weed out individuals who have alluring employment alternatives. At the end of the day, the coaches who stick around long enough to land top-level assistant and head coaching positions may be people who have a passion for coaching but who also had few good alternatives.

The classic example in business of adverse selection involves bank loans. Typically, individuals or businesses who are deemed significant risks are charged higher interest rates to obtain loans. The trouble is that at some point, the only people who are willing to pay very high interest rates may be those who face dire financial straits. In the end, if the bank does not set some upper-end limit on rates or have some other kind of sorting mechanism other than the price of the loan, it will end up attracting a bad pool of loans with almost certain likelihood of default.

A final foundational aspect of risk and uncertainty is the ability to assess honestly and accurately one's own attitude toward risk as well as the attitudes of others. Most people prefer to take on less risk than more given an equal payoff, especially when substantial sums of money or risk of personal injury are at stake. This aversion to risk is much keener in some individuals than others. Because most people, including managers, are risk averse when faced with important decisions, it's easy to see why managers sometimes bias their thinking about tradeoffs in favor of the costs more easily measured or estimated.

Outside of sports, these same ways of thinking can help managers. For banks, knowing exactly what will happen to interest rates or checking balances held by customers is impossible, yet movements in these kinds of things can have important effects on the bottom line. In spite of the uncertainty, past experience and current conditions do permit an evaluation of likely changes on average, an idea of a range for typical changes, possible but unlikely changes, and changes with a likelihood only slightly above zero. They also permit the assessment of the symmetry or asymmetry of these likely changes. In laying out the possibilities in this kind of analytical way and incorporating them with simulation software, the bank's decision makers can steer clear of extreme policies that either place the bank at far too great a risk or that steer such a safe course as to significantly reduce earnings in almost any possible future state of the world.

SPILLED MILK

A final fundamental aspect of management considered here is an understanding of sunk costs. A basic tenet of managerial economics stresses an age-old proverb, "there is no use crying over spilled milk." Put simply, sunk costs should not influence current decisions. The logic is simple. Bygones should be treated as bygones. Costs and problems of the past that have no bearing on the present should be ignored when determining the best course of action for the future. While on its face, this idea seems so simple as to hardly warrant discussion, astute management of sunk costs is a subtle matter for two reasons. First, the seemingly transparent principle of looking to the costs ahead rather than those already sunk is not always so transparent in application. Second, beyond the problem of properly recognizing costs that are in fact sunk are the personal and organizational recriminations that may go with those sunk costs.

On the problem of recognizing sunk costs as sunk, an episode with Western Kentucky University football in the late 1980s and early 1990s illustrates the confusions that can occur. The athletic department made the decision to play only ten football games even though the NCAA permitted an eleven game schedule. The thinking was that the revenues from an additional game at home could not cover the cost of an additional game. The flaw in the thinking was that the decision makers were including costs that were already sunk into their decision calculus. Rather than looking ahead to include only the additional costs that would be incurred from playing another game—stadium preparation and cleaning, security, electricity, athletic tape, and a few other minor expenses—the athletic director included sunk costs into his estimate. His means of doing so was not obvious to him or others. He estimated the cost of a future game by taking the average cost over all games. The trouble is that the average cost across all games included expenses that were already sunk such as coaches' salaries and equipment. As it turned out, this inflated the average cost of future games substantially because most of the costs incurred by the program were sunk while the additional expenses of another game were only a small fraction of the average cost per game.

An important distinction for the consideration of costs is the difference between sunk and fixed costs. Sunk costs are gone forever. Fixed costs, on the other hand, may be unavoidable for a given time period, but avoidable when a longer period is considered. For example, when a team decides to sign a player to a long term contract, those monies are fixed for the length of the contract or until another team is willing to make a trade and relieve the original club of the liability. Barring a trade, the player's salary represents an unavoidable cost to the team for the length of the contract. Decisions about other players signed over this same time frame must be made with regard to the budget, expense, or benefits of those players for this time frame.

While managers make mistakes with regard to thinking about sunk and fixed costs, there is a more complicated side than is indicated by the "don't cry over spilled milk" proverb.[13] In a cool, dispassionate world where all people look ahead in making decisions, the proverb would be sufficient. However, that is not the world of real management. Sunk costs may represent bygone decisions but these decisions live on in the minds of people. Regret, embarrassment, or fear of a bad evaluation over bygone decisions frequently permit sunk costs to influence thinking about current decisions. Rather than "cutting bait" with the past decision and moving on to the decisions at hand, attempts may be made to justify the past expenditures by continuing or even increasing expenditures on those projects. At the extreme, attempts may be made to cover up the very existence of the past expenditures and decisions.

In sports, these kind of scenarios have played out many times with regard to personnel decisions. A coach positions a player at a key position or a general manager brings in a coach in whom he has supreme confidence. The player or coach fails miserably. Rather than treating the past decision as a poor one and trying to make decisions based on current and future circumstances, the coach or GM continues to try to justify the prior decision and may even become belligerent when questioned on the matter. In the end, the team suffers and the coach or GM may suffer personal consequences for the inability to deal dispassionately with the past decision. The dilemma is that the coach, GM, or any manager is always going to be evaluated on the basis of past performance. This creates an incentive to make past decisions look better and the avenue for the past decisions to influence future decisions. Beyond the organizational incentives that may lead to sunk costs leaking into future thinking, some people place great pressure on themselves over past decisions.

Another element that complicates the matter of sunk costs are expenditures on long-lived assets versus short-lived assets or perishable goods and services. A past expenditure on a long-lived asset represents an investment. While the expense may never be recovered in dollar terms, the asset provides a stream of service to the organization. This is what makes personnel decisions difficult for athletic teams. Players' skills develop over time and as they do, the team can reap long-term benefits by sticking with a player. In contrast, a sunk expenditure on a short-lived or perishable item yields no such long-term benefits and should have no bearing on decisions about the future. While this is clear enough, knowing when an expenditure on an investment has been a bad one that will not likely be recovered through the lifetime of the asset is not very clear. It leads to guesswork—sometimes sending players off too soon only to see them succeed on another team and sometimes sticking with players too long. That is the nature of investing in uncertain assets. The problem centered on here is the tendency on the part of decision makers to treat expenditures on clearly short-lived assets or perishable goods or services as investments. "How can I not go on that cruise, I've already paid for it." Ultimately, dealing with sunk costs is not merely about juggling around numbers and parts, but it is also about dealing with people—a topic explored more in Chapter 4.

REPLAY

1. Key elements of managing teams and organizations often involve basic tasks such as motivation, assessing costs and risks, or coordinating activities. Failure to grasp the subtleties of these basic tasks have been the downfall of many intelligent managers inside and outside of sports.

2. The goals of organizations and teams do not perfectly coincide with the goals of the individuals within them. Successful coaches and managers recognize this and even coaches such as Vince Lombardi used a variety of tools to align individual goals with team goals more closely.

3. Every decision entails costs beyond those on the income statement. Assessing these "hidden" costs accurately may make or break a manager as the Babe Ruth history illustrates.

4. Key components of management policy must be integrated with each other. Otherwise, the result is much like the Reds or Rangers who acquired baseball's best centerfielder or shortstop only to flounder in league standings.

5. The uncertainty of the future, along with its associated risks, does not mean that all future states of the world are equally likely. Paul Westhead's Loyola team showed how to establish the characteristics of uncertain outcomes and make risk a tool to be manipulated.

③ Managing Markets: NASCAR and Southwest Airlines?

Television exposure is so important to our program and so important to this university that we will schedule ourselves to fit the medium. I'll play at midnight, if that's what TV wants.

—Bear Bryant, former University of Alabama football coach

During the 1990s, NASCAR's popularity exploded to rival baseball, football, and basketball and to become, arguably, the biggest sports marketing story of the decade. Stock car racing started in the late 1940s and early 1950s on dirt tracks and beaches. By the late 1950s and early 1960s it drew from the infatuation with muscle cars to move into larger venues and become a more structured sport. Still, through the 1960s and 1970s the sport attained little more than novelty attention on programs such as ABC's *Wide World of Sports*. In terms of car racing on the whole, only the Indianapolis 500 attracted sizable television audiences in the United States. As late as the early 1980s, NASCAR appeared to face few opportunities to challenge the major players in sports entertainment, operating in out-of-the-way venues such as Talladega, Alabama, Darlington, North Carolina, and Martinsville, Virginia. It appeared to be no more of a national sporting influence than Australian Rules Football and little more than one step up from "tractor pulls" and "mud bogs."

As the eighties merged into the nineties, the world turned upside down. NASCAR attracted new fans in droves.[1] Figure 3.1 indicates that the racing circuit has gained a status on a par with the traditional major sports, at least as far as television fees go.

Figure 3.1
Annual Revenue from Television Contracts (in millions of $)

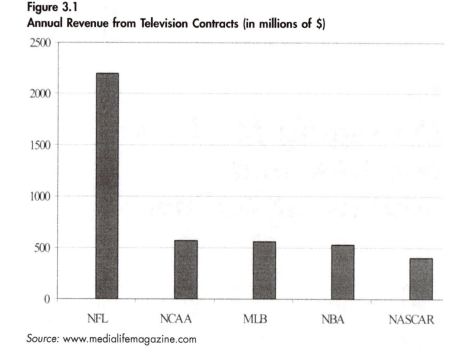

Source: www.medialifemagazine.com

By other measures, the growth of NASCAR is clear—attendance at Winston Cup events quadrupled from 1980 to 2000 and prize money to the points champion increased by a multiple of twenty in nominal terms. Even from 1990 to 2002, attendance at NASCAR events roughly doubled. By the late nineties, the "good ole boys" had moved beyond running their races in out-of-the-way places and mid-sized cities in southern states. New tracks and events popped up near major metropolitan areas including Dallas, Chicago, Boston, and Los Angeles. NASCAR's average TV ratings in recent years stands well ahead of MLB's rating and slightly above the NBA's. The 2002 Daytona 500 pulled a TV rating of 10.9 in comparison to 2000 NFL regular season shares of 10.7. The sport's most successful drivers such as Dale Earnhardt and Jeff Gordon, became as widely recognized and as wealthy as superstars in any professional sport. Joe Gibbs, an NFL coach with three Super Bowl rings, retired from football and purchased ownership of a racing team—a move that left many fans as well as observers in the sports media dumbfounded and thinking that Gibbs would only use the stock car ownership stint as a brief sabbatical before returning to football. In fact, his return to football took ten years.

Whether through NASCAR or other examples, the sports industry provides an open laboratory for examining the relationship between a product and its market including the decisions, accidents, and outcomes that shape this relationship. Names such as Roone Arledge, Bill Veeck, Lamar Hunt, Pete Rozelle, Tex Schramm, and David Stern are closely linked to the history and legend of market making of sports teams and leagues. The questions faced by these sports and media owners and managers precisely mirror the questions facing typical business managers. What are we going to make and sell? How broadly or narrowly are we going to define our product? How we are we going to package and distribute our product? What are we going to emphasize in promotions and advertisements? What changes will we consider in order to encourage repeat customers as well as to draw and develop new customers?[2]

WHY DO GAMES MATTER?

Baseball's 2002 All-Star Game attracted considerable but undesired attention because of an unprecedented tie, where the teams ran out of pitchers. MLB Commissioner Bud Selig displayed obvious frustration in front of the TV cameras as the two league managers explained the situation to him prior to the last inning. The fans went far beyond Selig in voicing their frustration when informed of the decision. The outcome became a public relations fiasco for the league as talking heads on television and writers in newspapers debated the nature of the All-Star classic and prompted changes to its structure, ultimately hinging home field advantage in the World Series on the outcome of the game.

In reality, the embarrassment to MLB had been in the works for at least a decade as the "production" of the game lost touch with consumer value. Historically, the game featured elite players from both leagues who played the game as if the outcome really mattered. In the era of Willie Mays and Hank Aaron, star players stayed in the game for several innings if not the entire game. The best pitchers frequently threw for two or three inning stretches. By the early nineties, the game began to play out differently. Star players would start the game, get an at-bat, play a couple of innings, and then exit the ballpark to depart on private jets, if they had not skipped the game altogether due to some minor injury. Lesser known players began to play as many or more innings as the biggest stars. Managers of the game began to be or at least feel pressured to play all of the position players on the roster. Maybe most telling, the players openly referred to the game as an "exhibition"—by which they meant to imply something akin to a softball game at the company picnic.

What the players overlooked along with the league executives in twiddling their thumbs while the All-Star Game devolved is the fact that all baseball games—even Game 7 of the World Series—are exhibitions. Baseball games and all sporting events played in large stadiums and televised across the nation exist only for the purpose of entertaining fans who are willing to spend money to see the games or support them by watching the games on television with the attendant advertising revenues. The games attract fans not because war and peace hang in the balance, but because fans root for their teams as if it did, and the players play as if it did. That is the very core of the value that sports provides as an entertainment vehicle whether it is the Super Bowl, the NCAA basketball Final Four, the World Series, or MLB's All-Star Game. Watching players, even elite players, horse around in an "exhibition" and then decide to go home because the hour is late does not provide much entertainment value to fans. Baseball games do not hang in the air with their value determined by some kind of philosophical debate by the likes of Howard Cosell or Bob Costas. Game 7 of the World Series or the Super Bowl are not intrinsically more valuable than any other game. It is all a matter of the importance that baseball consumers, all summed together, place on the event. Historically, fans had highly valued baseball's All-Star Game much more than the all-star games from other sports, and the players and managers played it accordingly. Without a change in the basic value that consumers placed on the game, there was no reason for MLB to devalue it, but that is exactly what began to happen during the 1990s.

The All-Star Game episode is just one example of where the people involved in producing a sporting event lost sight of what it is that they are really doing. Maybe Dick Allen, an All-Star caliber baseball player of the 1960s and 1970s, most clearly expressed the backwards understanding of sports as entertainment when he said that he wished that games could be played with the fans and media locked out of the stadium. Similar attitudes toward those making decisions regarding products and markets are frequently observed in sports. Coaches—the rough equivalent of production and operations managers in nonsports businesses—sometimes openly vent their hostility toward "front office" decision makers. The front office people making decisions about products and markets are somehow greedy money grubbers because they mess around with the games in order to try to make more money. Sports traditionalists among fans and media express similar views of the marketing decisions and the people making them, "the suits," blaming them for steering the attention of fans away from the game itself with gimmicks and sideshows, or worse, by tinkering with the rules of the games in order to try to stir fan interest.

The "jockacracy" inside of sports probably contributes to the tendency for players and coaches to not see themselves as entertainers in the entertainment industry. After all, a growling and sweating middle linebacker hardly presents the same picture as Britney Spears prancing around a video or on stage. Most players would not take well to the comparison. Instead, they frequently see themselves living in their own world where the tackles they make or the home runs that they hit are valuable in and of themselves apart from their entertainment value. It is this kind of thinking that leads coaches to go on diatribes about cheerleaders, music, scheduling, and other matters they find bothersome. In their minds, the actions of players and coaches create value independent of consumer reaction. To be fair, many athletes and coaches understand their role as entertainers, but the sports-as-entertainment outlook frequently gets buried beneath macho and personal agendas.

Yet, without fans who highly value the entertainment offered, no sports star would make $10 million per year. No coach would become a celebrity whose advice was sought on leadership, running a business, or any other matter. College coaches are often the worst to express views that seem to view their jobs as existing in a vacuum. They live in a world where the players turnover regularly so the coach becomes the celebrity in an environment that blends education and entertainment. Despite the not-for-profit organizational setting of college sports, no one can deny that it is a money-driven entertainment business. The fan who shows up along with 18,000 others to watch a Knicks game attends the game for the same reason that the fan shows up with 30,000 others at the Carrier Dome in Syracuse to watch the Orangemen play. Syracuse's Jim Boeheim's players are providing exactly the same entertainment that the Knicks' players are providing—the difference lies only in how the dollars are distributed. How long would a university such as Indiana have endured an abrasive figure such as a Bob Knight if college basketball were more like intramural games and attracted only 20 people?

Surprisingly, this disconnection between decisions regarding the product or service being offered and the production of the product or service also occurs in business settings as well as in the study of management decisions. Although widely recognized as part of the business landscape, marketing decisions and personnel are sometimes viewed with suspicion if not outright contempt. In everyday businesses, executives on the operations–production side often belittle marketing personnel, seeing them on occasion as merely sucker fish living off the more substantial efforts of others—after all, marketing executives do not make anything, they just sell what others make or so the thinking goes. In fact, managers often fall in love with their skills in overseeing people, production processes, or financial practices of companies or in hammering out deals with other companies to the point of forgetting who really drives the wagon—buyers who are willing to shell out money for whatever is being offered. Among academics, faculty in areas such as finance, accounting, and economics occasionally diminish the efforts of marketing faculty because of perceived shallowness and lack of rigor.

Despite these unflattering views of the personnel who make decisions regarding markets or of marketing as a discipline, the very core of successfully managing a business centers on making sound decisions concerning bringing value to consumers through a combination of attributes of the product or service including, but not limited to, the price.[3] In the big picture, marketing, at least in the best sense of the term, zeroes in on the connection between customers and these product or service attributes, collecting and deciphering information about markets and the connection (or lack of it) between the product and the consumer. Without proper marketing decisions, the operations side of a business, for all its seeming alleged substance, amounts to little more than the production of unsold goods or unwanted services. Companies with great products but marginal operations can still succeed, where those with great operations but marginal products rarely do. This fact holds true whether the business under consideration produces automobiles or provides entertainment in the form of athletic events. Viewed in this light, the discussion of innovating new methods considered in more detail in Chapter 7 is really just an extension of this discussion of the ongoing challenge of matching products and services to markets.

While it might seem that these kinds of points would go without saying, managers inside and outside of sports often lose sight of the central importance of the product or service. As with the All-Star game, the lack of attention to the product sometimes occurs due to a series of events, such as labor bargaining agreements that steer the focus of both labor and management away from the ultimate source of value to both. In other circumstances, egos of managers are inflated by success to the point that they fall in love with their own skills and forget to consider consumers. On other occasions, it may stem from nothing more complicated than laziness. Success begins to breed shirking and inattention. In any and all of these cases, managers have failed to give due attention to a continual emphasis on product or service.

TAPPING LATENT MARKETS

Finding ways to offer value to customers sometimes involves big technological leaps or radically new products. NASCAR's emergence as a major player on the U.S. sports scene is both interesting and astounding because it involves neither of these. As with many successful enterprises, stock car racing benefited from the missteps of its competitors. NASCAR tapped into consumers whom the existing Madison Avenue and Armani-clad league executives of the NBA, MLB, and NFL ignored, even though they were producing similar kinds of entertainment services. It would be mistake to credit all of NASCAR's success to great market-based decision making. No doubt, NASCAR's growth may owe as much to serendipity as to insight and foresight. In part, they stumbled into their success doing much of what they had been doing before it grew in popularity. Yet, being in the right place at the right time is no crime and is frequently part of the story of successful business ventures.

The NASCAR customer has evolved over the years. Even though some might still define the consumer base for NASCAR as solely a bunch of Southern rednecks, the customer base has grown beyond good-ole-boy homemade mechanics from Alabama and North Carolina. While the clientele is not dominated by citizens of the Hamptons, about 40 percent are reported to have college experience, almost 60 percent are under 45 years of age, and nearly 40 percent are female.[4] They are the result of the massive economic expansion in America starting around 1982 and proceeding through the 1990s. Pundits and social critics tended to fixate on how this boom loaded the pockets of corporate executives and affluent suburbanites from large metropolitan areas who sank their growing fortunes into stadium luxury suites, granite countertops in their sprawling new homes, trips to The Gap, expensive restaurants, and exotic vacations. These same writers often lamented the supposed stagnation of incomes for the middle class and below. However, these writers were much like NASCAR's competitors in that they were missing out on an economic transformation among America's rank and file. By the late 1990s, the stagnation of the middle class began to be exposed as more folklore than fact.[5] The burgeoning economy pumped up incomes in mid-sized cities, working-class suburbs, small towns, and rural locations across the country just as it was enriching those on the upper end of the income spectrum. Just like their wealthier neighbors, these working-class consumers searched for entertainment venues to spend their fattening pocketbooks, and NASCAR provided a custom fit.

Counting precisely the number of people and incomes of people comprising this group of middle-class suburbanites, mid-sized and small city dwellers, and rural residents is not easy because Census figures are not broken down along these lines. Still, ballpark estimates are possible. Out of the 280 million people in America, about 60 million people live outside of metropolitan areas—a sizable number of people itself. More telling, though, only about 100 million people live in the twenty largest metropolitan areas, and of these, only about 20 million live in the core of these cities. Beyond population alone, the working class in America carries substantial clout in terms of income. About four-fifths of U.S. households, comprising about 225 million individuals, make less than $75,000 per year, and three-fifths, covering about 170 million individuals, make less than $50,000 per year.

The bottom line is the size of this group of consumers who reside outside of the largest urban centers and below the most affluent income levels is huge, numbering between 100 million to 200 million. Moreover, even though these families may not own time share condominiums on Maui, their economic muscle became considerable during the 1990s. Some of the increased financial wherewithal went into new or larger homes, new cars and pick-up trucks, bigger televisions, and the like. The economic upsurge also began to evidence itself in the leisure expenditures outside of their homes. Almost half of U.S. food expenditures are for food outside the home. Mega-outlet malls began to spring up across the country in locations such as Woodbridge, Virginia (near Washington, DC), Grapevine, Texas (near Dallas), Tempe, Arizona (near Phoenix), and many others. Vacation destinations for working-class families exploded in places such as Orlando, Atlantic City, the panhandle of Florida, near the Smokey Mountains, and many others.

The combination of millions of potential fans with money and time to burn lit the NASCAR fuse. NASCAR offered a ready-made target for these consumers to indulge their sporting preferences and a clear alternative to the traditional big-time sports. Probably no greater contrast could exist than the one between NASCAR and the NBA. NASCAR and its clientele represented nearly everything that the NBA was not. The NBA pushed a slick, ultra-hip, urban, star-powered image both on-the-court and in its promotions. NASCAR fed fans a down-to-earth, driver-mechanic-next-door image. With little doubt, racial composition factored into the consumer equation also. Black players dominated the NBA while NASCAR was very, very white. Yet, race comprises only one part of a broader story. To lean on race alone as the key factor simplifies the story far too much. A league such as the NBA and NASCAR offered opposite cultural alternatives— ultra-urban, celebrity-focused versus working-class suburban, small-town, or rural.

Beyond the cultural differences, the enormous financial success of the NBA and the other traditional "major" sports spawned negative by-products. In many respects, the leagues became victimized by their own success. Through the 1960s and much of the 1970s, star athletes in professional sports made above average but not astronomical salaries. For instance, in the mid-1960s, two Hall of Fame pitchers, Sandy Koufax and Don Drysdale, held out of spring training until management agreed to salaries in the $100,000 range—a large sum of money but not an amount to place them among the highest rollers of society. Growth in television audiences, along with live attendance and free agency, vaulted salaries to un-precedented levels. The contrast can be seen by the fact that a solid but not spectacular short stop for the Oakland Athletics, Walt Weiss, made more money in the nineties than the sum of the salaries for the starting eight po-sition players for the Athletics championship teams of the early 1970s. The average salary in MLB by the turn of the century stood close to one mil-lion dollars with star-caliber players hauling in tens of millions per year.

As a result of these changes, by the 1990s competitions in the tradition-ally dominant sports took place between millionaires who stood apart from the common man not just in athletic ability but in behavior and attitude. The heroes among legendary sports figures such as Joe Louis, Babe Ruth, Joe DiMaggio, Willie Mays, Hank Aaron, Mickey Mantle, Wilt Chamber-lain, Bill Russell, Michael Jordan, Larry Bird, Magic Johnson, Johnny Uni-tas, and Jerry Rice had been replaced by anti-heroes such as Mike Tyson, Allen Iverson, Barry Bonds, Randy Moss, and Ray Lewis. These star play-ers exalted in petulance and posturing if not outright criminal activity. No doubt, expanded press coverage over athletes' lives alters the public's image of current players relative to some of the earlier players, but nonetheless, many star players in the major sports struck fans as aloof if not altogether spoiled. Beyond the problems of aloof athletes and lack of effort, the fi-nancial success of the major sports leagues presented a source of dispute that tarnished the players not tarnished with this kind of image, the on and off disputes between millionaire players and billionaire owners turned off fans. MLB suffered strikes and work stoppages in 1981 and 1994, even canceling the World Series in 1994. The NFL used replacement players for the first part of the 1982 season.

By comparison, NASCAR's heroes came across as the guy-next-door-made-good. They might push and shove each other over race tactics, but they showed up for work, drove their cars hard, and exhibited interest in and respect for their fans. In contrast, whether out of a sense of privilege or just as a justifiable response to the crush put on them as celebrities, su-perstar athletes in other sports frequently gave signals indicating that they represented an aristocratic elite with fans as their admiring and subservient peasants.

Ironically, now NASCAR has grown to the point where it may begin to face some of the issues that tarnished other sports. With growth in money, will NASCAR be able to hold on to its guy-next-door image or will its driv-ers begin to exhibit the spoiled-rich-athlete syndrome? Some would suggest that the emergence of figures such as Tony Stewart as a Winston Cup cham-pion may have already signaled a new era. Although drivers such as Richard Petty or Dale Earnhardt may have had a tough-as-nails reputation on the race course, they were endearing to many fans off of the race course.

Stewart, in contrast, whether on purpose or as an accident, developed the reputation as temperamental personality on and off the race course, finding himself in scrapes with reporters and other drivers that have brought reprimands and probations from both NASCAR and his primary sponsor—The Home Depot.

Beyond the missteps of other sports entities, NASCAR also benefited from evolving tastes of American consumers, especially those outside the Harvard Club. Before NASCAR exploded, professional wrestling had already grown out of its sideshow status and blossomed into a television phenomenon during the 1980s. Its growth signaled changes in tastes as well as the growing economic power of nonurban working families and individuals. The WWF and WCW started drawing large audiences by offering a combination of staged violence coupled with realism, athleticism, and, ultimately, sex. In this context, NASCAR's emergence as an entertainment force tapped into the same sort of extreme-entertainment of professional wrestling by offering the life-on-the-edge appeal of thirty men driving inches from each other at nearly 200 miles per hour.

While the details of the sports share little in common, the growth of the NHL during the 1990s probably owes itself to some of the same forces that have vaulted NASCAR into the spotlight. Until the 1990s, the NHL labored in relative obscurity in the United States. With several teams in Canada and no teams in the south or southwestern part of the United States, the sport hardly seemed poised for growth. To be sure, it had an avid following in Canada and parts of the northeast, but few people outside these regions followed the sport, knew much of its rules, or could recognize its athletes. The move of the NHL's most prolific and recognizable player, Wayne Gretzky, from the Edmonton Oilers to the Los Angeles Kings in 1988 definitely stirred interest in Los Angeles, especially with Gretzky leading the team to the Stanley Cup Finals in 1993. Many NHL insiders and observers credit his move to a major market outside of traditional hockey territory as saving the sport and positioning it to expand. Attributing the NHL's growth in popularity to Gretzky's move to LA exaggerates its importance and overlooks the market dynamics at work. No doubt, Gretzky's relocation attracted a lot more attention to hockey in the mega-media market of LA, but it would be an overstatement to suggest that this made much difference outside of Southern California. Instead, the economic growth of the working class mentioned above provided sports fans in many more cities with the financial wherewithal to support hockey in addition to creating millionaires and billionaires who could bid teams away from smaller markets in the United States and Canada.

Beyond the income influence, though, the NHL also benefited from the same heightened interest in "extreme sports" entertainment as did pro wrestling and NASCAR. Although a game with players of great skating and stick handling skill, hockey is a game that has traditionally attracted a working-class following. Moreover, while the league has adopted rules to limit bench clearing brawls, it still supports fighting as a means of attracting and entertaining fans. Whereas fighting leads to expulsion and sometimes suspension in basketball, baseball, and even football, it generates little more of a penalty in hockey—4 minutes—than holding a player illegally or interfering with the goalie—2 minutes. The NHL's limitation vis-á-vis NASCAR, though, is that hockey does not transfer very well to television. In terms of live attendance, hockey holds its own with the other team sports, but the speed of the puck makes viewing on television difficult, so that the fact that NASCAR has left the NHL in its television dust is not surprising in spite of similarities in the demographics of their fan bases. This topic of television and the NHL is discussed more later in the chapter. The league now finds itself mired in a labor dispute.

The lessons of these sports examples for managers at large is that untapped markets lay ready for someone to meet the needs of consumers in those markets. In a growing economy, people are looking for places to spend their money. Consumers, sometimes millions of them, are overlooked by seemingly well-managed companies. Southwest Airlines might be one of the most obvious cases that parallels a NASCAR. The company was completely off the radar screen of the airline industry when it started flying routes between Dallas, Houston, and San Antonio in 1971 and as it expanded to other Texas cities in the 1970s. Even as it expanded to cities such New Orleans, St. Louis, and Chicago during the 1980s, it was viewed as a minor, regionally-oriented carrier. Much like NASCAR, the company exploded during the 1990s, expanding to serve over fifty cities with 2,500-plus flights per day and revenues increasing from $1 billion in 1990 to over $5.5 billion per in 2002.[6]

Much has been made of particular parts of their formula for success—short-haul, point-to-point flights with high frequency, low ticket prices, quick turnarounds, utilization of many "second-tier" airports, casual ambience, and employee recruitment and development. Each of these tactics is interesting by itself, especially the point-to-point route system that flaunted and continues to flaunt the hub-and-spoke system practiced by other major airlines. However, focusing on a single element or two of their operations misses the bigger picture being emphasized in this chapter and what links them with the NASCAR story—their ability to find a marketplace full of millions of consumers with money to spend right under the noses of existing producers. Like NASCAR, the product being offered involved no important technological breakthrough or practice that would be admired (at the outset) by the *Harvard Business Review*. Instead, the success that Southwest found was available to almost any existing airline, but just like NASCAR's competitors, United, American, Delta, and the other major carriers were too busy dividing up an existing pie to develop other parts of the marketplace, to worry themselves with these consumers, or with the operational changes needed to make the product appealing to them.

Yet, consumers are not held by force. Market success can be very transient. Successful companies can quickly lose customers or lose out on potential customers by not managing their success in a way that continues to see consumers as the driving force of value for the company. MLB is a prime example in sports of this problem while business entities such as IBM and The Gap learned this lesson the hard way in the late 1980s and 1990s. Bill Gates and Microsoft also illustrate the slipperiness of grasping changing market conditions. He accurately anticipated the explosion in microcomputing and positioned Microsoft to take advantage of it. Yet, a few years later, he underestimated the Internet revolution, a mistake Microsoft quickly worked to rectify.[7] Those experiences show that even for forward-looking managers and companies, managing to the marketplace is not all or even mostly about holding the best divining rod or "vision." In the long term, possessing the ability to quickly recognize mistakes and adapt to changing markets is critical—a subject of more attention in Chapter 7.

RISK TAKING

In spite of the success of NASCAR and the NHL, successful marketing requires more than recognizing trends in consumer sentiment. Vince McMahon, owner of professional wrestling's WWF, decided to go after more of the extreme sports dollar by offering a spiked version of football called the XFL. Most of the basic rules would be the same as the NFL but with a few exceptions intended to increase excitement and entertainment value. The executives at NBC liked the idea and heavily promoted its first season during the spring of 2001. Unfortunately for the XFL and NBC, consumers did not care for the experience very much. After the initial weekend of games, viewership dropped off precipitously and NBC did not renew the league's contract for 2002.

Forty years before the XFL, a group of businessmen pieced together another fledgling football association, calling it the American Football League (AFL). The idea then was also to offer fans a more exciting alternative to the relatively sedate NFL. Like the XFL, the AFL tried to market its product primarily in cities that had been ignored by the NFL including Buffalo, Boston, Houston, Dallas, and Denver. They did place teams in the megamarket of New York as well as across the bay from San Francisco in Oakland and in Los Angeles. By 1962, the Dallas team moved to Kansas City and the Los Angeles team to San Diego. The league got off to an inauspicious beginning vis-á-vis its older rival. In 1960, the AFL averaged only 16,000 spectators per contest versus the NFL's 40,000. Even by 1963, the numbers had only grown to around 20,000 per game. By 1964, though, the league started to catch on with fans in increasing numbers. By 1965, they averaged more than 31,000 per game and had signed an agreement with the NFL that would lead to the first Super Bowl in January 1967 and a full merger by the 1970 season. During the last season in which the AFL operated as a separate league, it crossed the 40,000 fans per game threshold.

Why did the AFL succeed where so many other sports league ventures after it have failed including the XFL, WFL, and USFL? Details of the AFL history have been recorded in books and documentaries. Because the AFL succeeded, it is easy to cast the AFL success into a positive light while discrediting the efforts of McMahon as an ill-conceived venture by a media huckster. Yet, the contemporary evaluations of Lamar Hunt and his co-owners in the AFL were often as scathing as those directed toward McMahon. Like the AFL and unlike the WFL and USFL, McMahon did not start his league by trying to compete for high-profile NFL players at NFL level salaries. Instead, he tried to start primarily with marginal NFL players and rejects and instituted strict salary containment measures. In spite of these efforts, the venture failed because it was unable to sustain enough of an audience.

This uncertainty about the specific product or service offerings that will spark consumer interest is at the very heart of what makes start-up business ventures risky. In trying to get a handle on the combination of product attributes that builds value among consumers, academic study has laid out only the broad boundaries. Depending on the kind of data used, about 40 to 60 percent of consumer purchases tend to be driven by price of the product itself, prices of closely related products, expectations of these prices in the future, and consumer income. While a good start, a lot of the specific details influencing consumers come from other sources. The trouble is, that once the study of consumer sentiment goes beyond these basic influences, it becomes more difficult to come up with generalities. This does not imply a lack of effort given to the accumulation and analyzing of data. Just the opposite happens—data analysis takes place *ad nauseam*. Businesses highly value the information collected and studied by marketers that tries to make sense of demographic factors as well as psychological nuances. Focus groups, consumer surveys, test markets, and other methods are employed to ever refine the level of knowledge about what makes consumers tick.

In spite of an accumulation of data and analysis of it, finding reliable, general conclusions on which to base product and marketing decisions remains the search for the Holy Grail. It is not a lack of data in some cases, but just the fact that consumer responses are not always consistent. While the price of a good, such as a ticket or income changes may exhibit relatively stable effects on purchases over several years, the influence of a particular product attribute or characteristic may be more fleeting. As a result, many key marketing decisions boil down to a shot in the dark.

The entrepreneur whose seemingly good idea succeeds may eventually be built into an object of admiration and clairvoyance. His opinions become revered pearls of wisdom appearing on book jackets, periodicals, and on televised interviews. However, the difference between his success and the anonymous entrepreneur whose seemingly good idea flopped may boil down to little more than luck. Both were willing to take risks. Both may have done as much planning and homework as feasible. Both may have been financially responsible and utilized effective production methods, yet one succeeded and one failed, as with the AFL and the XFL. For high-ego, driven people in business or sports, suggesting the difference between a marketing success and failure owes much to luck is heresy. Nevertheless, when choices reflect hunches about consumer appetites in the near and distant future, it would seem that too often the difference between success and failure is over-rationalized. In the end, new business ventures and significant changes in strategy require risk taking, planning, and then plenty of good fortune.

MYOPIA AND MEGALOMANIA

In the 1980s, NBA fortunes turned around. The waning fan interest and TV revenues turned into growing billions. The renewal of the rivalry between the Los Angeles Lakers and the Boston Celtics sparked fan and media interest along with the superstar appeal of Magic Johnson from the Lakers and Larry Bird from the Celtics. In 1984 Michael Jordan entered the league and dazzled onlookers with his acrobatic skills and lightning-quick moves. Although his teams did not experience a great deal of success during the 1980s, the league under David Stern began to center its marketing efforts more and more on Jordan and a few other stars. During the 1990s, Jordan's Chicago Bulls won six championships and with no consistent team rival, Jordan became *the* marketing vehicle for the league.

After the 1999 championship series, Jordan retired (for the second but not last time). The league had already been searching for heirs to take over the marketing poster-boy mantle after Jordan, such as Shaquille O'Neil of the Lakers or Allen Iverson of the 76ers. However, no one captured the public's fancy to nearly the extent that Jordan had. The league that had lived by Jordan for a decade now was not necessarily dying without him, but it suffered from a bad cold. Without a great rivalry among teams such as the Celtics and Lakers, the marketing of the league as competition between teams had taken a backseat to a star-based marketing strategy. Now without *the* star, the league struggled to retain customers.

The NBA's experience illustrates a fundamental principle discussed back in Chapter 2 and applicable here to marketing strategy—recognizing and effectively managing tradeoffs. The tradeoff faced in this context is between a narrow-focus marketing strategy and a broad-focus strategy. Managers easily become entranced on one side and not recognize the tradeoff. The tendency to become too narrowly focused and not take advantage of broader business opportunities closely related to your original focus was emphasized by Theodore Levitt, former *Harvard Business Review* editor. He coined the term "Marketing Myopia" for this problem and used it as his book title. He cites examples such as the railroad industry which suffered because it did not recognize that it focused too narrowly on traditional rail service rather than realizing its real service was transportation. Likewise, the movie industry dragged its feet on entering the video market because it also viewed its product too narrowly—insisting it was about in-theater movie making rather than more broadly in the business of entertaining people through all kinds of film and video products. In the sports industry, horseracing tracks fell prey to the same narrow-mindedness in their initial opposition to the simulcasting of races. Rather than seeing simulcasting as a means to widen their market base, they saw it as a threat to live attendance.

Long before the NBA's marketing coup on a league-wide basis, Tex Schramm led the Dallas Cowboys from a winless new franchise in 1960 to a sport entertainment powerhouse by broadening the appeal of the team. The two hard-luck losses to the Green Bay Packers in the 1966 and 1967 NFL Championship games helped to boost the team into the limelight. Schramm paid attention to the essentials of securing a talented coach along with gifted players. Yet, he pursued many angles to set the team apart other than its performance. He adopted sleeker uniforms, scantily-attired cheerleaders, and other attention-grabbing ideas.

The moves by the Cowboys during the 1960s and 1970s as well as the NBA during the 1980s and early 1990s fall in line with ideas promoted by Levitt. He stresses the importance of a business constantly asking itself, "what are we in the business of doing." While sports traditionalists might roll their eyes at modernized uniforms, cheerleaders, halftime rock concerts or time-out skits, the evolution of a team or a league from merely a sports competition to broad-based entertainment vehicle seemed to make financial sense. The NBA appeared to gain consumers and David Stern gifted with a golden touch when the league steered toward broadening its appeal beyond merely the competition between teams and into an entertainment based entity emphasizing star players, entertaining half-time and time-out shows and music. During the 2001 championship series between the Lakers and the 76ers, the league took this progression into full-service entertainment one step further by presenting a live concert performance during halftime of one of the games.

The trouble is that executives can go so far in expanding the scope of the products or services offered that they lose sight of the implicit trade-off in this expansion. As with most any business decision, there is usually a point beyond which further expansion of the scope of the business will reduce value. In fact, short term successes may lead to an overvaluation of the benefits. One might call this "market megalomania." Sometimes narrowing the business strategy rather than expanding it will build additional value among a customer base. Coca-Cola stands out as a prime example. The company had broadened its scope during the 1970s. In the 1980s, the company refocused its efforts around being a worldwide soft drink provider, and the company's value soared as a result. Using this episode as a template would lead the NBA in the opposite direction that it is currently headed. Rather than trying to duplicate or even broaden what might have been a unique period with Michael Jordan during the 1990s, the league might gain from refocusing its attention and marketing efforts toward its historical core—the competition between teams.

In the sports world, success by pursuing a focused strategy has precedent. The NCAA, especially with regard to its basketball tournament, illustrates the benefits of a narrow strategy. Although a not-for-profit entity, the NCAA and its member schools for practical purposes operate much like any professional sports league except for the fact that players are not explicitly paid. As a sports business entity, it has been tremendously successful by developing and focusing on the competition between member basketball teams. The NCAA tournament has grown into a part of national culture—"March Madness." Between office pools, online contests, and wall-to-wall television coverage, the three-week event generates attention rivaling anything in professional sports by placing emphasis on nothing more than the win-you-advance, lose-you-go-home competition between teams. The tournament began in 1939 with only eight teams. By the 1970s, the field had expanded to 32 teams, but still the event attracted little attention beyond the Final Four except for the fans of teams directly involved.

Only from the early 1980s onward has the end-of-season tournament began to grow into a cross-country cultural happening. The growth of cable television provided the technological impetus. Before the 1980s, fans across

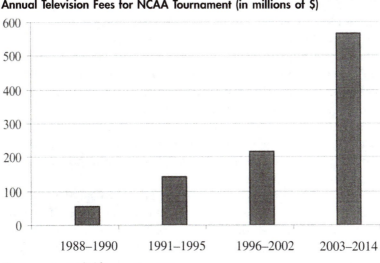

Figure 3.2
Annual Television Fees for NCAA Tournament (in millions of $)

Source: www.medialifemagazine.com

the country would find only limited coverage of early round games. Cable TV and coverage by ESPN brought the entire tournament into focus for fans regardless of geographic location and "cut-aways" to close games heightened the drama and underdog story lines. The tournament grew in size from to 40 teams in 1979, to 48 teams in 1980, and finally to 64 teams in 1985. The television contracts soon reflected the expanded fan interest. Figure 3.2 shows the growth of the television revenue from the tournament over the last 15 years from less than $60 million per year in the late 1980s to now almost $600 million per year. In terms of the point about marketing being under consideration here, the NCAA and college basketball stands in vivid contrast to the NBA. While the NBA pushed individual stars and nonbasketball entertainment, NCAA basketball presented team competition.

For executives, these episodes identify the importance of avoiding extremes. Whether in railroads or football, company strategies can be so nearsighted and narrow-minded that they miss out on developing closely related products and services or fail to make appropriate adjustments in their product as technology changes. In the other direction, executives who taste success by expanding their horizons have often become too far-sighted, imagining synergies at every turn where none, in fact, exist. The 1960s, 1970s, and 1990s saw a large number of conglomerate mergers, such as General Mills and Parker Brothers in 1968 or Time, Warner Communications, and Turner Broadcasting, based on supposed synergies that turned out to be merely illusory.

INCREASING VERSUS DIVIDING THE PIE?

Three decades before the growth of NASCAR, the emergence of the NFL as a major player in entertainment also combined luck with a bit of entrepreneurship to tap huge unfolding markets. Entering the 1950s, the NFL lagged far beyond Major League Baseball in attendance and national interest. The emergence of television set the table for a breakthrough by the league in that the essence of the game translated well onto television as college football had already shown. The nationally televised 1958 NFL championship game between the Colts and Giants that went into overtime is often credited with the birth of the NFL into a new era of popularity and exposure through television.

In spite of standing on the brink of a market breakthrough, the NFL hesitated to capitalize fully by moving into new population centers. This foot-dragging by the NFL opened the door for the American Football League. Rather than seeing the AFL as an entity capable of tapping into the football interests of millions of Americans, NFL owners largely viewed it as a financially unstable kid brother likely to fold soon. The NFL owners were much more concerned with dividing their pie than in seeing and grasping the opportunity to increase it. By 1965, though, this kid brother had grown into a major rival. The New York Jets signed University of Alabama quarterback Joe Namath for the seemingly outlandish sum of $425,000. Art Modell, owner of the Cleveland Browns, thought the salary to be only a publicity stunt. Yet, in his first season, Namath's Jets doubled attendance from 20,000 to 40,000 per game, not only providing plenty of money to support Namath's salary but giving the league a permanent foothold versus the NFL. Within a year, the NFL owners agreed to a merger with the AFL that would begin with interleague championship after the 1966 season and culminate in full integration by 1970.

What the NFL owners probably saw as a surrender ultimately accomplished what they had been unwilling to do on their own—expand the league to take advantage of emerging markets. A second team in New York as well as teams in places such as Denver, Oakland, Miami, and Kansas City did not hurt the league. Instead, it brought in a boatload of new consumers. The final step in setting the NFL on the course to the top of sports entertainment was another way to tap untapped markets. Often Roone Arledge of ABC sports is credited with the birth of Monday Night Football. While his production of it broke new ground, NFL Commissioner Pete Rozelle was the one to envision that a Monday Night primetime telecast of the league would broaden the league's markets. Many owners and the networks had scoffed at the idea. Rozelle was right on the mark, however, in seeing that the future of sports as a revenue generator lay in making it a television presence.

The NFL's experience reflects a constant challenge for unit managers within a single business entity, parties to business relationship, whether competitors linked in a joint venture, managers of units of an organization, or personnel involved in management–labor relations. The challenge is to try to keep focused on increasing the size of the overall pie rather than just fixating on how the pie is divided. Because leagues usually divide up monopolies over professional competitions in their specific sport in a particular area, owners often cannot resist the urge to become fixated on protecting their wedge of the monopoly pie. Interestingly, even many observers and analysts of sports also get entangled in the obsession with brokering the slices rather than making the pie bigger. Yet, the monopoly power of a specific sports franchise is not broad. Instead, in the marketplace each team faces competition from other sports leagues as well as other forms of entertainment and recreation. Ultimately, even with some flexibility granted by their limited monopolies, teams and leagues must pay attention to customers in order to pad their own pockets.

This is not widely recognized because sports leagues are so often seen as such different creatures from other kinds of business relationships. However, they are really not so different. Many businesses become overly concerned with the breakdown of market share between themselves and their closest competitors so much so that they can lose sight of the effects of their decisions on the market and their competitors more broadly considered. Similarly, a company can become so embroiled in disputes regarding the shares of revenue divided up among management, labor, and ownership that it loses sight of the objective—increasing revenue for all the groups involved.

Probably few matters reflect this fixation on slicing up a given pie more than competitive balance and free agency in MLB. Much has been made of the New York Yankees championship run from 1996 to 2001. Over that time frame, they appeared in five World Series, winning four of them. In assessing the "competitive balance" in baseball a "Blue Ribbon Panel" established by Congress determined that such balance was lacking, basing their finding on this recent Yankee run. For some reason, the panel failed to take into account or have any interest in the Yankees experience from 1981 to 1996, when they went without a visit to the World Series and took only one trip to the playoffs. Likewise, from 1982 through 2002, the Los Angeles Dodgers made only one trip to the playoffs and one to the World Series. From 1980–2002, the New York Mets visited the World Series only two times. In contrast, the Oakland Athletics made three trips, the San

Figure 3.3
Percentage of Pennants Won by Teams from New York or Los Angeles by Decade

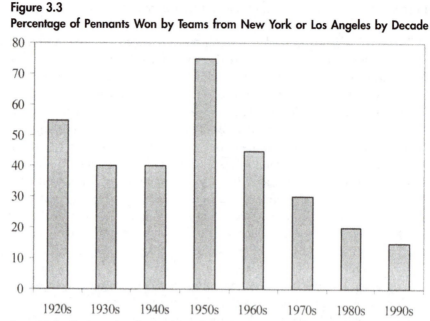

Source: John Thorn et al., eds., *Total Baseball* (New York: Viking, 1997) and www.mlb.com.

Diego Padres, Minnesota Twins, Toronto Blue Jays, and Cleveland Indians each made two.[8]

The subtext in these kinds of "competitive balance" discussions is usually player free agency. In the eyes of many fans, media, and owners, free agency is the beast killing the game. Yet before free agency, teams from New York (including Brooklyn) and Los Angeles dominated the World Series. Figure 3.3 shows the history by decade. From the 1920s through the 1960s, teams from the megalopolis won between 45 and 75 percent of the pennants each decade.

In contrast, the percentage over the era of free agency has slipped each decade to a low of 15 percent during the 1990s. On the other side, the free agent era has seen MLB attendance explode. Figure 3.4 displays this growth since 1945. It would not be proper to attribute all of this increased interest to free agency since incomes and populations were also increasing. One thing is clear—the advent of free agency, whatever it did to competitive balance, did not lead to dominance by the big market teams or diminish fan interest.

It is indeed possible that even free agency itself may have built fan interest in a sport such as baseball, although no one has really explored this possibility. Up until the 1970s, MLB teams that had players under contract retained the exclusive rights to sign those players in that league even after

Figure 3.4
Attendance per MLB Team, 1945–1999

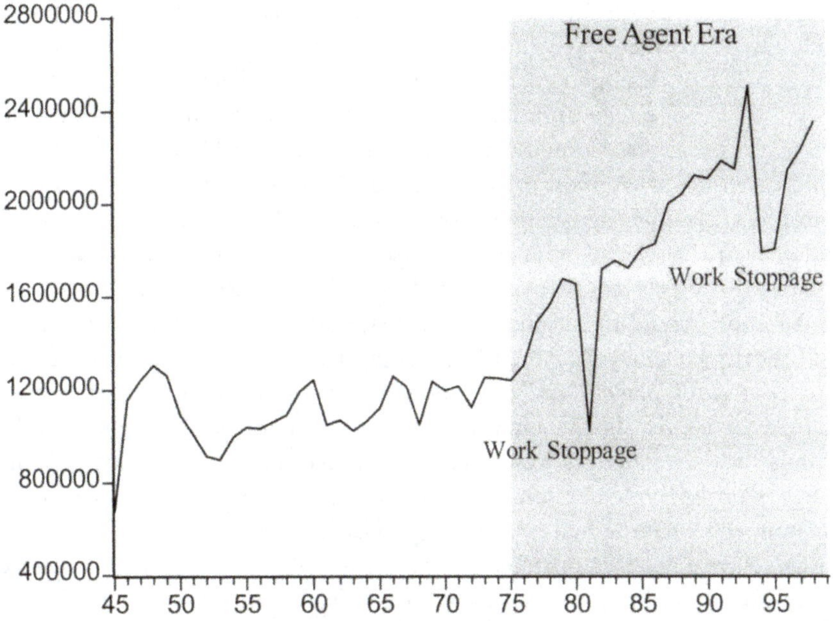

Source: John Thorn et al., eds. *Total Baseball* (New York: Viking, 1997) and www.mlb.com

the contract expired. The only players free to sign with any team, "free agents," were typically marginal players—those unconditionally released by a club or never drafted in the first place. These kinds of systems bound valuable players in all major sports to one team. During the 1970s and 1980s, labor movements in sports won battles that permitted varying degrees of free agency with more generous policies won in baseball, significant gains in basketball, and much more restrictive policies in football. Among the majority of sports team owners, player free agency is an evil without parallel. To them, the issue is cut and dried—free agency means higher salaries to players, and therefore, less money to owners. Probably no single issue unites owners more than hatred of free agency, leading to the adoption of all kinds of methods to limit its impact such as salary caps. A large number of sports media and fans have bought into this kind of thinking. In contrast to the majority, Bill Veeck liked and supported free agency.[9] Al Davis, the independent-thinking owner of football's Oakland Raiders, also advocated free agency. He declared, "Just cut all the players and make everybody a free agent."[10] Of course, many would write off Veeck's or Davis's support for it as merely another half-baked idea from a maverick. Whether all of Bill Veeck's or Al Davis' ideas were sound or not, on the matter of free agency he understood that it posed an important but often unrecognized tradeoff in marketing strategy for owners.

What the free agency naysayers fail to incorporate is the distinct possibility that free agency may actually build the customer base. Under the Reserve Clause system, owners with income from their teams or greater personal fortunes can and did merely purchase players from other teams. In fact, this was so common that the Kansas City Athletics of the 1950s and early 1960s were on occasion called a "Yankee farm team." As University of Massachusetts Simon Rottemberg noted many years ago, it is not at all clear that the advantage of wealthier owners to use their funds in acquiring better players would be any less under the Reserve system.[11]

Yet, how would free agency ever increase fan interest? One advantage to MLB of free agency that even Rottemberg left out of his calculus was the preferences of players and the long-term development of fan interest. If players care only about money, then the outcome under free agency will be similar to that under the Reserve Clause as described by Rottemberg. Some players probably do care almost exclusively about the dollars. They would switch teams for the highest offer regardless of other factors. Nonetheless, other players, just as other employees in general, value characteristics of job offers in addition to the salary offered. For example, location of a job is important to many people as is the opportunity to play with a championship team.

A good example from MLB is pitching legend Nolan Ryan. Between the 1971 and 1972 seasons, Ryan was traded from one large-market team, the New York Mets, to another one, the California Angels, under the Reserve system. After becoming a free agent in 1980, Ryan signed with the Houston Astros and later with the Texas Rangers in 1989. In both of these cases, he received significant sums but not necessarily the highest offer possible. Instead, his choice was influenced by his desire to play for a team in his home state of Texas. Many players, especially those well into their careers, share Ryan's desire to stay with a team near their home. Others highly value the chance to play with a contending team. What this means is that many players such as Nolan Ryan do play in different locations under free agency.

When players such as Nolan Ryan exercise their freedom to play outside of New York and Los Angeles, free agency helps MLB to build a fan base across the country. Star players such as Ryan draw fans for reasons beyond the performance of the team during the course of the season. Ryan pitched to sellouts or near-sellouts regardless of the Rangers' record. During the 1998 home run chase by Mark McGwire and Sammy Sosa, neither the St. Louis Cardinals nor the Chicago Cubs were involved in the pennant chase, and yet fans turned out in droves in those cities. When marquee players choose to distribute themselves across a wide number of teams, fans are drawn to the game that would not be otherwise. In contrast, during the Reserve Clause era, the Yankees, Dodgers, and Giants held onto many of the premier names in baseball—DiMaggio, Mantle, Mays, Reese, Robinson, Schneider, and others. Fans in other cities saw these players only during their occasional trips as visiting players.

Free agency is really only the most recent example of this diversion of baseball owners away from the real business of building a fan base. In days gone by, owners and analysts reacted much the same way to new ways to market their products such as night baseball, radio and television broadcasts, and cable broadcasts. In each case, the cry went up that this new thing would likely take fans away from one team or another. The common problem in all of these episodes is that owners and analysts sometimes forget that baseball teams not only compete with each other on the field but they also compete with other entertainment offerings. Often, the innovation and entrepreneurship spurred on by competition for consumer dollars that makes the biggest differences in owners' profits, players paychecks, and umpire salaries rather than particular settlements over how the shares will be divided among these groups. For instance, MLB owners and executives have found themselves at odds with umpires over compensation issues. Possibly much more important to MLB owners and executives in meeting the challenges of the market is the definition of the strike zone and who is going to determine it—the league or individual umpires—or issues over the evaluation of umpire performance. Ceding power over the strike zone or over the evaluation of umpires directly influences the product presented to consumers. When management cedes control over the product, it has given up something much more critical than higher salaries.

The fixation on dividing up the pie has even led highly respected economists to forget that all kinds of things go into building fan interest. Financial returns to clubs, individually and in the aggregate, are not just a matter of wins and losses and whether all teams are as likely to win the World Series in a given year. (In fact, complete parity in this regard may diminish fan interest as discussed below.) For example, developing hitters who can hit more home runs or longer home runs is valued by consumers, even though this does not change balance of competitiveness within a league. The pursuit of Roger Maris' single season home run record by Mark McGwire and Sammy Sosa in 1998 stimulated tremendous interest for these teams even though the teams were not very successful in those years. Moreover, MLB teams in general gained because these players drew large numbers into stadiums at visiting parks and on television. Nolan Ryan drew fans into Arlington Stadium and into other American League parks even when the Texas Rangers were an average ball club on the chance that fans might see another no-hitter by the all-time strikeout leader.[12] Beyond the performances of star players, fans enjoy seeing high-level perform-ances—great defensive plays, long home runs, and the like—that go beyond just winning and losing. It is unlikely most people would pay as much to watch Little Leaguers playing in big league parks wearing the big league uniforms.

The location of franchises is another example where MLB may have be-come overly concerned about dividing up the pie. The Montreal Expos have struggled as a franchise for much of the past 20 years. While the team hov-ered near and sometimes above average league attendance from the origi-nation of the franchise in 1969 until 1983, they have not equaled average league attendance since that time. After drawing more than 2 million fans in four seasons from 1979 to 1983, the team has averaged less than 1.5 million since with less than 1 million since 1998, even though league av-erages have risen to about 2.5 million. In spite of this fact and in spite of no MLB team in markets such as the Washington metro area or in Latin American cities, the league made no move until the 2003 season when it began a half-hearted experiment with Expo games in Puerto Rico. In many cases, the obstacle to expansion is another team, such as the Baltimore Ori-oles, who see such a move as dividing up their share of the pie. Whatever the effects on a specific team like the Orioles, the rest of baseball suffers because the concern about dividing the pie diminishes the total number of new fans likely to be drawn from areas further from Baltimore but closer to Washington, DC.

Even some degree of competitive "imbalance" may help build the size of the pie and not just how it is divided. The viewpoint and rhetoric by base-ball owners on free agency issue has steered all of the attention toward the idea that more balance in competition is always better. What is missing in most of these discussions is a recognition that a league can have too much or too little of either. Correctly seen, competition and cooperation must be balanced. In other words, there is an optimal amount of competition-cooperation. While everyone is often worried about the Yankees winning too much, from the standpoint of the league, the Yankees can win too lit-tle. After all, the Yankees are the most visible team in what is the largest media market in the country. If some other business, such as retail cloth-ing sales, were under consideration, no one would consider it to be out of line for sales in New York to exceed those in Kansas City.

From the club standpoint, sometimes people think in terms only of com-plete dominance being in a team's interest. They do not realize that there can be parity even from a fan's perspective. Walter O'Malley, longtime Dodger GM, recognized this problem. During the 1990s, the Atlanta Braves began experiencing this very problem. A long run of playoff appearances and National League pennants began to develop fans who took such appearances for granted. By contrast, when the run began in the early 1990s, Brave fans had been so starved for success by the team that they embraced the team with a collegiate-like fervor.

In spite of its ongoing success in drawing fans, the NFL may have put itself in a position of finding too much parity as one writer has suggested.[13] A league where teams bounce from terrible to the Super Bowl and back to terrible over just three or four seasons, as have the Falcons, may not stir the most fan interest. Clearly, there can be too much dominance by a team, but teams such as the Steelers and Cowboys of the 1970s not only spurred interest among their fans, but they provided an infrequent but intense rivalry followed by football fans who loved neither. Genuine rivalries that attract the interest of fans in general only tend to build between teams that are good over an extended period.

The importance of relative performance to profitability has encouraged some analysts to favor a greater degree of cooperation between teams. Relative performance within a league is measured by winning percentages, conference titles, and championships. If the Yankees perform better, then some team or group of teams must perform worse to offset the Yankees' wins— one Yankees win means one loss for another team. Because winning and losing in leagues has this "zero-sum" characteristic, the spending of money to in the pursuit of better performances offers no net benefits to the league as a whole. In their view, such competitive spending by teams and individuals in the pursuit of better performances merely siphons water out of the well.

This kind of thinking suffers from a fatal flaw—while win-loss standings for teams in leagues, by their very nature, offer no net benefits, the competitive struggle to outperform the other team can increase the overall size of the financial pie. The situation is not so different from common business competition between clear rivals such as GM and Ford. Over a particular year, GM, Ford, and other car manufacturers must divide up a market share pie that remains more or less fixed. In a given year, the amount that consumers spend on new cars may not be entirely fixed, but it is certainly limited. Relative standing among the manufacturers is extremely important over the course of a year. An additional sale by GM is a reduction to Ford—maybe not on precisely a one-for-one basis but there is a close tradeoff. The preface to Red Auerbach's book puts it this way, "If there's more than one company in your business, somebody is winning and somebody is losing, just like in the NBA. Somebody's got a bigger share of the market, somebody is making more money, somebody is beating somebody else."[14]

However, most consumers and analysts view (relative) competition between companies as a healthy rather than a disastrous situation because the competition to build better cars for the dollar—increased absolute performance—provides huge benefits to consumers over the long haul. Even more to the point here, the short term gains in market share of one company vis-á-vis a rival company does not tell the whole story about the measurement of organizational performance. Over the long haul, whatever the relative standing of Ford versus GM in terms of market shares, the profits of both companies may well flourish if their battles against each other prompt them both to improve their cars—an increase in absolute performance. When consumers respond favorably to improved automobiles, both GM and Ford gain. Whether one of the companies gains 33 percent of the marketplace to 30 percent for the other is in many ways inconsequential. Both companies as well as their employees and shareholders benefit.

MARKETING FOR THE PRESENT OR FUTURE?

The NCAA basketball tournament provides a stark alternative to the NBA's post-season structure. The NCAA tournament contains six stages with the winner advancing and the losing going home based on single game outcomes at each stage. The NBA setup moves at a snail's pace by contrast. Although there are only four stages, all of the stages are based on the best of seven games—until 2003, the first round was a best of 3 series. The NCAA tournament sets its schedule over three weekends while NBA playoffs extend about two months, sometimes with three days in between games. In spite of the lengthier NBA setup, rights paid to telecast the tournament by CBS to the NCAA ($545 million per year) rival those paid by ESPN–ABC to telecast all regular and postseason NBA games ($765 million).[15] Beyond the direct revenues, the NCAA event has become much more of a cultural event involving millions of people involved in office pools and fantasy brackets. The NBA playoffs generate no such widespread cultural impact.

Where does the NCAA tournament draw its market strength? Clearly, the sense of urgency, excitement, and importance for each game strikes a chord with fans. The tournament offers great drama. Aside from matchups of "1 seeds" against "16 seeds," most games produce uncertainty about the ultimate outcome and generate rooting interest for underdogs from people who are not rabid fans of those teams. Seeing "the little guy" like Gonzaga take Arizona to double overtime or North Carolina State defeat the mighty Houston team in 1983 is the stuff of legend. In contrast, the NBA playoff setup of the "best of seven games" accomplishes two tasks. It sharply reduces the likelihood of upsets by weaker teams, generating champions who achieve their result due more to skill and less to luck than in single game tournaments. Also, it strings the playoff sequence out over more games. However, it is not at all clear that as entertainment, it poses nearly as desirable a product. Playing seven game series waters down interest in the early games of a series. Rabid fans may tune in for each game, but more leisurely fans may only tune in once they see that the series is competitive. One could easily imagine the NBA cutting all series down to the best of three games to try to generate more of the atmosphere of the NCAA tournament.

Why does the NBA not adapt its postseason product to imitate the NCAA tournament, given the obvious success of that tournament? They may have the sense that the college environment and spirit uniquely contributes to the NCAA tournament's success. The NBA playoffs in a shorter form might have a hard time enjoying the same effect. However, the reluctance to cut the playoffs down may also stem from the dilemma and risk faced by sports leagues and other businesses in trying to adapt products to attract new customers for fear of turning off the old customers. Policies that drive up current revenues must be balanced against policies that build revenue over the long haul. The lure of adopting policies for today is strong. While it is true that the total market value of a business accurately measured includes an estimate of the future profit streams to the business, the more distant those streams are, the more those revenue streams are likely to be difficult to project and heavily discounted. NBA executives' planning horizons may extend beyond the current year, but given their tenures, these horizons likely extend out to a few years.

MLB has faced a similar dilemma. Before night baseball became so popular, the World Series was an afternoon event, attracting attention from school-age children. In recent years, the starting time for many weeknight World Series has been pushed back to 9 PM on the east coast so that the games do not end until midnight or well beyond. The reasoning behind these start times is obvious—to maximize television audiences across the country. Earlier starting times mean fewer West Coast viewers, at least for the first couple of hours of the game. No doubt, the late-starting time is intended to boost current TV audiences, ratings, advertising dollars, and, ultimately, offers from the networks for the rights to televise the games. Yet, what comes in one pocket of the owners today may be leaving tomorrow. The World Series games start so late on the east coast that many children will not be among those audiences. The bond between these children and baseball is never established to the same degree as their parents or grandparents. As a result, the paying baseball customers and TV audiences of 2015, 2025, and beyond are diminished.

For businesses that are living hand-to-mouth and wondering whether there will be a next year, all decisions must be oriented toward the present. However, for businesses on solid financial footing and a broad customer base in place, long term development of customers is important. This fact is especially true in businesses, such as sports, where the customers frequently develop a life-long relationship with the business. For a business where long term customer relationships are established, such as baseball, the negative consequences of this present orientation may be severe.

This balance of the present and the future abounds in sports. Another example where the right balance is required is in the selection of locations for franchises. The prevailing thought is that it is a great thing for a relatively small city such as Green Bay Wisconsin to host a franchise in the NFL. Probably, the NFL does benefit from having a smaller city rich in tradition and nostalgia such as Green Bay among its members. Yet, some analysts commit the classic "fallacy of composition," thinking that if only the league were more like Green Bay, things would be better. In fact, if many or most of the league were made up of Green Bay type cities, not only would the fan base and financial results for the league deteriorate severely, but even Green Bay would lose the unique characteristic that makes it the darling of NFL traditionalists. Similar questions crop up in the question of regular season versus playoffs. The NBA and NHL expanded their playoffs to the point where well over half of the teams made the playoffs. For both leagues the playoffs extend over about two months and do not finish until June. In contrast, only about 40 percent of NFL teams qualify for the playoffs, and these playoffs extend over four weekends. In MLB, only eight teams qualify for the playoffs, which start and finish within the month of October.

In all sports, the playoffs tend to be more heavily watched by television audiences, so expanding them to include more teams and extending them attempts to turn this consumer preference into cash. Also, keeping more teams alive for the playoffs means, at least potentially, keeping fan interest higher in more cities throughout the regular season. This clearly drives the decisions adopted by the NBA and NHL. The other side of the coin, though, is that longer playoff seasons with more teams diminish the importance of regular season games and may reduce fan interest. Although fan interest may be higher for the playoffs, the interest in early round games may be less when more games are played. Even NCAA basketball may have focused so heavily on the end-of-season tournament that interest in the regular season has been diluted. In the major conferences, as many as half or more of the teams are frequently invited to the tournament, so that many if not most of the games played by the teams involve little more than a contest for a slightly higher or lower seeding in the tournament. The net result is that while the end-of-season tournament has continued to grow in popularity, regular season games have diminished in importance and popularity.

Professional hockey also presents an interesting example of the potential for alternative marketing strategies that involve a short term versus long term tradeoff. Based on rules and their enforcement, hockey presents varying degrees of scoring, speed, hitting, physical play, and even fighting. While all hockey incorporates these attributes, the balance between them is not constant across all "brands" of the game. Two alternative versions are presented by the NHL which has traditionally marketed the "Canadian" style of hockey versus the "European" style played during the Olympics and World Championships.

Relative to rink sizes for international matches, NHL rinks are narrower with less room in the area behind the net. The NHL game includes a center or "redline" that in conjunction with the two blue lines constrains "two-line passes." As a result of these differences, the NHL product tends to be lower scoring and emphasizes close-checking defense, frequent scrums for the puck along the boards and in the corners of the rink, and neutral zone "traps"—defenses geared to make it difficult to carry or pass the puck through the neutral zone between the blue lines. In contrast, international matches, even when played by NHL players, look different. Players skate the puck up ice more than dumping it into the other end and then chasing it down, passes tend to be longer because of both the increased spacing of players as well as the removal of the centerline restriction on two-line passes.

Over the years, the NHL has tinkered with rule changes to move the balance a little more in the direction of the European style as the fan appeal stagnated. During the late 1990s, the league cracked down on impeding other players through holding and hooking. Earlier, it instigated rules to limit fighting to two people at a time by levying much more severe penalties for other players joining a fight already in progress. However, these changes have been incremental at best. The bigger changes, such as removing the center redline, moving the blue lines closer to each other to open more room behind the net, expanding the width of the ice, or adopting more severe penalties for all fighting have been resisted.

In choosing its current path, the NHL has continued to be very successful in attracting live attendance at games. Yet, it still struggles to find a sizable television market and the advertising megadollars that accompany larger television audiences. Figure 3.5 illustrates this problem.

The NHL generates only about five dollars in television revenue for every live fan in attendance. By comparison, the NFL pulls in over $100 per live attendee, the NBA over $30, and even MLB, with all of its television woes,

Figure 3.5
Television Revenue per Live Performance

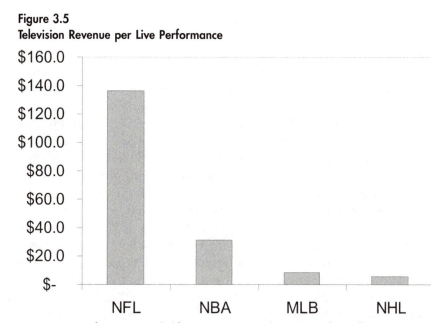

Source: Revenue from www.medialifemagazine.com and attendance from official websites of particular league.

pulls in over $8. The alternative path of the NHL game played under international rules holds the potential to help solve the "doesn't translate to TV" problem that has dogged professional hockey in the United States. Arguably, the European style translates to TV much better. The action is faster, transitions from offense to defense occur more frequently, less of the play takes place in the neutral zone or with the puck stuck in the corners along the boards, and scoring tends to be higher. Maybe the most important potential for the European style is that with players skating the puck over longer stretches of ice and making longer passes, the puck is easier to follow, helping to diminish one of the biggest complaints of NHL hockey on TV—"I can't see the puck."

Even though moving toward a style of hockey more like the international game might well reap rewards for the NHL, the league faces two obstacles in moving in that direction. These were mentioned in the previous chapter in the context of innovation and make change difficult for many large organizations. First, there is the natural aversion to risk. The NHL currently draws well at the gate, so why place these live attendance revenues at risk to pursue only the chance—not the certainty—of increased television revenues from a different style of hockey? When decisions must be made by a super-majority of owners or directors, those owners who are relatively more risk-averse carry the decisive votes. Second, many "purists" within the game, coaches and players, as well as commentators on the game and some outspoken fans, have strong preferences for the traditional NHL style. Even though they themselves might even enjoy watching matches played under international rules more, there is an attachment to the past and a reluctance to change. With these obstacles, the case for moving to international rules has to be supported by a nearly insurmountable amount of evidence to reach the threshold at which the change is made.

The decision making dilemma faced by sports leagues find many analogous situations in everyday business. A business that is attracting customers and turning a profit may well find it wise to keep up the strategies that have granted a degree of success. Certainly, many managers have sunk their businesses by determining to pursue a go-go growth plan that stretches the resources of the firm, alienates existing customers, and fails to produce the newly anticipated markets. By staying its course, the NHL protects what it already has, at least over the next several years. However, if it is the intent of a business to expand and reach broader markets, then the tyranny of the status quo must be overcome and some risks must be undertaken. In the NHL example, if it is to climb up the ladder to reach the same level television exposure as football, baseball, and basketball, a few fundamental changes in the product offered must be considered.

REPLAY

1. A product or service is what makes or breaks a business or sports league. Organizations with strong products and average operations often make money. Those with strong operations and weak products do not.

2. Incredibly, the importance of the product is often underappreciated as with the NFL's success versus other sports such as MLB in recent years. Management's role in evaluating and adapting the attributes of their product or service to the interest of the marketplace matters a lot more to long term success than secondary financial issues.

3. Untapped markets almost always exist right under the noses of existing producers as shown by NASCAR. Such opportunities are especially abundant where population and income are growing.

4. There is no general formula regarding how narrowly or widely to define the target market. Sports leagues have gained and lost by going in either direction.

5. Managers must keep competition from other markets at the heart of their decisions. Otherwise, managers will fall into the trap of internal pie divisions rather than development and care of the product as with MLB.

6. Product has value only because of appeal to consumers. Sports leagues with long term growth such as the NFL evolve with consumers.

4

Managing People: The Men Behind Dean Smith and Bobby Knight

The number one reason why one team outperforms another is people.

—Red Auerbach, former NBA coach and general manager

The tragedy of our times is that we've got it backwards. We've learned to love techniques and use people.

—Herb Kelleher, Southwest Airlines CEO

As the epigraph indicates, former Boston Celtic Head Coach and General Manager, Red Auerbach, equated success and people. Whether selecting players, developing their skills, or placing them together in the right mix, much of his advice about successful management centers on the people factor. Long time NFL coach, Marty Schottenheimer, echoed this conviction during a stint as an ESPN analyst when he repeated a motto he preached and that had been preached to him, "Don't just think plays, think players." Within football circles, this bit of wisdom means that schemes and strategies must not overshadow thinking about the talents and limitations of the people playing the game. Whether Schottenheimer consistently remained true to this philosophy as coach of the NFL's San Diego Chargers or former coach of the Washington Redskins, Cleveland Browns, and Kansas City Chiefs, it highlights the critical importance of people to success on the playing field.

Even though athletics is highly labor-intensive, the insight about the vital importance of people to success still holds weight even for organizations where machinery and materials play a much bigger role. As General Electric CEO, Jack Welch, put it, "You wouldn't want to field a Super Bowl team that didn't have the best athletes."[1] In his workshops for top-level corporate executives, MIT Sloan Management School economist Shlomo Maital drives this point home. He goes so far as to pronounce productive people within a firm as the most crucial versus all other resources and as the main source of long-term advantage.[2] This does not mean that all businesses are or should be highly labor-intensive or that use of equipment, location, materials, or technology are not important to the success of a business. The point is, however, that even in business settings where equipment completes many of the tasks, the people operating and maintaining the equipment, those purchasing it, those determining how to arrange it, and those organizing and managing the other people make or break the business. Where location matters, a person must select that location. Where technical processes are vital, a human being must develop those processes or be aware of their existence and see their applicability to the given situation. Where flipping hamburgers is important, then someone has to see that responsible people are hired to do this job if it is to be done right.

As on any athletic team, specific individuals and groups of people in a business do not all impact team outcomes equally. A CEO's contribution to overall company performance for good or bad swamps the influence of the mailroom entry level employee just as the quarterback's does the back-up right guard. Still, throughout an organization, the overall impact of mailroom employees or mid-level managers may be large. Without their effective input, the company will sputter just as a team will if the punter or long-snapper performs poorly. In addition to differing contributions made by specific individuals, as with positions on-the-field, certain jobs have a much larger pool of capable people readily available, making the departure of a given person less onerous to the team. Certain tasks, for example a quarterback in football or a mechanic in industry may require more training or specialized knowledge than others so that workforce problems in these areas create more havoc. The decisions of a pitcher in a baseball game or the CEO of a large corporation may directly influence overall team performance more directly and by a greater magnitude. Regardless of the relative contributions across team members, though, as a unit, highly productive and reliable people provide the backbone of any team and its scarcest resource.

Sports teams provide a clean and accessible picture of the main functions of management of a workforce. First, coaches and general managers must assemble team members, an important job in itself. Second, they must find ways to motivate the players effectively. Third, they must make decisions that are sometimes obvious, but in other cases are complex and subtle about how best to combine and utilize these team members. The simplicity of enumerating these main duties masks a difficult job. Managing people likely poses the most difficult jobs for any manger. Devising successful strategies to deal with another team or a rival company requires skill and luck. Developing successful plans to market a team or company to consumers takes creativity. Juggling expenses and keeping everything running with budgets takes technical abilities and organizational abilities. Still, equipment does not have family problems. A plant does not become eligible for free agency. Balance sheets do not go into rages. However complex these or other aspects of management may be, the personal and emotional aspects that go into dealing with human beings can stretch the abilities of even the best coach or manager. People are a resource for an organization, but they are not a resource just like any other one. Unlike land, equipment, buildings, and money, people think, feel, and react.

Management in a sports context is almost all about managing people. In fact, the sports-to-business books and seminars by coaches focus almost exclusively on the human relations aspect of their jobs. This myopia on the part of coaches may arise, in part, because the human relations part of coaching most easily finds mileage in business settings. Although coaches employ strategies, they may think these not very transferable beyond the bounds of their sports. Also, because many of the organizational issues are less complex, given the sizes of sports teams and because most coaches do not deal directly with the financial matters of their teams, the human relations aspect takes center stage. Beyond the attention which coaches give to the people side of their jobs, they often deal with them right out front for everyone to see, unlike other organizations where human relation issues, problems, and squabbles are usually handled behind closed doors. Even when the confrontations take place behind closed doors, events and quotes usually leak out due to the intense media coverage given to sports organizations.

GETTING GOOD PEOPLE

The 1976 Indiana Hoosiers accomplished a remarkable feat by winning the NCAA championship with 32 wins and no losses. Their coach, Bob Knight, received credit for his skills and jumped to the status of sports celebrity. While Knight in previous and subsequent years demonstrated considerable expertise in developing players into a cohesive team, ultimately winning two additional national championships, maybe the most underappreciated factor in the high level of success of his 1976 team was in attracting so many talented players together on the same team. Not widely recognized, the 1976 Indiana team rivals any college team of the past in terms of talent. Writers may neglect this fact because no single player from that team achieved NBA stardom. In spite of having no future NBA superstar, all five starters played at least two years in the NBA with significant minutes, rarely duplicated by the starting five of any other college team, even the great UCLA juggernauts.

Beyond the 1976 Indiana squad, many other coaches probably receive too little credit for their recruitment or acquisition of players relative to the credit they receive for their strategy or development skills. While this imbalance in attention occurs across nearly all sports, no where is it more in evidence than in college basketball. With the revolving door of players, coaches become the main celebrities and garner a lot of attention for their schemes and styles. Yet, no coach—not Wooden, Krzyzewski, or Bob Knight—has won very many games for very long without great players. In fact, Louisville coach Rick Pitino has commented that the way he assesses his and other teams' chances to reach the Final Four is to estimate the number of future NBA players on their rosters. Table 4.1 drives the point home by listing the number of NBA players on NCAA championship teams and runner-ups from 1964 through 1989. With only one exception, Texas Western in 1966, these teams placed at least two players in the NBA and 48 of the 58 teams contained three or more NBA-caliber players. After the 1960s, four or five future NBA players on a team became common. Knight's 1976 Hoosier team compiled over 2,600 total games in the NBA, rivaled only by the 1989 Michigan and 1982 North Carolina team including Michael Jordan, James Worthy, and Sam Perkins.

Table 4.2 uses similar data but looks at specific coaches, the number of Final Four appearances they have made, and the number of Future NBA players they had during their tenures. In addition to the total number of future NBA players, the table also lists the number of players who would go on to log more than 10,000 minutes in the NBA. The table makes clear that the coaches who have made repeated Final Four appearances have been loaded with talent—some more than others but all with significant talent pools. John Wooden and his UCLA teams are some of the most widely recognized as talent-driven because of highly publicized players such as Kareem Abdul Jabbar and Bill Walton. On his ten championship clubs, Wooden had 23 future NBA players including 13 with more than 10,000 minutes, and two of the best players of college players all-time in Abdul Jabbar and Walton. In terms of NBA talent, Dean Smith's teams top the list. He nearly doubled the number of future NBA players of any other coach. All of the coaches appearing in five or more Final Fours had more than 20 future NBA players. Even though he has not had a player of that caliber, Mike Krzyzewski, a coach widely noted for his "teaching" and game management skills, has succeeded with a large number of future NBA caliber players—on the order of 20 NBA players in 23 years of coaching. Bob Knight had nearly 30 future NBA players during his 30 years at Indi-

Table 4.1
Future NBA Games for NCAA Champion and Runner-Up, 1964–1989

Year	Champ-Runner-up	NBA Players	NBA Games	Median NBA	Max NBA
1964	UCLA-Duke	3-3	2521-1734	724-73	1031-849
1965	UCLA-Michigan	3-3	1843-1082	46-42	1031-817
1966	TX Western-Kentucky	1-4	163-1713	0-224	163-960
1967	UCLA-Dayton	3-2	2284-433	22-0	1560-379
1968	UCLA-UNC	3-4	2284-1380	22-145	1560-747
1969	UCLA-Purdue	3-3	2284-916	22-283	1560-578
1970	UCLA-Jacksonville	5-2	2475-1391	590-0	760-1329
1971	UCLA-Villanova	4-2	2375-505	590-0	760-457
1972	UCLA-Florida St.	4-3	2486-274	515-2	828-263
1973	UCLA-Memphis	4-3	2092-952	468-72	828-752
1974	NC State-Marquette	3-4	1153-1635	115-262	592-855
1975	UCLA-Kentucky	5-5	1432-1561	281-211	691-672
1976	Indiana-Michigan	5-3	2609-1538	536-7	719-946
1977	Marquette-UNC	4-5	966-2059	96-407	679-1033
1978	Kentucky-Duke	3-4	1200-1760	156-259	531-938
1979	Mich St.-Indiana St.	3-2	1787-1053	305-0	906-897
1980	Louisville-UCLA	4-5	2109-2104	408-325	768-648
1981	Indiana-UNC	4-3	1944-2565	261-417	979-1222
1982	UNC-Georgetown	3-2	3078-1996	926-0	1222-1039
1983	NC State-Houston	4-4	1160-2350	36-96	928-1119
1985	Villanova-G'town	3-4	1137-2466	45-599	793-1039
1986	Louisville-Duke	3-3	818-1589	53-325	465-723
1987	Indiana-Syracuse	4-4	490-1989	64-586	255-706
1988	Kansas-Oklahoma	2-4	841-2009	0-438	747-785
1989	Michigan-Seton Hall	7-2	2683-378	638-0	825-352

Source: Jan Hubbard, *The Official NBA Encyclopedia* (New York: Doubleday, 2000).

ana. Another fact regarding Knight that shows the importance of talented players is that almost all of these future NBA players attended IU before the mid 1990s. Once the players of this talent level dried up for Knight, his teams became only very average in their performances over his last seven seasons.

Ironically, some coaches are denigrated because of their success in recruiting or acquiring players. Fans and analysts seem to prefer to judge coaches based on what they did given the level of talent they possessed rather than on their overall performance regardless of the particular combination of talent and coaching. This implicitly undervalues evaluation and recruitment or acquisition skills and overvalues "coaching" skills. Few coaches have received more criticism from fans on this basis than Dean Smith. Smith sometimes receives less credit than one of his successful contemporaries such as Bob Knight because Smith successfully recruited so many highly talented players. Over his years as head coach at North Carolina, Smith recruited more than 50 future NBA players with whom he won 17 ACC regular season championships, made 11 appearances in the Final Four, and won 2 national titles—the number Final Four appearances far placing him second only to John Wooden and far exceeding Bob Knight's. Yet, the thinking goes, "given equal talent, Knight's or

Table 4.2
Final Four Appearances and Number of Future NBA Players of Selected NCAA Coaches

Coach/Years	Final Fours	Seasons	NBA Players	NBA> 10,000 min.
John Wooden	12	28	23	13
Dean Smith	11	36	52	20*
Mike Krzyzewski (Duke)	10	24	19	5*
Denny Crum	6	30	29	5*
Bob Knight	5	30	27	8*
Guy Lewis	5	30	20	8
Lute Olson	5	29	20	5
Jerry Tarkanian	4	19	21	7
Rick Pitino	4	16	12	2*
Jim Boeheim	4	27	17	6*
Nolan Richardson	3	18	8	4*
John Thompson	3	27	18	5*
Dale Brown	2	14	14	3*
Lou Carneseca	2	24	15	1
Al McGuire	2	14	13	2
Eddie Sutton	2	34	15	6
Bobby Cremins	1	16	16	7*
Wimp Sanderson	0	15	15	6*
Norm Stewart	0	32	14	3

Note: *indicates that the coach has players still active in the NBA.
Source: Jan Hubbard, *The Official NBA Encyclopedia* (New York: Doubleday, 2000).

Krzyzewski's teams will beat Smith's." Even if this is true, it ignores the fact that evaluating and recruiting players is part of the overall management job of a coach. Finding and attracting the talented players is not a factor that can genuinely be "held constant."

The tendency to overvalue the strategy and development part of managing or coaching and underappreciate the player evaluation-acquisition part of coaching extends beyond college basketball to great coaches in other sports and to business managers. One renowned coach whose methods have received nearly all the credit for his success while his player evaluation-acquisition skills have received little to none is Vince Lombardi.

Upon taking the Green Bay job in 1958, he first set up a film room to study old Packer films. As an assistant with the New York Giants in a different division of the NFL, he had seldom seen the Packers play. In pouring over these films late into the nights, he appraised the veterans, reaching pivotal conclusions that would lay the foundation for Green Bay's dominance in the 1960s. Among them, he recognized the potential in Paul Hornung. Although Hornung had been a college Heisman Trophy winner, he had been seldom used in the pros and had become disillusioned with football. Lombardi saw Hornung as the centerpiece of his power running attack, saying, "There's my offense" and "You're my Frank Gifford [the star runner for the Giants]." Between revitalizing veterans like Hornung, bringing in other veterans such as Emmel Tunnel, and seeing the capabilities in future Hall of Famers such as defensive back Willie Wood, Lombardi pieced together a core unit that won five NFL titles from 1959 to 1967 as well as two Super Bowls.[3]

Even though the importance of evaluating and acquiring players may be underappreciated by fans and media, it does not escape the attention of most successful coaches and sports teams. College coaches and their assistants expend enormous amounts of time and energy sifting through potential recruits and then trying to lure particular ones to their institutions. Professional sports teams employ scouts, hold individual and group workouts, and spend countless hours evaluating draft prospects. However, such diligence was not always practiced. Teams such as the Dallas Cowboys of the NFL expanded the resources spent to evaluate players. Even now, a few teams still do not seem to get the point, such as the Cincinnati Bengals who do not even employ a full-time scouting network.

As among sports teams, there is considerable diversity among businesses in how seriously they take getting the right people. Some diligently screen applicants or aggressively recruit workers. This not only includes companies paying top salaries to high-level executives but also some companies who are careful even when hiring unskilled workers for relatively low paying jobs. In contrast, other businesses take an amazingly slipshod approach to hiring people, even when the pool of applicants is broad. In effect, they send the message that they view workers as merely interchangeable parts so that it really matters little who gets hired. Even where companies spend resources to initially screen applicants, they may not necessarily put forth much effort to identify the people most likely to help their companies succeed based on more in depth study of their backgrounds and meaningful interviews, pushing almost all of the duties off on the human resources department.

The job of any manager in dealing with people becomes much more doable if the organization attracts the right people in the first place. Attracting and screening the kinds of people suitable for the situation alleviates many future headaches. In contrast, poor hiring practices can make the job of managing next to impossible. It's easy to fall prey to hiring practices that place too much attention on only the most obvious attributes without enough attention given to other personal characteristics that contribute to success. The problem frequently reflects either a type of adverse selection or agency problem or both. Adverse selection is the tendency to make poor purchasing or selection decisions because of false or misinterpreted signals. It surfaces because the person buying the service or product does not have full information as to the nature of service or product offered. Agency problems occur when the agents (employees, players) within an organization pursue objectives that are not in line with the principals (owners, managers) of the organization.

The recent saga of the Portland Trailblazers attests to the potholes into which many managers fall in acquiring their workforce. During the late 1990s, the team loaded up on players with tremendous raw athletic talent, yet many of the players they acquired top the list of "great athletes" who have not figured out that the objective of a sports team is winning games and championships. For instance, in one of their past moves, the team traded to acquire Isaiah Rider from Minnesota. When he arrived, Rider already had a reputation for erratic work habits, unexplained absences, and petulant behavior, but at times, he could dominate a game with his talents. By the 2000 season, the team had tired of Rider's antics had traded him to Atlanta for "good citizen" Steve Smith. At power forward, they played a budding star in Rasheed Wallace who replaced Rider as team bad boy. Wallace had been drafted in 1996 as a sophomore out of North Carolina. Upon entering the league, he quickly gained a reputation as a superstar in training but also gained a reputation for being temperamental. To the mix, the team also added Scottie Pippen, the second best player from the Chicago Bulls six championships but a player known for his moodiness and sulking. They traded a solid-performing and hardworking forward, Brian Grant, to Miami. Then, for a finishing touch, the team decided to add guard Rod Strickland. During the 2001 season, Strickland would rival Wallace for the title of best player with the worst attitude; only Strickland has displayed his bad behavior over a much longer time span.

Over these years, the team showed promise, owing to its considerable athletic prowess. Blazer coach, Mike Dunleavy, earned the 1999 NBA Coach of the Year Award for helping the team reach the Western Conference Finals that year. Their player moves had been seemingly so adept that an April 2000 *Sport* article called it "The Blazers Monopoly" and heaped high praise on general manager Bob Whitsett's moves in skillfully working with owner Paul Allen's millions and dealing with the salary cap.[4] Yet, after a disappointing end to the 2000 season, the team imploded during the 2001 season. Rather than improving on his reputation, Wallace only worsened. He not only led the league in technical fouls, which he did the year before also, but set a new NBA record. Moreover, he sometimes berated teammates, throwing a towel at center Sabonis in a timeout huddle during a game. Poor performances in the last two months of the regular season placed them facing the Los Angeles Lakers in the first round of the playoffs. The Lakers bounced the Blazers in short order, precipitating a shakedown of the team, including the firing of head coach Mike Dunleavy. Unfortunately, the team had not learned its lesson, filling its roster with players that repeated these episodes during the 2002 and 2003 seasons with the same outcome. Finally, with little prospect for improvement, the team finally traded Wallace to Detroit during the 2003–2004 season.

A general lesson can be learned not just for sports teams but for most any organization. Accurate screening of potential personnel to assess character can be just as important as assessing pure knowledge or skill. References and employment history are not just items to pass over on the job resume but do, in fact, contain important signals. Properly screening these signals become more important as the length of the employment relationship is longer and as the cost of getting out of the relationship is higher. Incredibly, some managers bypass deep searches into references or employment history even when the hiring involves long-term employment relationships or relationships not easily severed.

In fact, a common thread among coaches with long records of success is the ability to strike the right balance of athletic talent with mental skills and character. John Wooden, for one, placed high priority on academic skills in his recruitment of players.[5] Mike Krzyzewski says that he typically looks for players that demonstrate attributes beyond their vertical leap or height. In particular, he looks for players that display a respect for authority. In spite of these examples, many general managers and coaches become allured by the siren's song of raw athletic talent. A few teams have seemingly institutionalized the kind of player acquisition mentality that goes after athletes of great "potential" but with poor work habits, limited grasp of the mental aspects of the game, or little commitment to team objectives. In the NBA, the Los Angeles Clippers seem to have perfected this formula for finding athletes instead of winners. The point for managers of all types is that getting the right people is crucial, but one must dig below the surface in looking for the qualities that make for enduring, productive workers.

Keeping the right kind of people goes hand-in-hand with attracting the right kind of people. In sports, as with other business, there is going to be turnover—an issue discussed more below. Yet, when possible and productive for the organization, keeping players or employees content requires managerial attention and skill. The era of free agency in sports has been opposed by most of the old guard of sports managers, who liked the idea of getting a player who had no other playing options. Retention of the player was rarely a problem under that kind of system because the player had no other options in sports. The free agency era placed retention of players more on a par with the retention of employees in any business. In spite of some forms of free agency being present in all sports leagues now, some owners and general managers still operate as if they held exclusive rights to all players.

Mark Cuban, owner of the Dallas Mavericks, stands out as person who understands the importance of managing personnel retention so much so that he garnered a front page article in the Wall Street Journal.[6] Cuban has been a whipping boy for the press because of his questionable outbursts against officials during games and active participation with the interests of the team. In spite of this, Cuban has overseen his team with a keen eye toward attracting and retaining players. He understands that salary matters, and matters a lot. As he said, "Am I crazy to spend [millions] in contracts when I have a chance to get three layers deep into the playoffs. That's dirt cheap. I'll sell more seats, more merchandise."[7] Yet, he also sees other factors in addition to salaries that influence retention. Rather than paying millions to players in payroll and then trying to pinch pennies by skimping on other player-related expenses, Cuban has tried to use non-salary items as compensation also. The team's locker room facilities, for instance, offers players state-of-the-art amenities with personal televisions for players, top-flight equipment for physical therapy, luxury hotels on road trips and other things. In general, he wants his million dollar players to be treated as million dollar players rather than trying to weasel a few thousand back by pushing poor locker room facilities on them. He even lavishes similar treatment on visiting teams under the thinking, "some of those guys may want to play for us some day."

The contrast between the thinking of many owners and general managers in sports versus that of Cuban mirrors what is seen outside of sports. Many business managers suffer from the "pennywise and pound foolish" syndrome. They will pay salaries and wages as the market demands but then skimp on minor and relatively inexpensive details of the work environment that do influence the outlook of employees. Many comedic satires of this kind of activity have cropped up from the Dilbert cartoon series to the Staples television commercials. In contrast, other managers seem to understand, as Cuban does, that beyond basic compensation, other expenditures for employees that may not be very expensive can, in fact, create much goodwill in the workplace.

A leading firm in this respect is SAS, a comprehensive data and software developer and consultant out of Cary, North Carolina, and once labeled "the most important company that you have never heard of." They set a top priority in building a workforce based on establishing long-term relationships with talented employees. To accomplish this goal, SAS provides amenities that are in line with the kind of stable, long-term employees that they seek. They constructed a pleasant lunch facility, on-site health care and schooling, individual offices, relatively short work weeks, and other benefits to employees while at the same time expecting productivity from their workforce. Not all of these perks are cheap and some are not practical for other kinds of businesses. Obviously, a fast-food chain such as Burger King is not going to the same kind or level of amenities as a top-end software provider. Yet, even in low-pay, low-skill, high-turnover jobs, the workers care about things other than just their paychecks. These things may be flexible scheduling, not having to wear silly-looking uniforms, humane treatment, or other things. The point is that whether the example is Mark Cuban or SAS, these mangers are clued in to the fundamental importance of trying to attract and retain productive employees.

USING PEOPLE EFFECTIVELY

Nobody remembers the 1980 Arizona State Basketball team, although it rivaled any college team in history—at least as measured by the NBA careers of its members. The team's floor general was Lafayette "Fat" Lever who played nearly 24,000 minutes in the NBA, averaging 6 assists, 6 rebounds, 14 points, appearing in two All-Star games, and making the NBA All-Defensive team once. Byron Scott played in the backcourt with Lever. Scott played over 30,000 minutes in the NBA, averaging over 14 points per gain and winning three titles with the Lakers. At seven feet in height, Alton Lister was the center. He played nearly 19,000 minutes in the NBA. The other two players, six-eleven Kurt Nimphius and six-eight Sam Williams, were less well known for their NBA careers, but Nimphius played over 11,000 minutes over eight seasons and Williams 4,500 minutes over four seasons. In total, team amassed almost 89,000 NBA minutes. By comparisons, most college put no players in the NBA. For better college teams with two or three players of professional caliber, the typical range of NBA minutes would be 20,000 to 40,000 in total.

Not only did the team log many professional minutes, but it possessed a balance of height, quickness, shooting, defense, and rebounding. Yet, it did not advance beyond the second round of the NCAA tournament. A good, but not great, Ohio State team whose players logged about half as many NBA minutes beat them soundly, 89–75. The next year, the same team except for Nimphius lost to Kansas in the second round 88–71, even though Kansas possessed little NBA talent and probably did not have a single player who could have started for ASU.

Few NCAA teams have underachieved as much as Ned Wulk's 1980 and 1981 squads. Wulk coached Arizona State from 1957 to 1982 and won a whopping 79 percent of the games. Yet, he never could "get over the hump" to win the big matchups. His 1980 and 1981 teams illustrate the fact that while having talented people may be necessary to performing well, it is no guarantee. The way that the manager pieces together the players along with the adjustments to strategy made on an opponent-by-opponent basis can have a big impact on the outcome. In other words, great managers do not win without great players, but great players often fail if not managed properly.

Earl Weaver illustrates the role of a manager who helped his teams reach their potential. He managed the Baltimore Orioles over seventeen seasons, becoming one of the most successful managers in baseball history. Because of his occasional antics with umpires, mastery of game tactics, and his intensive use of information, the picture of Earl Weaver as a player-oriented coach is often lost. Moreover, his player skills did not include making them feel warm and fuzzy or always liking Weaver himself. Nevertheless, he excelled in getting the most from his twenty-five man roster. As one baseball analyst put it, "He used everybody and cared about his players."[8] Rather than constantly harping on the deficiencies of his players, he focused most intently on what they could do for his team, leading baseball in the "platooning" of players based on the game or situation. His abilities to draw from the full talents of his roster permitted his Orioles to remain highly competitive even as free agency began to reshuffle many star players away from teams like Baltimore.

Once the right people are on board, the next issue is how to utilize them to their fullest potential. Like Earl Weaver, Mike Krzyzewski, the most successful college basketball coach over the past two decades at Duke University, casts a big presence as a strong-willed leader, yet he eschews the fascination that most media analysts, fans, and even other coaches have with "positioning" players. For instance, it is common to refer to the tallest players who mainly play inside as playing at the 5-spot (center) and the smallest, ball-handling guard as playing at the 1-spot (point guard). Krzyzewski sarcastically stated that his team contains "players not numbers." No doubt, Duke has some means of identifying and segmenting roles for players on the court, yet Krzyzewski's emphasis on avoiding hemming in his players too much highlights a key ability he displays for using people at or near their highest value to the team, whatever that may be. As he put it, "I try to find some way to integrate everybody, allow them to improve, and have them understand their places."[9]

Krzyzewski's statement is a working example of Marty Schottenheimer's "think players, not plays." Successful leaders must think in terms of utilizing the abilities of their players and not just in terms of plugging players into a set of plays. Managers in all kinds of businesses would do well to learn such ideas. Trying to plug people into slots as if they are robots may work out fine in some instances. If a machine needs an operator, then it needs an operator. If a fork lift needs operating, then someone needs to be plugged in who can operate a fork lift. Yet, at times, a good manager must stop and actually think about how to adjust plans and roles to best utilize the abilities of people and not just how to plug one person into another person's slot.

Even if an organization acquires a talented and motivated workforce, for performance to reach its highest levels, managers must put people in the right places. This fact cuts across managers who oversee businesses or a sports team. Utilizing people effectively requires an emphasis on flexibility. Coaches and other managers must avoid locking people into certain slots when their value may be higher somewhere else within the organization.

Table 4.3 presents data regarding showing some of the most underachieving teams in NCAA history. It lists the team, the team that defeated it in the NCAA tournament, and the number of future NBA games for the players on those teams. The reason for underachievement—poor decisions by the coach, bad luck, poor officiating—are not identified. Still, the point that talent is necessary, but not sufficient for success, is made clear in the table.

Guy Lewis' 1983 Houston team, often thought to be the biggest bust of a talent-laden team, was stocked with substantial NBA talent but was not close to being the most talented team defeated, especially considering the level of the competition. In fact, Dean Smith's 1984 team that was defeated in the Sweet 16 by Indiana, featuring Michael Jordan, Sam Perkins, and other future NBA players, easily takes the top spot for biggest upset of a great team. In fact, Smith places 4 teams among the top 10. Certainly a 2-point loss to a team with talented players of its own is no big indictment of a coach. However, the 96–73 drubbing suffered by North Carolina in the Sweet 16 tournament to a team that logged only half of the NBA minutes is surprising. The point here is not to bash Dean Smith. The earlier sections record his achievements. Rather, it is to point out that getting the most out of a talented group is not an easy task. Injuries, intra-team rivalries, a few missed opportunities, or poor decisions can sour a team's chances.

Table 4.3
NCAA Teams with the Most Future NBA Games Not Winning Championship

Year	Teams	Players	Total Games	Median Games	Maximum Games
1984	North Carolina-Indiana	5-2	4029-404	737-0	1031-235
	National Semifinal: 68-72				
1978	Notre Dame-Duke	7-4	2840-1760	707-259	1068-938
	National Semifinal: 86-90				
1990	North Carolina-Arkansas	5-3	2696-1393	508-445	652-496
	Regional Semi-final: 73-96				
1975	Indiana-Kentucky	6-5	2525-1561	536-156	719-672
	Regional Final: 90-92				
1976	North Carolina-Alabama	5-4	2472-1889	482-438	1033-993
	First Round: 69-74				
1985	Georgetown-Villanova	4-3	2466-1137	599-45	1039-793
	National Final: 64-66				
1983	Arkansas-Louisville	3-6	2464-1600	720-201	965-768
	Regional Semifinal: 63-65				
1982	Houston-North Carolina	4-3	2455-3078	153-926	1119-1222
	National Semifinal: 62-68				
1983	Houston-North Carolina St.	4-4	2350-1160	96-36	1119-928
	National Final: 52-54				
1974	UCLA-North Carolina St.	6-4	2376-1153	468-115	828-592
	National Semifinal: 77-80				

Source: Jan Hubbard, The Official NBA Encyclopedia (New York: Doubleday, 2000) and Jim Savage, The Encyclopedia of the NCAA Basketball Tournament (New York: Dell Publishing, 1990).

While utilizing people effectively is an issue for sports managers and coaches, business managers sometimes face limits not encountered by their coaching counterparts. For example, in some cases work rules negotiated through collective bargaining agreements restrict the options open to managers in moving their workers around. Barring such rules, the situations between sports and typical business settings are very comparable. For example, as organizations grow larger, they tend to hire people to fit particular job descriptions, and usually, these people are not repositioned within the organization unless major restructuring occurs. This is not unlike sports, especially at the professional level, where players drafted as quarterback, running back, or some other positions usually stay at those positions for their entire careers. Occasionally, college players find new positions in the pros, but once repositioned, further changes are rare or are minor changes such as cornerback to safety or a third baseman moving to first base. With such job positioning, the task of the manager in effectively using the human resources on hand, short of a general "reengineering" of the organization, is more one of tailoring and customizing responsibilities than completely altering job tasks.

Coaches with long track records of success also avoid the fascination with fitting square pegs into round holes. When Lew Alcindor (Kareem Abdul-Jabbar) came to the UCLA Bruins, John Wooden scrapped his entire offensive scheme. By his accounting, he spent hundreds of hours talking to other coaches about plays for post players to more fully utilize Alcindor's unique and impressive abilities. Wooden also changed the defensive "rules" for his teams. Previously, one of the team's staple axioms was to never let a player drive toward the bucket along the baseline. With Alcindor in the middle, such drives usually turned into blocked or missed shots, so Wooden discarded the old rule and encouraged his players to force opponents along the baseline.[10]

A model of success in flexibility and adaptation over the longest stretch of time in the NFL is probably Don Shula, who started as head coach of the Baltimore Colts and then moved to the Miami Dolphins in 1969. Shula's teams in Baltimore in the 1960s and Miami in the 1970s were relatively conservative teams, emphasizing running the ball and strong defense. In 1973, the Dolphins finished the season undefeated. By the 1980s, the rules concerning pass defense had changed considerably, making passing more effective. Also, in 1983, the Dolphins drafted Dan Marino out of the University of Pittsburgh. Shula quickly grasped the incredible talent of his young quarterback and adapted the offense to take advantage of the rules and Marino's arm. Although the Dolphins reached the Super Bowl only in 1985, they continued to be successful and could not be described as a team inextricably tied to a particular system.

At the college level, Lou Holtz has made a career out of building football programs or rebuilding programs that had fallen upon hard times. Various attributes of Holtz as a leader might be cited as contributing to his success at these projects, yet Holtz teams have not been known for their complicated offensive or defensive schemes. Instead, Holtz excels in recognizing talented players, motivating them to play hard, and moving players around so as to extract the most from them. At the University of South Carolina, for instance, he used one of his most talented players, running back Derek Watson, not only as a running back in the offense but as a wide receiver, punt returner, kick returner. He even used Watson as a punt-block specialist on occasions. Few coaches use players so broadly in this era of hyper-specialization. Yet, Holtz recognized that his team's best chance to win came from trying to use Watson in as many valuable ways as he could find.[11]

At times coaches like Holtz, who try to utilize the entire array of a player's abilities, receive criticisms for unduly exposing a valuable running back to injury. Similar comments have cropped up in the 1990s when a stellar defensive back such as Deion Sanders has been used as a kick or punt-returner or in the 1970s when St. Louis defensive back, Roy Green, began to play at wide receiver also. As with any activity, the question must be considered as to whether the additional benefit derived outweighs the additional costs and risks encountered, but a blanket rule of thumb that limits a player to doing only one thing on a team is unlikely to arrive at the best solution. After all, it is not the player's contribution as a defensive back or running back, *per se*, that matters, but his overall contribution to scoring points or holding the other team from scoring. Coaches such as Holtz help to make up for some of their team's athletic deficiencies versus the powerhouses such as Florida or Tennessee by using the talents of his most gifted players more intensively.

To use people most effectively, coaches or managers must avoid the temptation to view people as interchangeable parts in a big machine with the coach twisting the knobs. So often, managers handcuff the people they have on staff, even when many of these people are capable of making a difference themselves. Nowhere can this be more easily seen than in sports. Coaches fall in love with their systems and schemes. An example of this kind of thinking occurred with the University of Houston football program in the early late 1980s and early 1990s. During the 1980s under head coach Jack Pardee, the team installed an offensive scheme known as the "run and shoot"—a system that Pardee had run adopted as coach of the USFL Houston Gamblers. The offense spread four wide receivers all over the field, emphasized no-huddle play calling, and racked up points left and right. In spite of NCAA probationary status with restricted scholarships and no television appearances, the Cougars were becoming a novelty. Andre Ware, the team's quarterback, won the Heisman trophy in 1989, passing for over 4,600 yards and 46 touchdowns in one season and leading the team to a 9–2 mark. After Ware graduated, David Klingler inherited the quarterbacking responsibilities and experienced even greater statistical success, passing for over 5,100 yards and 54 touchdowns.

Pardee departed to become coach of the NFL's Houston Oilers. John Jenkins, offensive assistant coach and mastermind of the run and shoot scheme, took over as coach. Jenkins was completely enamoured of his offensive schemes. He flatly stated that he did not think anybody could stop the offense. What Jenkins failed to realize, though, was that other factors had contributed to the Cougars' success. The Houston defense had played well, and the players, including the offensive line doing the blocking, had been well suited to the offense. Soon, opposing defenses devised effective counter-strategies, and the Cougars did not have the compliment of players needed to defend the quarterback or the receivers to make it work as well. By the 1992 season, Houston took several sound beatings. Shortly, Jenkins and his unstoppable schemes vanished—a victim of managing solely in terms of plays and not players.

DEVELOPMENT AND TURNOVER

Nurturing and developing inexperienced talent defines another part of the role of a manager in being able to utilize the resources of the people around him. In sports, few leaders accomplished this better than Walter Alston of the Los Angeles Dodgers. Alston experienced an incredibly long and successful run with Dodgers, managing them from 1954–1976. His unprecedented longevity, in large part, owed itself to his ability to recognize raw skills of younger players and inspire confidence in them. Over Alston's tenure, players such as Don Drysdale, Sandy Koufax, Maury Wills, John Roseboro, Ron Perranoski, Frank Howard, Willie Davis, Tommie Davis, Steve Garvey, Davey Lopes, Bill Russell, and Ron Cey—all household names during their playing era—broke into the majors with the Dodgers and flourished. Koufax, recognized as one of the great pitchers of any era, especially benefited from Alston's patience. As one writer put it, Alston waited six and one-half years for Koufax to find home plate.[12] Alston acquired some of these skills as a protegé himself of Branch Rickey, a seminal figure in the player development system that has come to dominate professional baseball. Certainly, some sports coaches and managers such as George Allen with the Los Angeles Rams and Washington Redskins have flourished by using predominantly older players. Yet, the tenure of these coaches is often cut short because of their aversion to younger players. When the string runs out with the veterans, there is no supply of younger talent ready to carry on. The longevity of a Walter Alston is really only possible if younger players are infused among the older players.

Integrating younger players and handling the turnover or reassignment of team members is one of the most complex jobs faced by any manager and fraught with land mines. In athletics, players go through productivity life cycles. For players who remain in professional sports for sizable stretches of time, performance usually increase over a few years, reaches a plateau at which productivity may hold for several years, and then output begins to decline, ultimately leading to either retirement or release. While these facts are well known, making decisions with regard to individual players can be quite difficult because of the uncertainties of future performance as well as loyalty issues. How quickly should young players be integrated? How long should veteran players be kept on? Maybe the most commonly cited gaffe in recent years was the Boston Red Sox cutting loose Roger Clemens after the 1997 season only to see him win over 100 games the next six seasons, including three American League Cy Young Award. Yet, only hindsight makes this decision a "no-brainer." Clemens had already played 13 seasons and his earned run average in three of his prior four years had been one run or more per game higher than his career averages.

Looking at these numbers as well as observing Clemens pitch, one could have easily concluded that he had dropped off of the plateau and was going downhill, as almost all athletes do who play long careers.

The coaches and general managers who handle these questions the best are those who handle the situation incrementally—striking a balance between integrating young players and utilizing older players. Coaches and general managers whose decisions lead to bad outcomes usually lean toward an all-or-nothing approach. One of the best cases of successful balancing of veteran and younger players comes from the NHL's Colorado Avalanche. The team moved from Quebec in 1995 and won the Stanley Cup in their first full year in Colorado, 1995–96. In 1998, Bob Hartley took over as coach and guided the team to appearances in the Western Conference Championship and another Stanley Cup in 2001. On integrating younger players, an ESPN announcer transmitted Hartley's philosophy, "old players get older; young players get better." On his teams, rookie and second year players received considerable playing time, even during the playoffs. Yet, Hartley's statement does not imply that he steers entirely toward the use of younger versus older players. In a highly publicized move, the team traded for 20-year veteran defenseman Ray Borque from the Boston Bruins late in the 2000 season. Then, during the 2001 season, the team acquired 10-year veteran defenseman Rob Blake from the Los Angeles Kings. In both cases, the Avs gave up younger talent in favor of the veteran players, and Hartley utilized both extensively.[13]

In contrast to this incremental mixing of old and new, one of the downfalls of Rick Pitino as coach of the Boston Celtics was his inability or unwillingness to see the importance of veteran players and the stability they bring. When he took over, he took an extreme approach to integrating new players. As one article put it, "When it comes to personnel matters, [Pitino] acquires and discards players the way a stock trader does."[14] A former Celtic player noted, "He didn't want veteran players when he got there. Now he realizes that wasn't right."[15] As an opposing example, The New York Yankees under Joe Torre have expertly balanced the integration of older and younger players. Torre has been very willing to utilize young players and rookies extensively including Derek Jeter, Bernie Williams, Jorge Posada, Mariano Rivera, and Alfonso Soriano. Further, he has been willing to do it at what are thought to be the most critical defensive positions of shortstop (Jeter), catcher (Posada), and centerfield (Williams) where many managers reluctantly place young players. At the same time, though, he has used veterans to balance these young stars.

On the other side of the coin, it is very easy to be too slow in integrating fresh people within an organization, even for good managers. The Pittsburgh Steelers languished at the bottom of the NFL until coach Chuck Noll arrived, and the team drafted several key players during the late 1960s and early 1970s including Terry Bradshaw, Joe Greene, Franco Harris, L.C. Greenwood, Lynn Swann, Jack Lambert, and others. The Steelers built a dynasty, winning Super Bowls in 1974, 1976, and 1980. Injuries and retirements of the 1970s veteran core began in waves and soured the Steelers' fortunes during the 1980s. First, the team dropped to being just average. Then, from the mid 1980s on, they lost many more games than they won. The other dominant team of the 1970s, the Dallas Cowboys, closely marked the fate of the Steelers. The Cowboys had built a solid team from the mid 1960s into a 1971 Super Bowl winner. Then, in 1975 they experienced an exceptionally good draft and excelled through the 1970s and early 1980s. By the mid 1980s, however, this core of players began to drop and the team's winning percentage slid. By Tom Landry's last year, they were one of the worst teams in the league at 3 wins and 13 losses.

Based on their dominance and Super Bowl victories, one might easily argue that riding the veteran core of the teams paid off. However, the other side could be argued also. At some point during the late 1970s or early 1980s, had the teams begun to more rapidly integrate younger players, they likely would have avoided the downfalls of the late 1980s. Such a strategy may have led to fewer wins in the early 1980s, but greater success over the long term. Ironically, the Cowboys had pursued such a strategy through the mid 1970s. They made room and gave playing time to the players in their 1975 draft into an already successful team.

MOTIVATION—BEYOND THE BASICS

Bo Schembechler coached the Michigan Wolverines from the 1960s to the early 1990s. As a disciple of Ohio State legend Woody Hayes, Schembechler's team won games by athletic talent and brute force. There was seldom anything tricky or subtle about their strategy—run the ball a lot and throw once in a while. The Wolverines under Schembechler were not pretty but highly successful. Schembechler excelled in his ability to obtain maximum effort from players. While all coaches emphasize effort, Schembechler did it in a way that translated obviously into game situations. Although it might seem that players' sloughing off might be a problem only in practice, slight declines in effort occur frequently in games. Players fatigue and back off a bit. The play runs long, and a player backs off a bit. The main focus of a play moves away from a particular player, and he may ease back. Anyone who watched a Schembechler coached team in person could see that the Michigan coaches instilled a culture where the players went at full speed from the beginning of the play until the whistle blew to stop the play—even to the point of continuing a second or two beyond the whistle in many cases. Defensive backs ran hard even when the ball was completely across the field. Offensive tackles completed their downfield blocks whether the play was nearing an end or not.

These seemingly minor differences in effort have huge differences on outcomes over the course of an entire game or season. The defensive back who thinks his teammates are sure to tackle a runner and slows up by only 10 percent will likely be correct in most situations and his team will suffer no ill effects of his slightly diminished effort and his coaches will likely not even notice. In fact, as he becomes accustomed to doing this, the player not even be aware of his slightly reduced effort. However, in a game or over a series of games, the 10 percent reduction in effort may be the difference in a 20 yard gain and a touchdown in the one or two times that the runner breaks through the seemingly sure tackle of the teammates. Likewise, in business, a 10 percent reduction in effort compounded over weeks, months, and years makes a large difference in overall productivity that may seem trivial at any given moment in time.

In work settings ranging from construction labor requiring exhaustive physical labor to office labor requiring mental effort, lost productivity due to diminished effort may be the most common problem plaguing businesses. As the quote from Pete Carill indicated in Chapter 2, people, in general, would rather do something less difficult than something difficult. This is not to indicate that "optimal" effort is always at break-neck speed. In a game played in short bursts, such as football, all-out effort may be optimal. In games with continuous action or long seasons such as basketball or hockey, some amount of "pacing" is necessary just as in a long distance run. Likely, business settings more closely approximate these kinds of endurance events than they do football. Yet, even in these situations where an all-out sprint is not in order, consistently strong effort will pay dividends over the long haul.

The question is, how does a coach or manager motivate people to provide strong effort levels toward company objectives rather than personal objectives?[16] Chapter 2 covered a few of the basics regarding motivation of people. The theme of that chapter was that effective coaches and managers recognize the divergence of individual and team objectives. With only a paycheck, some players or workers will fully integrate their objectives with those of the team or company. Others will pursue the team or company objectives with a bit of personal pursuit, while others will seek their own objectives to the fullest extent possible. Astute leaders are aware of and seek to find ways to meet the need for individuals to subjugate themselves to the needs of the team while continuing to recognize the importance of individual. In Chapter 2, Vince Lombardi's practice of handing out five and ten dollar bills at weekly meetings to call attention to excellent performance became a ritualistic practices that surprised Packer Gary Knofelc in "how prideful you would become" in receiving such small rewards.[17] Lombardi understood player motivation in terms of "the player produces for himself and the team as an extension of himself."[18]

Finding ways to address this divergence between team goals and personal objectives presents an ongoing challenge for coaches and managers, and many methods have been utilized to deal with it. Most coaches rely, to a some extent, on verbal harassment. In some cases, this becomes almost the sole means used usually to their detriment. Although a coach as successful as Lombardi used this method a lot, he is frequently misunderstood to have leaned on it solely. In reality, he factored in the personal goals and satisfaction of his players. Other coaches and business leaders attack the motivational issue by attempting to build a culture of groupthink that mimics some aspects of family culture. In some instances, this method amounts to little more than sloganeering with more of a perceived than real effect. Although Lou Holtz is a big proponent of developing a positive, goal-oriented outlook, he forcefully notes, "Talking ain't doing." In his view, neither pep talks or attempts to inspire a false sense of confidence improves performance, and the latter may actually reduce it as reality takes hold.[19]

Those who study management or lead in business or athletics sometimes embrace an overly simplistic view on motivation and incentives. The mention of "incentives" may cause some to fixate only on cash bonuses. Simply put, an incentive includes any benefit that rewards players for good performances or punishes them for bad performances, whether it involves the exchange of money or not. In this light, incentives include contractual performance targets, prizes, or awards for exemplary performance, promotions, titles, preferred treatment, special honors, embarrassment, undesirable duties, additional training, and just about anything that a coach can dream up that is legal. The key to effective use of incentives of whatever stripe is that they are closely linked to the desired or undesired behavior and are of sufficient size to illicit the desired response without going far beyond that point. Lombardi's weekly awards ceremony struck this balance. A manager or coach who hands out too many awards quickly diminishes the value of them and their effectiveness. Players or employees must find them meaningful.

Beyond the mere recognition of the need to motivate players or employees, one of the most difficult questions is how much should a leader attempt to customize motivational policies? Should all players be treated alike or should policies be tailored to fit individuals and particular circumstances? The difficulty of this question is seen by the diversity of approaches adopted even by very successful coaches. On the one hand, nearly all coaches who have written or spoken on this matter espouse some form of consistency in their policies. In practice, though, what they mean by consistent or fair policies across players differs widely. Individualizing of rules and incentives is needed while recognizing that limits to individualization must exist. As good managers realize, people are not like a bunch of homogeneous nuts and bolts. In terms of external motivation, some people require little in the way of pushing or enticing once they sign on. They can be counted on to put their best effort forward, and may, in fact, bristle at paternalistic oversight. At the other extreme, some people will take any opportunity that the boss turns his head to goof off even when given incentives otherwise.

At the one end of the spectrum is the approach taken by Marty Schottenheimer when he took over the reins of the Washington Redskins in the fall of 2001. For instance, he required every player to participate in a notorious practice exercise called the "Oklahoma Drill" where runners and tacklers face off in one-on-one situations. Even 40-year-old veteran players such as Bruce Smith and Darrell Green were not exempted from the drill. As Smith later noted, "I don't think I've ever done the Oklahoma drill, maybe in high school." However, this kind of extreme is not very common among successful coaches. It may not even be typical policy for Schottenheimer. There may be reasons beyond the immediate moment why he chooses to make all players engage in a particularly challenging drill. In taking over a team that he believes underachieved or was lacking in discipline, he may think that the importance of establishing a culture of hard work and discipline is greater than individualizing his policies for the time being. If in the same job after two or three successful season, he might not make the same one-size-fits-all decision.

Even a coach such as Vince Lombardi, known for being tough on every player, individualized his approach. He stopped yelling at quarterback Bart Starr in front of the team after a conversation with Starr where the quarterback said such criticism undermined his on-the-field leadership. Wide receiver Max McGee referred to him as "the greatest psychologist" in knowing how to tailor his approach to different players. David Maraniss notes that because of Paul Hornung's ability to shrug off criticism, Lombardi often used him as a whipping boy. Marv Fleming needed constant riding. Willie Davis was so self-motivated that he received very little reproach. Lombardi even cut McGee slack on some of his curfew breaking that he would not have tolerated from just any player.[20] Another NFL coach often noted for his inflexibility with regard to players, Tom Landry, customized his policies to some extent. Former fullback Walt Garrison said that Landry permitted defensive standout Bob Lilly to just jog around in shorts for the first few weeks of training camp.

UCLA basketball coach, John Wooden, was also known for his consistency and fairness across players. In regard to his handling of racial differences at a time when racial issues sparked great controversy, one of his black players, Curtis Rowe, said, "Coach Wooden doesn't see colors. He sees players."[21] In spite of this even-handed culture, Wooden openly criticized the idea that treating all the players alike made sense. He flatly stated, "They knew I never treated them all alike in every respect, and I never professed I would."[22] For instance, because of Lew Alcindor's height, race, and abilities, he viewed Alcindor as facing pressures unlike those faced by the other players on the team, so he adjusted some of his policies accordingly. In spite of his rationale and candor on this matter, Wooden recognized that his differential policies sometimes stirred negative feelings among other players.

While it may be surprising, some of the greatest coaches of all time are at the extreme end of the spectrum when it comes to individualizing team policies. The most glaring example may be Red Auerbach as coach of the Boston Celtics. Auerbach made no secret of his special treatment of star player Bill Russell. He felt that Russell was so valuable to the team and played so hard during games, that he often permitted Russell to sit out practice drills or to go at less than full speed to conserve himself for games. For many athletes, the long-standing coaching maxim, "you play like you practice" is true. Yet for some, it is not true. Bill Russell often played nothing like he practiced.

The optimal degree of individualization of policies by a manager depends on the situation. For instance, greater individualization is likely more critical in a sport such as basketball than in one such as football. A football coach has to interact with fifty players, where a half dozen may be considered stars. In contrast, an NBA coach has a much smaller set of players, a twelve-man roster, to oversee with maybe one or two star players. Further, the impact of a single player such as a Bill Russell is considerably greater than any one player on a football team, also giving the basketball coach a greater incentive to make adjustments. On the other hand, the degree of individualization needed may change over-time create difficulties for a coach. As coach of the Phoenix Suns, Paul Westphal took Auerbach's tack and treated veteran players such as Charles Barkley and Danny Ainge differently than many other players. The policy worked fine until Barkley's skills diminished, creating a situation where players who had resented some of the differential treatment became more important. Westphal ultimately lost his job as this shift in power took place.

COMMUNICATION AND CONFLICT

Bill Parcells identifies the idea that "confrontation is healthy" as his "Rule Number Two" in turning a team around. He goes so far as to say, "If you want to get the most out of people, you have to apply pressure—that's the only thing that any of us really responds to. . . . Creating pressure in an organization requires confrontation, and it can get very intense, very emotional. I've seen coaches avoid confrontations with their players because they don't like conflict, and I assume the same thing is true among the leaders of business teams. . . . Without confrontation, you're not going to change the way they think and act." He goes on to praise directness in communication because it is much more valuable to people and the organization to have a leader who is extremely clear and open than one who vaguely talks around subjects.[23] For Parcells, communication and confrontation may not be one and the same, but they are first cousins. Mike Krzyzewski supplies a similar outlook, "Confrontation simply means meeting the truth head on."[24]

No doubt, for a team to succeed, people must know what it is that they need to do. In one way or another, nearly every successful coach emphasizes the importance of "communication." However, what this means can vary widely across coaches. One thing is for certain, most coaches do not refrain from direct confrontation. The clarity and direct communication embraced by a Bill Parcells or a Mike Krzyzewski have been an important component in their success as team builders. Many organizations, in fact, flounder because their leaders avoid clear-cut statements. This kind of avoidance may stem from a personal distaste for conflict, or it may merely reflect a leader who is pursuing personal agendas and playing political games at the expense of the organization.

However, Parcells, Lombardi, and other coaches who lean to the blistering end of the spectrum may superimpose their own personalities on the subject of clear communication by leaders. In examining the edges of Parcells' comments or in observing the behavior of coaches such as Parcells, Krzyzewski, or others, they fail to distinguish between direct communication and acerbic put downs. At times, they equate caustic with clear. Parcells is well known as not only making things clear to players but belittling them. Of course, in Parcells' view of the importance of applying "pressure," such humiliation may be intimately linked to directness. Here, the point is that they may succeed in spite of their harshness and not because of it.

Clear, direct communication may be a key component of successful management, but scathing tirades or biting shots are not integral part of clear communication. Joe Torre, for instance, lists straight communication as his "third ground rule" for success. However, he also places the treatment of players with respect as a key factor. As a general rule, he does not humiliate players or criticize them in front of other players, choosing rather to handle matters plainly but in private.[25] John Wooden is another example of a highly successful coach who used plain language with his players but avoided biting remarks. Wooden openly discussed the importance of discipline and communication, even noting the case of a specific coach he knew who had good talent and good knowledge but communicated very poorly to his players.[26] Yet, Wooden accomplished his objectives without the vitriolic verbiage. The examples of Torre, Wooden, and others who succeeded without the harsh communication, does not show that their style was superior. Instead, it suggests that, indeed, the Parcells and Lombardis of the coaching world, in spite of their success, may have overestimated the importance of their particular brand of direct communication.

The importance and role of coaches and managers in being able to interact with people has increased over the last few decades, especially in sports such as basketball and baseball. For a long time, coaches could subscribe to the "X" style of management—management by authoritarian decrees, intimidation, bullying, and so on. In bygone eras, many coaches have certainly won with this style whether Woody Hayes at Ohio State, Bo Schembechler at Michigan, Bob Knight at Indiana, and others. As professional players have become more mobile in recent years and pay for players has made them millionaires, this style of management has been eroded. More commonly now, successful coaches have to be able to sit down and talk to players and resolve disputes between themselves and players or between players, probably more so in sports with smaller rosters than in sports such as football with larger rosters.

Nobody exemplifies success at human relations better than Phil Jackson in his tenure with the Los Angeles Lakers and the Chicago Bulls.[27] Over a decade, he has coached teams to eight NBA championships. No doubt, it helps to have some of the best players in the league, or ever, in Michael Jordan, Shaquille O'Neal, Kobe Bryant, and Scottie Pippen. Still, Jackson has been able to mesh strong and often volatile personalities and egos into champions. In Chicago, he slowly convinced Jordan that developing offensive systems that integrated other players more would make them a better team over the long haul than just giving the ball to Jordan every time down the court. He prodded excellence out of a petulant player such as Scottie Pippen. He even folded the eccentric Dennis Rodman into the mix. In Los Angeles, he helped O'Neal make the transition from just an offensive force into an excellent defender, rebounder, and passer, and kept the childish outbursts of Bryant from derailing a run toward a second championship.

In accomplishing this, Jackson displayed the kinds of skills necessary to deal with people. He was not just a unidimensional figure all about "touchy-feely" talks and Zen philosophy. He displayed toughness, candor along with patience and restraint. He emphasized key basketball goals but made clear that life beyond the organization did exist. He demanded attention and effort but did not try to dominate players' lives.

The debate over the best means of communicating with players is really a subset of a broader debate concerning motivational methods and organizational discipline. A 2001 *Sports Illustrated* article entitled "Lords of Discipline" featured several college coaches espousing hard-line, retro ideas on discipline.[28] For instance, when taking over the helm of the University of Alabama football program in 2001, Dennis Franchione issued a 185-page policy manual to players and installed a nightly curfew for players not performing well academically even during the offseason. University of Missouri head coach, Gary Pinkel, banned earrings and hats worn indoors along with many other measures with the intent of instilling discipline. Northwestern coach Randy Walker, noted, "Lombardi talked about man's innate need for discipline. It gives people ease, because life is puzzling." He openly speaks of his admiration for former Ohio State coach Woody Hayes, legendary for his drill sergeant ways.

Throughout much of its history, team-based athletic training and discipline has modeled itself after military training from the junior high school level through the professional ranks. Winning and losing presented clear and unavoidable alternatives, portrayed akin to living and dying. The tenure of coaches and the careers of players depended on them. Winning, and therefore survival, depended on pushing individuals to the limits of their physical abilities and developing unwavering commitment to the team. In training and preparation for these objectives, coaches played the role of the drill sergeants with nearly absolute authority over the player's life. Practically anything short of death was acceptable. Screaming and verbal humiliation not only coincided with pushing players to the limits of dehydration, exhaustion, and pain but were thought by some to be indispensable toward reaching these ends. All of these tools were thought to develop not only physical skills but also built teamwork and character. Aside from maybe one or a few star players, the athletes represented little more than pieces of equipment at the disposal of coaches and general managers.

Countless anecdotes could be included from players from bygone eras at various levels about their experiences with this kind of treatment. For example, in 1954 Paul "Bear" Bryant left a successful football program at the University of Kentucky to take over a floundering program at Texas A&M. In his first year, he took the team an infamous 200-mile bus trip to a small "adjunct" facility of the university near the West Texas town of Junction. The episode has been documented in several written accounts and replayed in a film called *Junction Boys*. Out of 90 to 105 players that left on the trip (the exact number is not known), only 29 returned with the team to College Station for the season ten days later. During their stay in Junction, the team endured deprivation more akin to that imposed on military "Special Operations" recruits than the training of college players. The players slept eight men to a concrete-floored, tin-roof barrack and practiced for three hours at dawn and in the afternoon on a field of sand, rocks, and grass burrs. They received little or no water during practice and minimal medical attention, while being subjected to verbal and, according to some players, physical abuse. Bryant intended the experience to cull out the poorly motivated players, but even he was surprised at the size of the defections. Even those who defected feared Bryant to the point that most chose to hitchhike to town during the night and pay their own bus fare rather than have to quit to Bryant's face.[29]

Even though such over-the-top methods are more common at the college level, they have not entirely vanished from professional sports. When Tom Coughlin took over as head coach of the expansion Jacksonville Jaguars of the NFL in 1995, he immediately set out to develop an entire culture around the team to his liking. Beyond the usual—demanding effort and attention—he instituted several rules with which he intended to create discipline over the long term and attention to detail. These included such minute things as prohibitions on the wearing of baseball caps or sunglasses on the practice field and crossing of legs during team meetings. Nine-year veteran receiver, Darnay Scott, who jumped from the Bengals to the Jaguars during the 2002 offseason described Coughlin as a "mean guy" and "that military-type person."[30] The same kinds of complaints have surfaced when Coughlin took over the New York Giants for the 2004 season.

Although few if any coaches or former coaches will publicly criticize another coach for such tactics, some do voice more general disagreement with this view of discipline. ABC football analyst and former Oakland Raider coach John Madden recounts a very different approach toward team culture during his years with the Raiders, taking issue with the "yes sir—no sir" view of discipline. For him, discipline meant doing the right things on the field. He explained, "If a guy wears a tie and a sport coat, if he has a nice haircut, if he likes milk and apple pie, that's nice. But if he jumps offside, he's an undisciplined football player . . . The guy who says 'yeah' can be a disciplined player while a guy who says 'yes sir' may jump offside. He demanded just two things of players—that they listen to the coaches and go as hard as they could go. Otherwise, the Raiders' players faced few restrictions from their coaches. Raider players worked hard in practice, played hard in games, and paid attention in film sessions.[31] Yet, they did not look or act like Boy Scouts. While different in many ways from Madden, Duke coach Mike Krzyzewski defines discipline in much the same way, saying it is "doing what you are suppose to do, in the best possible manner, at the time you are suppose to do it."[32] He gives the players a generic rule, "Don't do anything detrimental to yourself." While this obviously covers a wide array of specific behavior, Krzyzewski consciously avoids assessing too many rules, even though he is very much a demanding and "in-control" kind of coach. In his view, "People set rules to keep from making decisions."

Pressures from society along with increased financial clout of players and free agency have influenced the militaristic culture, softening it a bit or limiting its extent over the last three decades. In some of these cases, the change in culture came about through externally imposed changes rather than changes in existing coaches. For instance, in the early 1990s, University of California basketball players successfully ousted coach Lou Campenelli for alleged verbal abuse of players. The widely publicized firing of Bob Knight as head coach of the Indiana University basketball program involved, in part, his brutal treatment of players, especially in the instance where his behavior was caught on a publicly-aired video tape. In a bit of irony, Knight was one of the most vocal defenders of Campenelli and biggest critics of the University of California administration.

However, the trend away from the militaristic coaching style has been initiated by coaches themselves without pressures from external bodies and sometimes without the support of their colleagues. Bill Walsh became head coach of the San Francisco 49ers in the late 1970s after serving as an offensive coach for Cincinnati in the prior years. While at San Francisco, Walsh compiled a regular season record of 92 wins and 59 losses, winning four Super Bowl titles. Although Walsh could be acerbic with his comments and demanded exacting attention to detail, he prided himself on the team's ability to succeed without creating an atmosphere of physical intimidation.

Even before widespread departures from the paramilitary culture in sports coaching became more common, some very successful coaches eschewed those kinds of methods. John Wooden, as coach of the UCLA Bruins won 10 NCAA basketball titles from 1964 through 1975, demanded attention and effort. His former players viewed him as a disciplinarian. Yet, he achieved the necessary amounts of effort and attention while steering away from verbal abuse or explicit intimidation. In his own words, Wooden viewed "the bench as a great teacher." Players failing to give expected effort or failing to follow instructions found themselves on the bench rather than being exposed to expletive-laden rages by their coaches. Even farther back in sports history, Bud Wilkinson, head football coach at the University of Oklahoma from 1947 to 1963, compiled an 81 percent winning percentage along with three national championships and winning streaks of 47 and 31 games. Like Wooden, Wilkinson placed high expectations on his players but was noted for his lack of temperamental outbursts. No doubt, both Wooden and Wilkinson could play more subtle games with players. Wilkinson was noted for treating injured players as outcasts, seemingly as incentive for them to return to action as soon as possible. Still, in contrast to the blustery, temperamental, drill sergeant tactics of most coaches, Wooden and Wilkinson behaved much more like contemplative business managers or teachers.

In addition to the ethical and philosophical issues surrounding debates over disciplinary methods, a key for managers or coaches is not whether discipline or managerial control is important, but how much control really helps the team or organization. Due to societal norms, the degree of control attainable in the sometimes para-military world of sports is frequently not usually possible in business settings. Although the leeway for managers to dominate the lives of employees was and is less, the domineering-militaristic managerial style so common in sports also has been present in other kinds of workplaces. Do these relatively extreme efforts to dictate behavior at a very minute level improve performance, or do they reflect more about compulsions and obsessions of the coach than meaningful policies for the team? What is discipline and to what extent is it really useful?

Coughlin and Madden represent coaches at the polar extremes in terms of the strictness or looseness of team culture. Which coaching style generated more success? Madden's teams regularly appeared in the playoffs, capturing a Super Bowl victory in 1975. Coughlin's Jaguars reached the playoffs in only their second season, made them the next two seasons, and reached the AFC Championship game in at the end of 1999 season. Based on those records, it would be difficult to pick one style over the other. Yet, Coughlin's star faded from 2000–2002 with losing seasons each year, resulting in his firing at the end of the 2002 season. In the end, his missteps in the general manager role may have cost him as much or more as his coaching or maybe his attempts to do both were the problem—an issue raised in Chapter 8. Still, even in comparing their successful years, their success in spite of these vast differences in style might suggest that the particulars of the coaching style were irrelevant in one and maybe both cases. Instead, these and other coaches shared other traits helping them toward their success.

Among the college football coaches listed in the "Lords of Discipline" *Sports Illustrated* article, Ralph Friedgen, rookie coach at Maryland, had a banner year. Under his guidance, the Terps won the ACC for the first time in over 20 years and secured a birth in the Orange Bowl. He followed up with highly successful seasons in 2002 and 2004 including major bowl appearances. However, the success of the others was more limited. Franchione's Alabama team finished at 6–5 up from 4–7 by his predecessor. In 2002 the Crimson Tide went 9–3 under his leadership—a solid but not outstanding year by Alabama standards. In 2003 he jumped shipped for Texas A&M, where his initial campaign was disappointing. Missouri finished the 2001, 2002, and 2003 seasons without enough wins to qualify for Bowl eligibility—not a very high standard. Northwestern finished 2001 and 2002 years abysmally, looking more like the doormat of the 1980s than the Big Ten Champion of the 1990s. Obviously, judging success based on just a few years has its limitations. Still, it is far from obvious that such narrow ideas about discipline are nearly as important as the caliber of the players and the offensive and defensive strategies employed. Coaches and observers alike can become overly enchanted with a particular personal style of coaching, and the culture the coach develops on the team. One thing is for certain—coaches with a variety of personalities and imposing diverse cultures on their teams have been successful. On the flip side, all kinds of coaching personalities have failed to find success. This is not to suggest that some aspects of the managerial style of a coach, and the culture he or she fosters, do not make a difference. Increasingly, a big part of the job of professional and even college coaches is the ability to go beyond the technical strategies and to be able to deal with players. Coaches who are not very good in their ability to deal effectively with players slowly seem to be waning.

Beyond the managerial style of coaches, sports commentators love to refer to the importance of team "chemistry," but does it really matter? The answer would seem to be yes, no, and maybe. The degree of interaction and integration necessary to complete required tasks is a critical factor in determining just how important chemistry is for organizations. For example, baseball has been called an individual sport for which a team score is kept. This may overstate the lack of interaction between players but it does highlight the fact that the degree of team coordination is low relative to other sports. A few positions such as pitcher and catcher or shortstop and second base demand close cooperation, but the left fielder and the first baseman or the third baseman and the right fielder hardly interact. When hitting, players need to respond to situations and coaching directions, but each batter faces the pitcher alone. The relative isolation and independence of baseball players in their productive capacities means that chemistry should not be a key influence on team performance.

No MLB team illustrates the unimportance of chemistry better than the Oakland Athletics dynasty of the early to mid 1970s. The team won 101 games in 1971, 93 in 1972, 94 in 1973, 90 in 1974, and 98 in 1975. They advanced the American League Championship series in each of these seasons and won the World Series in 1972–74, defeating a powerhouse Cincinnati team from the National League in 1972 and very strong Baltimore teams from their own league in 1973 and 1974 to do so. In addition, the team finished second in their division in 1969, 1970, and 1976. The team achieved these heights in spite of tumultuous internal battles between manager and players, owner and players, owner and manager, and the players themselves. For example, in spite of winning two World Championships, the tension between owner Charlie Finley and manager Dick Williams grew to the point that Williams was replaced with Alvin Dark for the 1974 season.

In baseball, an obvious recent case of the lack of importance of team chemistry is the San Francisco Giants. They advanced to the World Series in 2002 and came within a few outs of capturing the title. They achieved this success in spite of their two best players, Barry Bonds and Jeff Kent, disliking each other to the point of getting into a shoving match in the dugout during a regular season game. Both in Pittsburgh and in San Francisco, Bonds has been seen by some other players as a selfish and moody player, given to defensive lapses due to his indifference. Yet, over the last several years, he hit the baseball with power and batting average on a level or even surpassing greats such as Ruth, Mays, and Aaron. Kent, as the next best player on the team and representative of some of the other players' attitudes, took exception to Bond's effort. In spite of these tensions boiling into open hostility at times, baseball is a game where a player such as Bonds could play his position in left field decently and then step up to the plate and perform in a way that helped his team. As maddening as some of his attitudes may have been to Kent or others, they could largely do their jobs independent of Bonds.

In other sports, where the explicit cooperation between players is much greater, team chemistry likely plays a bigger role. For instance, in football, a player such as wide receiver Randy Moss of the Minnesota Vikings creates a dilemma for his team. His speed, quickness, height, and eye-hand coordination make him one of the most dangerous receivers of all time. Yet, by his own admission, he does not play hard on every play. He also throws childish tantrums directed at his quarterback not throwing him the ball enough. As talented as Moss is, he is only one of eleven offensive players on the field at a time and one of about 40 players who contribute during a game. While his contributions may be spectacular, he may only have the ball in his hand five to eight times in a game, and several of those contributions could be substituted by most any professional wide receiver. So, when Moss creates friction on the teams through his on-field or off-field antics, it can have a seriously detrimental effect on team morale and performance. One cannot be certain of the size of Moss' negative effects, but the poor performance of the team during the 2002 season were not helped by them.

The main thing that a manager must assess is how important is harmony among the labor force to the overall performance of the team or company. If people do their jobs largely independent of each other, a less than pleasant relationship between co-workers may bring about tension but affect productivity little. On the other hand, where cooperation is important, chemistry between workers is more than just a nicety.

REPLAY

1. People provide the foundation to long term success for any team or organization. People are a key if not the key resource for a firm. This point is obvious in athletics, but it is true for businesses even in an era of rapid technological use and innovation because people are always the decision makers.

2. Attracting and keeping the right people is an undervalued but critically important skill. Ironically, the success of coaches such as Dean Smith have sometimes been denigrated because of their skill in getting good people. Such thinking is backward and tends to overvalue manipulation of people and other resources over getting good people.

3. Incredibly, some managers appear to place a low priority on attracting and retaining their workforce, instead viewing them as interchangeable parts. At times, some pro sports franchises have skimped on scouting budgets just as some business executives pawn off hiring chores as a nuisance.

4. Motivating people requires thoughtful consideration of a wide array of incentives rather than a narrow, one-size-fits-all view. People, even highly paid professional athletes or mangers, are not robots. A mix of rewards, recognition, and other incentives are required.

5. Plain communication is essential to effective managing—practically all great coaches possess and develop this ability. However, the harsh or para-military methods employed by some coaches are not contributors to success.

5

Managing Information: Mike Krzyzewski as CIO

If I am through learning, I am through.

—John Wooden, former UCLA basketball coach

Beginning during the tenure of Bill Walsh as head coach, San Francisco 49ers offensive coaches would pencil in the first twenty offensive plays they planned to use prior to the game. This represents about 25 percent of a team's offensive plays in a typical game. Many coaches weaned on the San Francisco system as well some others adopted this practice such as Mike Shanahan, head coach of the two-time Super Bowl champion Denver Broncos, and Dennis Green, then head coach of the Minnesota Vikings. Of course, game situations frequently dictate deviations from the plan. For instance, a long return of the opening kickoff inside the opponent's ten yard line would usually spur an immediate revision of plans. Although Walsh admitted as much to a reporter by saying that "things never go as planned," he added that "sooner of later we'll come back to everything that's down [on the scripted play sheet]."[1]

At first glance, the practice of scripting so many plays before the game begins seems a bit strange. Purposefully restricting one's own flexibility would appear to make the job of opposing defensive coaches easier. While the practice has tradeoffs and even its advocates do not stick by it to the letter, its main advantages revolve around the acquisition and management of information. Professional football teams enter a game with a large number of plays in their playbook from which to draw. Planning in advance to call a particular set of plays helps reduce the uncertainty for one's team. As Walsh puts it, "Listing them makes me feel more secure and my quarterback feel more secure." In addition to this security blanket, drafting the plays also permits the offensive club to gather information about defensive planning and response. Of course, all teams, even those without a pre-planned set of plays, try to analyze defensive reactions to obtain important clues, but the practice of scripting plays permits this information to be gathered in a systematic, preplanned rather than haphazard way. This information acquired during the early parts of a game can then be utilized as the game progresses.

Although pundits during the 1990s frequently referred to an ongoing information revolution, decision makers in the twentieth century did not discover the importance of reliable information. Monarchs, military leaders, and merchants from antiquity have understood the value of searching out and carefully using information. They did not require twentieth century industrialists or academics to tutor them on how informed decisions are superior to decisions made in ignorance. The late twentieth century, however, ushered in staggering technological breakthroughs in computers, electronic networks, video retrieval, and other information technologies. These technological developments dramatically lowered the costs of collecting, transferring, and analyzing information, and thereby, compounded the amount of information on hand at exponential rates.

In fact, the information explosion occasionally recast the problem into one of too much information rather than not enough. It also infected some managers with an addictive fascination with information technology rather than a sensible and cost effective use of information. Regardless of how tight budgets might be for other kinds of expenditures, information technology expenditures often skirted through as if endowed with magical properties. Marking out a Web presence and finding a catchy ".com" name frequently took precedence over more serious matters as managers feared being left in the dust of information technology. As managers and companies have begun to learn, some more quickly than others, information and technological upgrades are only useful to the extent that they help to improve decision making within an organization or better position the firm to interact with untapped customers. Put a little differently, the value of information to any decision maker rests in its ability to help decision makers simplify the complexities and reduce the uncertainties of the world. The end result is a better foundation for decisions or to better connect with customers. While sports managers have not led the way in using new technology to manage and transmit information, their experiences with information do highlight several critical features of effective management of information.

INFORMATION, INFORMATION, INFORMATION

In real estate, the adage for success has long been "location, location, location." For most sports teams as well as many businesses, information can be substituted for location as the critical ingredient in success. Whether in football, on Wall Street, or Main Street, managers face a complex world. A multitude of causes and effects occur nearly simultaneously and situations change rapidly. In football, offensive and defensive personnel shift from play to play as do pre-play formations, blocking schemes, pass routes, offensive plays, defense schemes, position on the field, down, yardage to obtain a first down, and so on. On Wall Street, timely reports on raw material production, contractual agreements, technological developments, financial data, political developments, and other economic signals are deemed so critical that firms spend billions of dollars per year in the pursuit of this information. On Main Street, the habits and preferences of consumers, the reactions of rivals, availability and costs of materials and wholesale items, the cost of borrowed funds, and the reaction of shareholders all pose knotty and important informational puzzles not easily unraveled.

The Dallas Cowboys developed into one of the premier sports organizations of the sixties and seventies, in part because of their emphasis on information. During only their second season of operation, General Manager Tex Schramm hired a statistician to work with coaches to quantify performance factors and to use computers to record, organize, and analyze the data. The statistician paired an original set of 300 measured items down to a small set summarizing character, quickness, agility, strength, explosiveness, competitiveness, and mental alertness. Scouts used these metrics as the basis to assign grades from 1–9 to prospects. The team went so far as to search out and adjust for the biases of individual scouts in their grading. By 1963, Schramm and head coach Tom Landry began to exploit this wealth of information in drafting players and signing free agents.[2]

While sometimes reluctantly, other parts of the sporting world slowly crept into the information age. Baseball manager Earl Weaver kept compiled detailed statistics on the performance of specific hitters against specific pitchers and vice versa. Before his time and even beyond, many managers simply relied on the tried but not always effective "lefty against righty" strategy or on merely gut feelings about situations. Weaver recognized that a manager's judgment still mattered but that this judgment would be better informed by meaningful data. About the same time as Weaver, Dick Williams also pioneered a greater reliance on detailed information about situational performances of his players. He utilized this kind of analysis to help guide the Red Sox to the World Series in 1967, the Athletics to a dynasty in the 1970s, and the Padres to the World Series in 1984. As this kind of meticulous review of data become more acceptable, some later managers went even further with it. Tony LaRussa, for one, is widely noted for his attention to organizing and studying summaries of key bits of information about performance. LaRussa has won pennants with the White Sox, Athletics, and Cardinals. One writer goes so far as to call him "compulsive" in his attention to detailed information. LaRussa views information as not only one of his primary tools in making strategic moves against his opponent but also in rationalizing his decisions to players.[3] The movement toward the information age has swung far enough that now Brian Billick, head coach of the Baltimore Ravens, requires all of his assistants to utilize personal computers in the recording of certain details— a requirement hard to imagine even ten years earlier, especially in the macho culture of professional football.

Developing an organizational culture where information gathering and analysis methods, especially new ones, are embraced is no easy task in itself. Because it stepped so far out of line with common practice of the sports world of the early sixties, the intensive, computerized, data-oriented analysis of the Dallas Cowboys spawned derision from other teams, the media, and sometimes even from Cowboy players themselves. These detractors saw the computerized methods as an extension of Tom Landry's seeming impersonal ways and a triumph of cold methodology over more passionate leadership. Similarly, Earl Weaver often took abuse over his reliance on numbers. Even one of his ace pitchers, Jim Palmer, derisively referred to Weaver's data analysis. In several instances, the use of more intensive information gathering or analysis methods in sports took sizable leaps forward when leaders either came from outside of sports or had at least spent some time pursuing other careers or interests. For example, Tex Schramm had spent time working in network television in New York. During his time there, he became aware of how computers could store and analyze huge amounts of data. Tony LaRussa holds a law degree. Outside of sports, the same kinds of resistance to informational technology also emerge. Workers and managers involved in the day-to-day operation have frequently viewed data collection and evaluation as ivory tower edicts from detached executives. They may nominally adopt procedures forced on them but discard such tools for actual decision making, choosing to fall back on experience and gut feelings.

The critics of incorporating new information gathering and analysis methods often suffered from two common problems that frequently hinder the integration of better information collection and analysis in other kinds of organizations. First, many do not really understand the methods employed. With limited understanding of their workings, these critics view the new ideas as esoteric and suspicious. For example, the critics of the Cowboys viewed the methodology simplistically as merely a fascination with or reliance on "computers" rather than people. They could not see the intimate link between the methods used and gaining an informational advantage over the competition. Unlike the poorly informed critics, Tom Landry's background in engineering made him respect detailed data analysis rather than be suspicious of it. He quickly bought into the importance of quantifying and scientifically analyzing large amounts of relevant data. He recognized the advantage this information could provide to his coaching and scouting staff.

This same problem rears up in business settings. Often, the higher level managers' training in data analysis may have become stale and dated in the twenty or thirty years since they graduated from college. They may see basic accounting or finance data as useful but be suspicious of more sophisticated statistical techniques simply because they are unfamiliar with them. For information to be useful in an organization, key managers or leaders must fully "buy in" themselves. With the Cowboys, for instance, Tom Landry's acceptance and participation in the data-oriented analysis made it more than just a novelty. Even with his support, some coaches and players would still not grasp the relevance of the methods, but without his full support, the information, no matter how useful, would have been brushed aside as a lark of Tex Schramm and some pointy-headed statistician. Cooperation also increases when these tools and their uses are not just explained to those impacted by the methods but where the relevance and usefulness of the tools can be demonstrated in hands on ways.

The second hurdle to newer and better uses of information stems from an overconfidence in one's abilities to solve complex problems with little more than seat-of-the-pants decision making. Experimental psychologists have documented this behavior and labeled it "cognitive conceit." Among both sports managers and business managers, success can produce a culture of bravado where one's own gut feelings become over-valued. Promotion to higher levels of responsibility itself can sometimes breed this kind of overconfidence and contempt for more or better information.[4] The cognitive conceit problem, though, does not just strike executive-level personnel. It can run throughout all levels of an organization. It may influence players to think that they "don't need any stinking computer printouts to help make decisions." A successful baseball player, in part because of his success, may develop an inordinate amount of confidence in his ability to pick the right pitcher just based on a hunch and observation.

Probably the best way for managers to heighten awareness of this kind of problem among themselves and others is to use real examples or even borrow some of the experiments from cognitive psychologists. As a simple example, most people have considerable confidence in their ability to pick out a seeming "hot streak" whether it be by a hitter in baseball, a basketball shooter, or other situations. In fact, considerable evidence has been collected indicating just the opposite. Most individuals poorly distinguish between a random sequence and a non-random sequence. If a coin is flipped 100 times, it is quite common for sequences of several heads or tails to surface. When presented with these sequences disguised as shooting outcomes—made versus missed—rather than coin flips, it is common for people to impute "hot streaks" to these purely random sequences.

TRACKING INFORMATION WITHIN THE TEAM

During the 2001 Stanley Cup playoffs, Colorado Avalanche coach Bob Hartley's practice of consulting players concerning team decisions attracted attention. In Hartley's view, a coach who does not try to gain from the knowledge of the players is foolish. Duke University basketball coach Mike Krzyzewski echoes this idea, espousing a broad view of effective communication on a team.[5] He encourages dialogue between players and views facilitating and encouraging that dialogue as part of his or any leader's job. He even goes a step further than most coaches by prompting players to speak up in timeout huddles. As he notes, "I want players to talk in the huddle because they might notice something that I cannot see from the sidelines."[6]

Hartley and Krzyzewski either consciously or intuitively understand that information resides in the minds of many different people in an organization, sometimes in large chunks and sometimes in little pieces. Some information is held in common among almost all members of an organization and carries the label public information, but some information is held by one or a few individuals—private information. Private information may include facts that, in principle, could be known by others but in reality are known only by one or a few. Skillful management of information requires institutionalizing ways to collect this private knowledge residing among team members and using it for the team's advantage. In organizational parlance, the idea of trying to extract all information relevant to decisions within an organization is called the "informativeness principle."[7]

Instituting policies that promote revelation of key pieces of private information relevant for decisions is very important but often undervalued in management decision. Many coaches, for instance, appear threatened by the notion that their players may know as much or more as they do about some subjects. For them, suppressing rather than promoting the communication of information by team members becomes policy. Of course, these policies may not be explicitly considered. Instead, they tend to arise more or less by default as coaches may belittle attempts by players to share information or may impose such authoritarian regimes that players are afraid to offer any information. A person would be hard pressed to find a coach or manager any more "in control" of his team than Krzyzewski, yet he recognizes that seeking out and fostering the exchange of information does not threaten his leadership, rather it enhances his team's performance. This kind of emphasis on the acquisition and use of meaningful information is mirrored by successful leaders in business. GE chief executive, Jack Welch says, "Learn, learn, learn." As he explains, "We soon discovered how essential it is for a multibusiness company to become an open learning organization. The ultimate competitive advantage lies in an organization's ability to learn and to rapidly transform learning into action."[8]

In contrast, fostering the spread and use of information requires that a coach or manager actively foster and facilitate an environment in line with this objective. Players must be able to see that the manager values and expects truthful revelation of information. Yankee manager, Joe Torre, recounts a conversation with pitcher David Cone during Game Three of the 1996 World Series that illustrates the importance of drawing out information. Torre needed truth from Cone about the player's condition and whether he could expect to get left-handed power hitter, Fred McGriff, out. Torre also recognized that Cone's fierce competitiveness might encourage the player to alter the truth in order to stay in the game. Torre spoke very frankly with Cone in order to motivate honesty. Although intensified because of the circumstances, Torre's search for relevant and honest information was not just a one-time, ad hoc appeal. He ranked "straight communication" as his third "Key to Success" and actively cultivated truthful dialogue from players throughout the season so that he felt the response from Cone, with a little extra pressure, would be accurate.[9]

Simply put, coaches and managers who cultivate the truthful revelation of important information place themselves in a position to make much better decisions. A football coach at Southern Illinois during the 1950s, for instance, encouraged his offensive linemen to report back to him with regard to whether they could handle their assigned man by themselves or whether they might need help. This kind of search for information as a basis for adjustment was uncommon in the football world, especially in the 1950s. On most teams, a player unable to block his opponent by himself would be subjected to a barrage of harsh and belittling language as if the trouble lay only in the player's desire. In contrast, the Southern Illinois coach assumed his players were giving full effort so that blocking difficulties stemmed from a mismatch in abilities. With this information in hand, he could make adjustments in blocking schemes so that the opposing player could not disrupt the offense for the entire game.[10]

Unfortunately, the importance of the informativeness principle escapes many leaders. The author played high school football on a team ranked second for most of the year in the state of Texas in its classification. The ranking grew out of a solid basis—the team reached the playoffs the prior season, boasted almost forty seniors, included several college prospects, put up offensive and defensive lines weighing in at or well above 200 pounds across the board (large for the era and classification), and enjoyed highly skilled backs and receivers. After eight straight wins that came with relative ease to start the season, the team lost its final two games and missed the playoffs. No problem plagued the team more than underutilization of talent. Certainly, the coaches attempted to use players to their highest valued use for the team, but as with all managers, their evaluations fell prey to errors and biases. To the point here, the coaches followed the common practice of most coaches and did not develop a culture or institute mechanisms for players to transmit vital information to coaches about the relative abilities of other players at certain positions. As with most teams daily practices provided players with first hand knowledge of which players were undervalued and which were overvalued.

The problem on the high school team in restricting information occurred largely because of tradition and lack of insight by the coaches. However, in business organizations, maybe more so than on sports teams, managers sometimes suppress information in order to gain personal informational advantage. The proverb, "information is power," is true, and holding information closely can grant individuals within a company the ability to gain power and related benefits at the expense of the company. For instance, upper level leaders may utilize opaque internal accounting methods to disguise expenditures that benefit them. Unit managers may hold back pertinent information from other units because withholding it may provide strategic benefits to that manager's unit. In athletics, such opportunistic use of information is likely rarer but not without precedent. A positional coach, because of a friendship or dislike of a player under him, might misrepresent the player's performance or give the player more or less opportunity than another player.

Eliminating the opportunistic use of information by individuals within an organization is a difficult task. People not only find rewards from hoarding information in their paychecks but also in power. It comes back to the agency problem discussed in Chapter 2—the diverging objectives of the individual from the organization or unit. Even in organizations that institute structures and incentives and encourage the sharing of relevant information, individuals can often still gain from keeping useful information to themselves. One tactic is to go beyond incentives that reward sharing of information and punish those who withhold relevant information. The difficulty here is that it may be difficult to distinguish opportunistic use of information from innocent mishandling or overlooking of information. The problem grows only worse at higher levels within an organization. High-level managers may face near impunity for the discretionary withholding of important information for reasons of personal advantage. In addition, it may be relatively easy to claim that the information is sensitive and strategic in nature.

The opportunistic use of information is a big part of the mix in the accounting scandals that surfaced in recent years involving firms such as Enron and auditing firms such as Arthur Andersen. It may be true that contractual conflicts exists in situations where an auditing firm is part of a larger organization reaping big consulting dollars from the audit client. This may lead to tension between accurate audits and attempts to hide information to keep the consulting business going strong. Those kind of issues are interesting but aside from the main point here. Within firms such as Enron and auditing firms such as Andersen, individual executives sometimes pursue their own agendas and intentionally withhold relevant information from the scrutiny of others within their firms. At Enron, the CEO and CFO appear to have not only been aggressive risk takers but not inclined toward the informativeness principle. Some auditors from Andersen—whether because of company policy or because of individual decisions—were not inclined to push for more transparency and neither did Enron's board. As in many cases where the informativeness principle is flaunted, the consequences caught up with Enron.

While better rules regarding corporate board oversight or audit-firm relationships may help, rules such as these already exist. To really avoid opportunistic use of information requires policies along with people willing to carry out those policies. The selection of people who will be in positions to utilize information either to the organization's well-being or to their own is a critical choice within all organizations because there will always be room for discretion and opportunistic use of information as long as information is costly to obtain. The hiring process may be one of the few chances that exists to put in place people who will truly implement information-sharing policies.

MANAGING THE LEARNING CURVE

The AFC Wild Card Playoff game between Buffalo and Tennessee at the end of the 1999 season had been a defensive tug-of-war. With less than a minute left in the game, the Bills scratched out a field goal to go ahead 16–15. The next play became part of NFL lore. The Bills kicked a low "squib" kick that the Titans' Frank Wycheck fielded. He took a step or two to draw in the Buffalo kick coverage team, wheeled to his left, and threw the ball across the field to Kevin Dyson. Dyson caught it and ran down the left sideline for the winning touchdown.

This "Music City Miracle" involved considerable luck that everything came off just right as well as a razor-thin judgment by the officials that the pass to Dyson did not travel forward—a decision still disputed by Bills fans. While luck played a sizable role, the Titans had prepared for this contingency. Titans players note that Jeff Fisher, the head coach, is compulsive about devoting practice time to nearly every conceivable situation. One player says, "You name the situation and we'll practice it. Fair catch-free kick, intentional safety."[11] Fisher understands an important premise as a manager—while luck may play a role, desirable outcomes do not usually just happen by themselves. Players do not just naturally put themselves in the right places or make the right decisions. Instead, these things must be learned through realistic practice and not merely through classroom meetings.

Mike Krzyzewski repeats a motto speaking to this very point, "It is not what I know. It's what they [the players] do that really matters."[12] Albert Einstein put the same idea a little differently, "Information is not knowledge." While all athletic teams spend considerable time "practicing," several of the most successful coaches go beyond the ordinary and often mindless scheduling of practice drills. They comprehend that learning is a process requiring time and careful attention to what is learned and how things are learned. Even though the term "learning curve" has entered everyday vocabulary, many coaches and managers still do not get the point. Instead of recognizing that learning occurs along a path and that this path requires management, they treat people as if they were robotic machines into which knowledge can be programmed much like one would plug program code into a computer.

In effectively managing learning, skillful coaches do not mindlessly imitate the routines passed down by their mentors but carefully craft meaningful learning environments to mimic game conditions or to develop specific skills useful in game conditions. For instance, almost all sports teams practice "game situations" to varying degrees, some coaches not only devote much more time to it, but they take greater care in more realistically simulating game environments than others. Mike Krzyzewski follows his own advice to "plan for nuances of game situations," adding that "not all coaches do." In his team's practices, faux-officials not only call fouls on players but team and individual fouls are tracked so that players can learn to adapt their play to the number of fouls that they have. As a result, in actual games Krzyzewski does not automatically pull players out of the game in the first half when they get their second foul as do many coaches because he has confidence that they not only have a conceptual idea of what to do but practical experience in adapting their play to the situation. He credits his game-like tracking of fouls during practice with his team's ability to foul less than other teams and shoot many more foul shots.[13] In contrast, many coaches practice without any officiating at all, permitting and sometimes even encouraging players to engage in behavior almost certain to lead to a foul in an actual game. Such coaches seem to think that the behavior developed during practice will be turned off like a valve during the game, when in reality, they unknowingly develop foul-prone habits.

Long before Mike Krzyzewski conceived of his practice regimen, UCLA head basketball coach John Wooden intently simulated game situations in practice.[14] He preached, "Failing to prepare is preparing to fail." Yet, in his view, intensive preparation meant doing rather than thinking. He steered away from the use of a playbook, listing all the different sets and plays teams run. Instead, he preferred to get his points across bit by bit in practice accompanied directly by the players doing these things. He viewed five minutes of talk and twenty-five minutes of repetition in practice as much more beneficial than thirty minutes of chalk talk.[15]

The critical importance of learning and the necessity of managing emphasizes the flip side of the informativeness principle. That principle highlights the existence of decentralized bits of knowledge across members and units of an organization and the importance of establishing mechanisms for collecting and utilizing the information. Effective management of learning recognizes that central management possesses some of the useful information for the firm, residing in the minds of a few designers, planners, or managers. However, for this information to be utilized effectively, mechanisms must be established that permit the knowledge to be dispersed among members or units in such a way that the knowledge is able to influence productivity and not just as sterile ideas.

Another consequential but commonly overlooked aspect of managing learning processes encompasses the lessons to be learned when things go wrong. "Failure analysis" is the label commonly applied to this topic and comprises a small but thriving subfield of engineering. The area examines the collapse of buildings or airplane disasters and attempts to construct a meticulous autopsy depicting the reasons for the failure, helping to identify ways to avoid such a failure in the future. The National Transportation Safety Board's accident investigation team is an ongoing example. However, failure analysis is seldom examined from an organizational or managerial perspective. Only recently has the topic begun to appear in little bits in business education curriculum or executive seminars as a tool for organizational learning and improvement. As a result business managers not only obtain little training in how to analyze and learn from failures but do not appreciate its importance. Even worse, they may eschew the analysis of failures. The tragedy in this is that while most failures have some technical "point of failure" cause, there often exist deeper, managerial and organizational reasons for failures that if left unchecked, lead to future failures of the same sort.[16]

Attention to failures and problems can help a team or organization avoid what has come to be termed the "normalization of deviance" problem. The term refers to the situation where a problem develops and is recognized. However, it is ignored because seemingly successful outcomes continue to occur in spite of its existence. It is akin to the problem of incrementalism—the old frog in water that is gradually heated to the boiling point. A basketball team may get away with careless fouls for much of the season because it dominates other teams talent-wise or effort-wise. The coach begins to view these fouls as little more than a nuisance. Then, in a key game, the team plays another team that cannot be dominated by talent and effort alone. Now, these fouls become critical to the outcome of the game, but they cannot be easily controlled just by telling the players to foul less. They team has not worked on the problem. Both the 1986 *Challenger* disaster and the 2003 *Columbia* disaster have been cited as examples of this kind of failure to examine problems and rectify them.

In contrast to most business environments, learning from failures as well as successes has a rich history in athletics. Long ago, such learning developed even to the point of becoming regimented through the viewing and evaluation of game and practice film and video. When done properly, analyzing past problems is one of the best teachers. Red Auerbach learned from his coach while playing at George Washington University that there were "only two things wrong with a mistake: not admitting it, and not learning from it."[17] In athletics, film and video have provided a means of seeing the problem very clearly. Krzyzewski calls it the "truth of video." A player may not even be fully aware of unproductive habits or untapped opportunities that examining a video can highlight. During the 2002 season, Tennessee Titans head coach Jeff Fisher used such a method to help his players correct a persistent problem of lining up offsides and jumping offsides. He took the step of setting up a camera aimed directly down the line of scrimmage so that players were able to view their alignment themselves.[18]

As commonly employed in athletics, failure analysis has had its limitations. Some coaches use it to do little more than belittle players, somehow thinking that junior high school coaching tactics work at any time and on any level. In a similar way, coaches may be too quick to jump to the conclusion that a player was somehow slack in his mental attentiveness or effort. In contrast, a legendary coach such as Red Auerbach viewed mistakes exactly the opposite—not usually arising from negligence but rather arising from a system or process that needed improving.[19]

Possibly the most common weakness of failure analysis in athletics is that among the vast majority of coaches it steers nearly exclusively toward technical, player-related issues and not toward organizational and managerial issues. An inclination toward self examination, especially out in the open to players, does not come easily to highly confident coaches. Many coaches have uttered the phrase, "I take responsibility for this loss," only to mean "You players let me down, so I'm going to work you like never before to make sure you don't let me down again." Few coaches during a film session admit, "Here is where I made a terrible play call" or "I should have substituted differently here." In fact, many coaches may be inclined to view any such admission of culpability as weakness, inspiring players or employees to lose confidence.

Yet, outside of these high-ego, macho-laced cultures, the honest acceptance of responsibility and admission of mistakes normally comes across to others as a virtue. By contrast, the chest-thumping insistence on viewing oneself as right no matter how much evidence to the contrary builds up evidence of a serious character flaw. Certainly, employees and team members prefer competent leaders over incompetent ones. Ineffective leaders, no matter how self-effacing or honest, wind up losing the support of those they are leading even if they do maintain respect for their humanity. Nonetheless, statements such as "I wouldn't have changed anything" are just silly when any reasonable onlooker can see that a different set of decisions would have improved outcomes. It is refreshing when a Mike Shanahan, head coach of the Denver Broncos, admits that he would be crazy not to change his strategy against the Baltimore Ravens after being manhandled by them in the playoffs the prior year.

Beyond machismo, the hesitancy of coaches to evaluate openly their own failures likely owes itself to the potential consequences of failure. In sports or business, failure will sometimes lead to negative consequences for those deemed culpable. There is no changing that fact. Coaches who lead a team through two or three losing season in a row likely face dismissal, and even though most coaches like to view themselves as "stand-up guys," few desire to speed their departure. The tendency to reduce or forestall the consequences of failure will, no doubt, lead to some of the same kinds of posturing and deflecting responsibility.

The politicizing of failure can also play a role in diminishing honest evaluation of mistakes. This is especially true outside of athletics, the analysis of failures such as the *Challenger* shuttle disaster or the Enron collapse may look at organizational and managerial issues, but these investigations are often so highly politicized that the analysis may not highlight the issues that are of genuine and enduring value to decision makers who would desire to learn from the problems. Sometimes during the analysis of a major disaster, Congressional committees, other government entities, or policy analysts and historians will examine failure stemming from decision making and organizational perspectives. Such analyses, even when considering how to better structure institutions or incentives to avoid failures, nearly always possess an undercurrent regarding whether more or less government involvement is appropriate, who should bear the blame, and who should suffer the consequences for the blame. These facts lead to all kinds of posturing and spinning of the facts in order to try to deflect blame. In the end, such political posturing becomes the enemy of effective, critical examination of failures.

How can a manager reduce the haze that the politics of failure invokes? Managers must first open their own decisions and systems that they have put in place to examination. Next, the leaders must depoliticize communication within an organization as much as possible. This kind of direct, plain-speaking about problems and changes is emphasized by former NFL head coach Bill Parcells in his *Harvard Business Review* article. While Parcells' own personal style and the culture of football may have tended more toward harsh than just direct and plain, his main point is valid. Outside of athletics, however, such clarity is often missing. Matters with personal, social, or political sensitive implications may be side-stepped. Managers may intentionally leave ambiguity in order to leave themselves "wiggle room" later on. In addition, other members of an organization may tend to hold back information or minimize discussion for fear of embarrassment or recrimination. No doubt, organizations do not operate in a social, political, or legal vacuum. Discussions must be tempered with regard to these "rules of the game." Still, within these bounds, open and plain communication with regard to problems and concerns is vital to the effective operation of any organization.

INFORMATION BY EXPERIMENTATION

Woody Hayes once said, "Be a pragmatist. First, find out what works. Then keep doing it."[20] Bill Walsh's practice of crafting a long sequence of plays before a game squarely takes Hayes' advice to heart and develops it into to an ongoing practice of managing information. More than just laying out a predetermined plan for attacking team, scheming the first fifteen or twenty plays in advance is a device for information gathering in a way that simplifies complex situations and provides more accurate information. The practice permits the team to set up a series of plays intended to isolate the defensive team's reaction to a particular formation, motion, blocking scheme, or pass route. The idea is to hold a number of the variables on a given play steady and isolate the particular effects of just one two things at a time. Of course, some things such as position on the field, down, or yardage to gain a first down are constantly changing so that not everything can be held steady. To deal with this, the offensive planners can devise contingencies among their set of scripted plays that deviate based on down and yardage.

Still, the idea, in essence, imitates as much as feasible what a chemist does in a lab—focus on the effects of one or two items of interest at a time while filtering out the influence of other factors. The complexity of the world often makes things appear as though everything has some effect upon everything else. Sorting out the main, secondary, and trivial effects is by no means easy—especially if one tries to do so by just sitting back and observing. Actively manipulating the interaction of chemicals with each other and their environment while holding constant things such as temperature or humidity permits the chemists to better sort out the way things are working. Broadly speaking, these kinds of practices are referred to as experimental design. To many scientists and engineers involved in laboratory research, the principles are almost second nature. Every day, they try to isolate relationships and filter out the effects of other influences. The same principles, though, have also come to be utilized in business settings, and as the example above shows, even in sports.

Coaches or business executives trying to experiment in this way face major obstacles. For instance, the defense or a rival company does not always have to respond to the same situation, formation, personnel, or play the same way. This can create false signals from the experiment. Yet, that is one reason that a sizable number of plays, such as fifteen, is chosen. A larger sample of plays strains out some of the random noise from the rival. Experimentation in business or athletics often must take place during the normal course of operation and not in a laboratory, also muddying the ability to collect "clean" data.

In spite of these obstacles, in sports as well as business, analogues to laboratory experiments do take place. Practice sessions, simulated games, scrimmages, and preseason games provide controlled environments that do not "count" toward team performance where coaches can tinker with ideas and players in ways that is very similar to the chemist in the lab. Baseball managers, for example, commonly play around with the hitting order of their lineup during spring training games. They also commonly give young pitchers more opportunities or try players in new positions during preseason.

While the experiments performed in these controlled settings closely mimic laboratory experiments and provide valuable insights, they have their limits. They are not the same as information gained during games that genuinely matter for team performance. However, collecting information through experimentation occurs even during actual game settings, although probably with less frequency than during practice sessions or preseason games. One common occurrence is when an MLB club finds itself out of the pennant race in mid-year. The manager will utilize younger players more in order to evaluate their skills and give them big league experience. This is an experiment run during actual game conditions. In another case, a manager unsure as to the abilities of a hitter in the leadoff spot might give the person a two-week tryout and see what comes about. As with the practice of scripting plays to begin a football game, the information gained is more reliable when other influences can be filtered out as much as possible.

KNOWING INFORMATION'S LIMITS

During football games, analysts sometimes refer to a "chart" that determines whether a football coach should have his team attempt a 2-point conversion after scoring a touchdown (with less than a 50–50 shot at making it) or kick the usual "extra point" worth 1 point (with a nearly 100 percent shot at making it). This chart is based on the way scoring in football tends to be based either on touchdowns (6 points) or field goals (3 points). Although 2-point "safeties" sometimes occur, they are unusual events. As a result, a 1- or 2-point lead often matters little, so a coach who scores and goes ahead by 1 point may opt for the 2-point conversion so as to increase the lead to 3 points. Likewise, a team that goes ahead by 5 points, may select to go for the 2-point conversion to increase the lead by 7 points—equal to a touchdown and 1-point conversion by the other team. The same kind of logic works for teams that may be trailing in a game and attempting to catch up in the most efficient way.

The problem with relying on a simple chart showing when to go for the 2-point conversion is that it does not provide information as to another critical aspect of this decision—that is, how much time is left in the game. If trailing by 2 points after a touchdown with 20 seconds left in the game, the decision to go for the 2-point conversion is a "no-brainer." However, the same situation in the middle of the third quarter offers no clear-cut decision. Going for the 2-point conversion and failing at this point in the game alters future opportunities. For example, if the opposing team kicks two field goals, then they will lead by 8 points rather than by just 7, so that a touchdown and 1-point conversion will no longer tie the game. Managers cannot fall back on a hard and fast rule to indicate the point in a game when the "chart" should be used. In fact, across different games, this point will differ based on the likelihood of more scoring by either team. The "when-to-go-for-2" chart provides a useful tool, but it is only useful for part of the relevant decision.[21]

This example illustrates a much broader dilemma regarding analysis and information that all managers face. On the one hand, there may be hard data and analysis regarding a problem. However this information often encompasses only a segment of the entire problem so that it is of limited value. On the other hand, only sketchy understanding or data may exist with regard to the broader elements of the problem, so that trying to incorporate all of the additional elements create tremendous uncertainty. As a result, a tradeoff is created between using solid but limited information to analyze part of a problem versus using more conjecture analysis to consider the larger dimensions of a problem.

This fundamental dilemma of real-world analysis crops up in the terminology of disciplines that study decision making. For instance, economists may use "partial equilibrium" analysis to study the effects of a regulatory change that reduces emissions of automobiles on price and consumption of automobiles. Others may attempt to identify the "general equilibrium" effects, meaning the secondary consequences on prices and consumption in related markets such as other means of transit or fuel as well as feedback from these secondary markets back on to the automobile market. The "partial equilibrium" analysis is typically much more straightforward and capable of being examined with reliable data. However, by its very nature, it may miss important external effects just as the 2-point conversion chart misses a key component of that decision. Yet, while very sophisticated "general equilibrium" models may be built with mathematical equations and computer simulations, these are often little more than guesses dressed up in a baroque façade.

The complexity of the world requires managers to break the world down into digestible chunks and to try to analyze these chunks with logic and solid, timely information. Managers who attempt to make decisions without serious attempts to collect or analyze data or who may even hold such attempts in contempt, suffer from the "cognitive conceit" problem noted earlier and documented by experimental psychologists. Yet, information and logic do not form a magic elixir permitting thought-free decision making. Managers must recognize that complex decisions rarely boil down to a neat little formula into which the relevant data can be plugged and the correct answer extruded. For one thing, no amount of information, quantified or otherwise, will typically capture all of the subtleties that may arise.

How does a manager strike the right balance between a narrow but more concrete information versus broader but more conjectural information? The U.S. Naval Academy has held seminars among faculty members from diverse disciplines to address these very kinds of questions. They label these kinds of problems as "ill-structured." Their colloquium is devoted to helping future Naval officers strike a balance between using hard tools and data while utilizing judgment to incorporate less quantifiable aspects of decisions. The colloquium draws from experts in mathematics, operations research, economics, political science, linguistics, and other fields. Beyond the Naval Academy, the study of "ill-structured" problems has grown on many campuses as people try to understand better the nature of problem solving in complex environments.

In baseball, managers may ignore "the numbers" or rely on their "hunches." If this means that a manager insists on guessing rather than using extensive data about hitters versus pitchers, the manager is likely to cost his team wins over the long haul. A few short run successes are possible and may reinforce the manager's overconfidence on such hunches. However, over a 162-game schedule where the manager faces similar situations over and over, the long run averages implied by "the numbers" will provide a much better guide than seat-of-the-pants guesses. After all, such guesses are really no different than guesses at the roulette wheel. A player may go home with a big win on any given occasion, but over the long haul, the house advantage wins out.

On the other hand, a manager may gain an advantage in "playing a hunch" due to a lack of reliable information. New situations and contingencies arise that do not always neatly conform to prior experiences. If the situation under consideration has only surfaced a half dozen times, then an average computed from these outcomes is based on such few trials as to give no meaningful information. For example, a specific hitter may have faced a particular pitcher only a handful of times. Under such circumstances, the manager's impressions of batter performance are likely superior to trying to tease long run averages out of short run statistics.

Another reason that information does not substitute for decision making is that a human manager possesses the ability to weigh multiple dimensions of a decision that may not be embodied in a unidimensional statistic. Hurricane forecasters, for instance, have access to equation-based simulations (models) of weather events utilizing the power of computers and widespread weather measurements. However, a variety of models exist with each one placing a little more weight on a particular measurement. The human forecasters rely heavily on the models but also use their judgment and experience to merge divergent models into a single forecast that also draws from information that may not be fully implemented into the model. Baseball managers, even those who put much effort into the collection and evaluation of performance measurements, do much the same thing.

The "by the numbers" versus "playing a hunch" tradeoff finds its way into all kinds of decisions in business and sports. Generally speaking, it can be called the problem of "rules versus discretion." All managers—in business, sports, or government—manage more effectively if they establish policies that dictate what will happen under certain circumstances. For instance, if a baseball outfielder misses the cutoff man, he receives a $100 fine. If people do their jobs in a satisfactory way, they should have an idea of their compensation. Clear, rule-based policies help people affected by management decisions to make plans with some degree of certainty. Without clear-cut, rule-based policies, people are left to guess as to what the consequences of a certain course of action are.

On the other hand, no set of rules can completely foresee and specify all possible contingencies. In academics, this is referred to as "incomplete contracting," and it arises due to the dynamic nature of the world and the limits of knowledge. A baseball manager who establishes a pinch-hitting rule that never permits discretion implicitly must assume that he has figured out all possible circumstances that may arise regarding future pitchers and hitters and their performances on a given night. Clearly such an assumption stretches reality to the point of absurdity. The same is true in business. Organizations that become so procedure-based as to permit no managerial discretion are setting themselves up for problems—some small and some possibly large. For instance, air travel in the United States is highly procedure-based and regimented regarding takeoff, landing, and in-flight practices for flight crews. However, pilots are left with discretion regarding in-flight decisions involving weather conditions. In contrast, one snowy night in Detroit, with all but one gate closed and planes waiting on the tarmac to disembark passengers, the airport manager and airline managers became so rule-bound that they created major problems. Rather than listen to pilot request to offload passengers first and then worry about luggage later, they stuck "by the book." As a result, passengers waited on planes for eight hours and more as toilets overflowed and the planes ran out of food, water, and clean diapers—not to mention keeping passengers basically prisoners for hours on end. The problem with discretion is that it must be used with caution. If policies are chucked too easily, they lose their value in reducing uncertainty.

FACT VERSUS FOLKLORE

In his book, *One Knee Equals Two Feet*, John Madden relates several axioms that were once held as gospel among NFL coaches and insiders. One widely held belief was that teams "can't win with a scrambling quarter-

back. Just about every coach thought that."[22] As he notes, Roger Staubach poked holes in that dictum during the 1970s. Whatever truth the adage may have held in bygone eras, the advent of faster defensive players and more aggressive, blitzing schemes turned it on its head. By the 1990s, the ability to move around became a highly sought after quality of quarterbacks. Yet, people with pedigree as strong as former quarterbacking legend and coach, Norm Van Brocklin, went so far as to say a quarterback should run only from fear.

The "scrambling quarterback" axiom illustrates an important aspect of information—folklore often takes on the guise of rock-solid fact. An imperative to the effective use of information is the ability to distinguish accurate measurement from noisy information and outright nonsense. In business and sports settings, as well as in personal areas such as health and diet, managers and observers accumulate maxims and rules-of-thumb over the years. This kind of conventional wisdom develops through practical experience often by trial and error. In many cases, the wisdom passed down contains kernels of truth. The problem is that such received wisdom of this kind also passes along folklore that embodies half-truths as well as obsolete truths—ideas that may have once reflected reality but have not been updated as circumstances have evolved. For example, the ideas about scrambling quarterbacks may have been relevant in earlier eras but became less so as defensive schemes adapted. Or it may not have ever been correct. It may have only seemed that way because individuals with great running ability like Staubach had never been given a chance to show the idea wrong.

A prime piece of sports wisdom that has taken on the status of ironclad fact is the dictum, "defense wins championships." While many coaches and media analysts across a variety of sports invest this phrase with near scriptural importance, nowhere is it trumpeted more than in football. Even when the phrase is not being stated verbatim, it seeps out of the edges of statements. For instance, a *Sports Illustrated* writer discussing Jimmy Johnson's decision to go to the Dolphins and turn down an offer from Tampa Bay, added, "If Johnson were a prophet, he would have seen that a defense-oriented team with a caretaker quarterback could get farther than a superannuated team with a Hall of Fame quarterback."[23] The clear implication of the writer—defense wins. More recently, in analyzing the NFL playoffs in January 2002, new Dallas Cowboy and highly successful NFL coach, Bill Parcells, said, "Opposed to high-scoring games that you saw last week, you will see a little bit of tighter struggles. The defenses are now in these games with Tampa and Philadelphia ready to go, and Oakland played pretty good defense at the end of the year. You will see a little stronger defensive effort, and that is always *the key to championships is the ability of teams to play defense* [emphasis added]." Yet, the facts

Table 5.1
Offensive and Defensive Ranking of Super Bowl Teams Since 1970 (Ranked by Points Allowed or Scored Within a Season)

Season	AFC Team	Rank Offense-Defense	NFC Team	Rank Offense-Defense
2000	Baltimore	7-1	New York	7-2
1999	Tennessee	3-10	St. Louis	1-2
1998	Denver	1-4	Atlanta	2-2
1997	Denver	1-3	Green Bay	1-5
1996	New England	1-6	Green Bay	1-1
1995	Pittsburgh	1-5	Dallas	3-2
1994	San Diego	2-3	San Francisco	1-4
1993	Buffalo	4-1	Dallas	2-2
1992	Buffalo	1-8	Dallas	2-3
1991	Buffalo	1-9	Washington	1-2
1990	Buffalo	1-4	New York	9-1
1989	Denver	3-1	San Francisco	1-2
1988	Cincinnati	1-6	San Francisco	4-5
1987	Denver	2-3	Washington	3-4
1986	Denver	5-5	New York	3-2
1985	New England	7-2	Chicago	1-1
1984	Miami	1-5	San Francisco	1-1
1983	Los Angeles	1-7	Washington	1-5
1982*	Miami	6-1	Washington	6-1
1981	Cincinnati	2-7	San Francisco	5-2
1980	Oakland	3-5	Philadelphia	4-1
1979	Pittsburgh	1-3	Los Angeles	5-5
1978	Pittsburgh	4-1	Dallas	1-1
1977	Denver	8-1	Dallas	1-5
1976	Oakland	3-5	Minnesota	3-1
1975	Pittsburgh	4-1	Dallas	3-4
1974	Pittsburgh	4-1	Minnesota	2-2
1973	Miami	3-1	Minnesota	6-1
1972	Miami	1-1	Washington	3-1
1971	Miami	2-1	Dallas	1-4
1970	Baltimore	1-2	Dallas	7-4
Median 70-00		2-3	Median 70-00	2-2
Median 90-00		1-4	Median 90-00	2-2
Median 80-89		2-4	Median 80-89	3-2
Median 70-79		3-1	Median 70-79	3-3

Source: National Football League, *NFL 2001 Record & Fact Book* (New York: Workman Publishing, 2001).

show that, at best, the view that a defense-oriented team would perform better than one with a great quarterback is based on an obsolete fact.

Table 5.1 displays the winners of the American Football Conference (AFC) and the National Football Conference (NFC) every year since the teams from the old AFL merged with the NFL in 1970. Beside each winning team, the team's offensive rank and defensive rank within the Conference is shown based on total points scored and total points allowed during the regular season. Overall, 11 of the 31 AFC champions finished with higher ranking defenses than offenses, while 18 finished with higher

Table 5.2
Summary Season Outcome for Top-Rated NFC and AFC Offenses and Defenses by Decade

Ranking	In Playoffs	In Championship	Champion
#1 Rated AFC Offense			
90-99	10	7	7
80-89	8	5	3
70-79	7	5	3
#1 Rated AFC Defense			
90-99	9	2	2
80-89	9	3	2
70-79	10	8	7
# 1 Rated NFC Offense			
90-99	10	10	5
80-89	8	10	5
70-79	10	6	4
#1 Rated NFC Defense			
90-99	10	5	2
80-89	10	4	4
70-79	9	6	5

Source: National Football League, *NFL 2001 Record & Fact Book* (New York: Workman Publishing, 2001).

ranking offenses than defenses. In two seasons, the ranks were equal. The NFC also crowned 11 champions with higher ranked defenses, 12 with higher ranked offenses, and 8 with equal ranks. In recent years, the "defense wins" maxim falters even more. Since 1990, only 5 of the 22 champions between the two conferences had a higher ranked defense. Super Bowl champions are also identified in the table by an asterisk, supporting the same conclusion. Only 10 of the 31 Super Bowl winners had a higher ranked defense than offense, while 15 had a higher ranked offense than defense.

Table 5.2 provides a different twist on similar data by summarizing data for the most highly ranked offensive and defensive clubs within each conference each year.

For both the AFC and NFC, the number of times that the highest ranked scoring offense reached the playoffs, advanced to the Conference Championship Game, and advanced to the Super Bowl is shown by decade. From these data, one could mount a small argument for the importance of defense over offense during the 1970s as 12 of the best defenses across both conferences won conference championships to only 7 of the best offenses winning conference championships, and 14 of the best defenses advancing to the conference championship game versus 11 for the best offenses. Much of this is attributable to the early 1970s when great defensive squads such as the 1972 and 1973 Dolphins and the 1974 and 1975 Steelers dominated. However, during the 1980s and 1990s the numbers reversed themselves. By the 1990s, excellent offenses dominated. During this decade, 12 of the best offenses won championships and 17 advanced to the conference championship game, compared with 4 and 7 for the best defenses. Table 5.3 reinforces these results, showing the performance of the best ten offenses and defenses since 1970. Again, great offenses dominated the 1980s and 1990s, reaching eight Super Bowls and winning six. Great defenses were more common in the 1970s. Since 1970, only three of the best defensive teams reached the Super Bowl with each winning.

Instead of the "defense wins championships" slogan, a more accurate formula for winning championships would be stated as, "teams with solid offenses and solid defenses win championships." As the NFL game evolved over the 1980s and 1990s, one could legitimately claim that great offense and good defense won championships. To be sure, a few defense-based teams with mediocre offenses excelled, such as the 1990 New York Giants and the 2000 Baltimore Ravens, but these were the exception rather than the rule. Even a great defensive team such as the 1986 Chicago Bears also led the league in scoring offense. Although the 2003 New England Patriots played very good defense during the season, they won the Super Bowl in an offensive shoot-out with another defense-minded club, the Carolina Panthers. A rebuttal to these numbers might be that great defenses contribute to offense not only by scoring points themselves but by creating turnovers and short fields for the offense. While it is true that offensive output is not independent of defensive performance, this reasoning works the other way also. Great offenses help their defense by keeping the ball away from the opposing offense and by pushing the opposing offense deeper into their own end to start their drives.

Another common example of errors and myths in sports information is they attribution of "streaks" or "momentum." Players, fans, and the media are quick to impute a "hot streak" to a shooter who hits several buckets in a row, to a batter who has had an above average hitting streak, a golfer

Table 5.3
Performance of NFL's Top 10 Defenses and Offenses Since 1970 (Ranked Relative to Median Points Allowed or Scored Within a Season)

Team	% of Median Points Allowed	Result	Team (year)	% of Median Points Scored	Result
Rams (75)	47%	Lost NFCC	Rams (99)	177%	Won SB
Colts (71)	48%	Lost AFCC	Vikings (98)	177%	Lost NFCC
Ravens (00)	50%	Won SB	Rams (00)	175%	Lost NFCW
Vikings (71)	50%	Lost NFCD	49ers (93)	164%	Lost NFCC
Steelers (76)	51%	Lost AFCC	Redskins (91)	158%	Won SB
Steelers (75)	52%	Won SB	49ers (94)	158%	Won SB
Vikings (70)	54%	Lost NFCD	49ers (84)	156%	Won SB
Falcons (77)	56%	No Playoffs	Bills (91)	155%	Lost SB
Bears (85)	57%	Won SB	Denver (98)	153%	Won SB
Titans (00)	57%	Lost AFCD	Packers (96)	152%	Won SB

Notes: Season ranking relative to median is within each team's conference. SB = Super Bowl; AFCC, NFCC = Conference Championship; AFCD, NFCD = Divisional Playoff; AFCW, NFCW = Wild Card Playoff.
Source: National Football League, *NFL 2001 Record & Fact Book* (New York: Workman Publishing, 2001).

who hits several birdie putts, or to a goalie who strings several good games together. Likewise the hitter who is "mired in a 3 for 30 slump" is experiencing a cold streak, and the shooter who misses several shots in a row has gone "cold." It may well be the case that teams or individuals find themselves in "the zone" on occasion. The problem is that many observers are much too quick to impute a streak where the outcomes may be indistinguishable from random and very ordinary variations around a given value. For instance, in a sequence of ten coin flips with a 50 percent chance of a head or a tail, a run of ten heads in a row is unlikely on any given set of 10 flips, but becomes very likely over a series of 1000 sets of 10 flips. Similarly, a golfer who, on average, one-puts 7 greens during eighteen holds, will have rounds with 10 or more one-putts and rounds with 3 or fewer one points. These outcomes do not reflect streaks, per se, but usually just random variation around the average.[24]

Investors and analysts frequently make these same mistakes in tracking the behavior of stock prices. The likelihood of a given stock price going up or down over a day or month is very close to 50–50—in the United States the likelihood has been slightly in favor of going up. Although this is true, a chart showing the movements of a stock price over hundreds of days or many weeks often displays movements that look strikingly like up-trends, downtrends, and sometimes cycles. However, the apparent patters are usually only a mirage. The same kinds of movements can be generated on a computer where the outcomes are forced to have a 50–50 chance of moving up or down.[25]

Business management has been a fertile ground for all kinds of folklore about effective decision making. One classic example is the quality movement embodied by and pushed by Edwards Deming. Deming is mentioned here not because he was some fly-by-night management quack. Those kind of people are easy targets. Rather, Deming was a serious thinker with serious ideas. However, whether because of his fixation or the adulteration of his ideas by others, management concepts and practices that represented food for thought and useful tools started to be peddled as gospel. In particular, the phrase "quality is free" became a mantra for the movement. Under special circumstances where a firm is underutilizing its resources to a great extent, productivity gains can be found by instituting Deming-inspired procedures without giving up much. Over the long haul, though, quality along with the methods to improve process require expenditures that require giving up some other budget item at least in the short term. Many firms flocked to these quality-enhancing methods to find initial improvements but then experienced great difficulty in sustaining the improvements. The movement lost steam in the 1990s. In fact, the whole Japanese economy, which had been touted as the proof of these methods, stagnated in the 1990s.

The adoption of folklore as the way to manage a business runs the gambit from strategic-level ideas all the way down to personnel level decisions. It incorporates sound ideas garnered from serious people like Deming all the way down to the management-guru-of-the-month who landed on the *New York Times* bestseller list. Michael Porter, an eminent Harvard business economist, pushed the idea focusing on business strategy, the structure of competition in one's market, and not getting caught "in the middle" between quality and volume. Like Deming's contributions, Porter's ideas were serious but took on a life that far exceeded their value.[26] Other ideas acquired large followings but had much less going for them such as thinking that success was all about writing a really good mission statement, pursuing diversification through conglomerate mergers much like diversifying a business portfolio, and benchmarking. The lesson for managers to learn is to be wary of accepting the wisdom about managing without careful scrutiny. Even very successful and intelligent people fall prey to fiction that they begin to believe is fact. After all, Bill Gates once said, "64K ought to be enough [memory] for anybody."

REPLAY

1. Better information makes any manager better whether in sports or business. Coaches such as Bill Walsh and Mike Krzyzewski are prime examples in sports of the importance and use of information.

2. No individual possesses all the relevant information within an organization. Organizations and teams foster the sharing of relevant information shared up, down, and across units and individuals make the most use of the information. Mike Krzyzewski's Duke teams have built this kind of culture.

3. Information is required for increased learning and knowledge, but it is not sufficient to ensure learning and knowledge. Not all coaches transfer the knowledge in their heads to player performance equally. Managers must structure environments that convert information into usable knowledge.

4. Learning from mistakes is not a mere cliche, it is common practice of successful coaches and managers. To help the team the most, learning from mistakes must become a consistent practice.

5. Experiments provide a wealth of knowledge to scientists as well as to coaches. They can do the same for managers who possess the insight and creativity to utilize them.

6. Knowledge and information are dynamic. Rules-of-thumb and longstanding practices may arise for legitimate reasons but may have become obsolete as the "defense wins championships" mantra illustrates. Reevaluation of knowledge and practice is important.

6

Managing Games within Games: Do Baseball Managers Have Beautiful Minds?

A good hockey player plays where the puck is. A great hockey player plays where the puck is going to be.

—Wayne Gretzky, former NHL star

Late in a game during the 2001 National League Divisional Series between Arizona and St. Louis, Cardinals' manager Tony LaRussa faced a decision common in baseball—to let a right-handed hitter bat against a right-handed pitcher for the Diamondbacks or to pitch-hit with a left-handed batter. Commonly, hitters perform better against pitchers who throw from the opposite side than they are hitting. LaRussa chose to stick with the original hitter. After the game, reporters quizzed him about the choice. LaRussa's answer illustrated one of the most basic skills utilized by managers during the late innings in close games. To make an intelligent choice, he needed to look beyond the single decision at hand to the sequence of decisions likely to unfold, anticipate the likely outcomes of those decisions, and reason back to his most favorable decision at the present. In short, he had to put himself in Arizona manager Bob Brenly's shoes and consider the decisions Brenly would likely make down the line to determine his own best choice now.

Figure 6.1 depicts a simplified version of such a sequence of decisions using a basic flow chart. In the diagram there are only two sequences in the decision process—first LaRussa's choice about the hitter and then the reaction by Arizona manager Bob Brenly. However, the essential elements of the strategic setting would fall out the same even if another sequence or two were added as is often the case for MLB managerial situations.

Figure 6.1
A Strategy Game within a Baseball Game

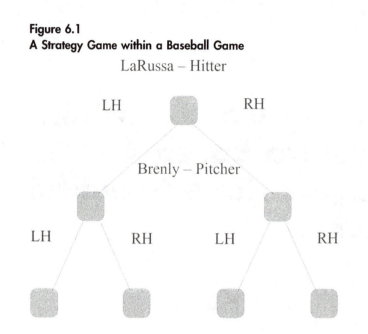

LaRussa – Hitter

LH   RH

Brenly – Pitcher

LH   RH   LH   RH

In the diagram, LaRussa looks ahead to the possible outcomes after Brenly's decision to determine the option most favorable to Brenly. Clearly, Brenly will not choose the two middle options that would lead to an expected batting average of 0.33. Instead, LaRussa can see that if he changes to a lefthanded pitch hitter, Brenly's move will be to bring in the lefthanded reliever. The stable outcome of this "game" and the best LaRussa can do is to keep the righthanded batter facing the current righthanded pitcher. In fact, this is the essence of the reasoning that LaRussa explained to the reporters inquiring about his decision. He chose at the first step by looking ahead at the different options for Brenley and how Brenly's would limit his own options. LaRussa determined his most favorable outcome by working backward from that point. The most strategically-minded MLB managers can look many moves ahead in an effort to manipulate the consequences of the fact that once a player is removed from a game, he cannot be reinserted.

A SCIENCE OF GAMES?

The reasoning processes described above and frequently required of MLB managers represents just one kind of strategic situation or strategic "game"—a decision setting where two or more parties attempt to select the best strategy based on a course of action taken or expected by another party. All kinds of strategic games crop up in athletics for owners, managers, and players as well as in other kinds of business and personal pursuits. In fact, an entire field of academic study called game theory has developed around the study of games defined in this way. The Ron Howard film, *A Beautiful Mind*, based on Sylvia Nasar's 1998 biography of Nobel Economics Laureate John Nash attracted attention to the field because of Nash's pioneering contribution to game theory as a graduate student at Princeton in the 1950s.[1] The term *game theory* arose from the study of games of skill and chance ranging from casino games to tic-tac-toe. During the twentieth century, great minds formalized these ideas with mathematics.

During the 1950s and early 1960s, hype about game theory's promise far outstripped actual work on making it applicable to analyzing real decision making. Some thought that it would come to dominate completely the technical analysis of decision making because it explicitly incorporated interactions between decision makers. By the 1970s the hype faded and the field fell into obscurity for twenty years. Critics assigned it to the trash heap of interesting academic ideas that failed to produce much in the way of tangible results (such as chaos theory). However, a few theorists and practitioners continued to plug away through the 1970s and 1980s. By the late eighties and early nineties, the range of applications swelled far beyond the nuclear deterrence models of the fifties and sixties. Economists and others studying management began to investigate its uses for business strategies such as pricing, location, innovation, and imitation. The applications widened to other business practices such as auctions, contracts, incentives along with a variety of non-business applications involving family relationships, politics, and everyday personal decisions. By 1994 enough momentum had gathered for the Nobel Prize to be awarded to Nash along with two other pioneers in the use of game theory in social science applications—John Harsanyi and Richard Selten—although Nasar reported that some on the Swedish committee still failed to see its importance. While game theory no longer holds out the promise to become the sole means for analyzing decisions, it has become a widely recognized and useful tool with which to consider certain kinds of decisions. More recent practitioners have even suggested utilizing it to estimate better the risks of terrorist threats to companies and their insurers.

The study of strategic games is now a staple course in the better MBA programs and is widely utilized in other graduate programs across the country. While the frontier level work and much of the academic use of strategic games tends to be dominated by extensive use of mathematics, the key features can be grasped by simple diagrams or tables along with some clear, logical thinking. The study of strategic games does not necessarily render a set of hard and fast rules that can be applied in every kind of decision-making scenario. Instead, it identifies the essential elements of particular games, effective means for finding the best strategy or best set of strategies, and common game scenarios and strategies.

For the concepts regarding strategic games to be of use, a few essential elements of a decision making situation must be clearly defined. First, the number of decision makers involved must be identified. In most sports settings this number is two—one coach or manager against another or one player against another. In business, the number maybe two or more, depending on the particular setting. Next, the timing of player decisions must be set out, whether simultaneous, sequential, or a mixture of the two. As discussed below, sport environments provide examples of all of these. Baseball pitching moves are sequential while steal-pitch-out decisions are more or less simultaneous. In addition, whether a game is to be repeated by the players with each other or with new players can matter for outcomes. Third, the information available to the decision makers must be specified, including whether players share the same information or hold private knowledge. In sports situations, much of the relevant information about player capabilities and the like is public knowledge, although information about injuries may sometimes be less than fully revealed. Fourth, the actions or decisions available to the decision makers along with the payoffs to the players must be laid out. These payoffs may include monetary or psychological benefits or costs, but for a game to be analyzed accurately, the payoffs must be relatively accurate. Generally speaking, the more a decision-making environment can be paired down to very simple terms, the easier it is to use the concepts from game theory to analyze it.

Even without technical, academic study of strategic games concepts, some individuals seem to possess an innate ability to analyze situations and make superior choices than other people. Great chess masters may not ever study game theory formally, but they exhibit great skill in the ability to look ahead and reason back through a series of potential moves and counter-moves. Likewise, among the managers in sports and business as well as everyday individuals who routinely face strategic game environments, some display an uncanny ability to pick out the key elements of the strategic possibilities and to make decisions that align with those suggested by a more technical and formal analysis.

This is not to say that the decisions of sports managers, entrepreneurs, corporate executives, or chess masters, fall perfectly in line with game theory. On the one hand, people have limited computational abilities so that not all possible outcomes or combinations may be analyzed. The advantage of IBM's "Big Blue" computer and its programmers in playing world champion Gary Kasparov lay primarily in exploiting this advantage in computation speed to weigh more moves than Kasparov. Managers of all kinds adopt rules-of-thumb and use hunches to bridge these computational gaps. On the other hand, the formal analysis of game-like decisions by game theory has its own limitations. Strategic game analysis models decision making and all models demand simplification of reality. As a result, these models do not incorporate all of the rich detail of complex decision settings. Accordingly, many situations are either not amenable for study by strategic game analytics or are only beginning to be studied. Further, decision making has and always will require judgment and discretion. Individuals possess creative, imaginative elements and the ability to judge fine nuances on-the-fly that no model can fully incorporate. This was actually one of Kasparov's advantages over Big Blue, and one of the major reasons why he could perform so well against a competitor with tremendous computational capacity.[2]

LOOKING AHEAD—REASONING BACK

The strategic setting where two baseball managers make moves and countermoves during the late innings of a game illustrates a sequential game. Their decisions resemble moves on a chess board where players alternate moves over some time frame. The means of solving for the best strategy involves looking ahead through the sequence of decisions and reasoning back, as was illustrated in Figure 6.1. The official term for this method is "rollback" or "backward induction." Chess masters attain their status largely because of their ability to look far ahead in the game, evaluate possible combinations of moves, and reason back to the implications for the current move better than their opponent. Their abilities in this regard stagger the mind. Baseball or business manages who perform better than others when facing a series of sequentially connected decisions possess the same kind of ability, if not to the same degree. Many other examples of sequentially-linked strategic decisions arise in sporting events. For example, in an America's Cup sailboat race, the skipper of the leading boat typically chooses to imitate the trailing boat's maneuvers at least toward the closing part of the race. By pursuing this second-mover strategy, he may reduce the speed of his boat, but he also reduces or eliminates the opportunity for the trailing boat to find a more favorable wind. The America's Cup example also illustrates that choosing first is not always the preferred position. Moving second permits the skipper of the lead boat to maintain an informational advantage over the second boat's captain.[3]

The quote from NHL legend Wayne Gretzky that heads this chapter subtly generalizes the kind of thinking discussed here. Great players have either the ability to reason quickly or the innate ability to assess situations and see situations unraveling before they actually do so as to take action now that results in a desirable outcome. This ability, described by players like Gretzky, permits them to see the game as if it were being played at a slower pace—everything is happening at the same speed for them but their foresight allows them the sense of a more leisurely pace. In fact, effective strategists across all kinds of decision making areas—business, military, politics—share this trait in common. While some individuals probably possess a greater or lesser gift for sequential strategy from birth, the talent can be nurtured and sharpened through study and practice. In part, writing out the possible decisions in the game tree format noted above can be quite useful in bringing a decision into better focus. Writing down sequential decisions in this way is not as simple as it may appear at first glance. It requires the ability to collect and condense the key information and decisions while excluding extraneous facts. However, the process of parsing the information itself promotes clearer thinking about strategy.

STICKING WITH A STRATEGY OR MIXING STRATEGIES?

Former University of Texas football coach Darryl Royal was fond of the expression, "You gotta dance with the one that brung ya." He usually meant that his team needed to stick to a particular strategy that had been successful in the past regardless of the game situation or moves by the opponent. Similarly, some coaches are fond of saying, "We are just focusing on what we do best and not worrying about the other team" or some variant of that statement. John Wooden, for instance, often paid little attention to the particulars strategy and tactics employed by his upcoming opponent, choosing instead to work on his own team's strengths and weaknesses independent of the opponent in most, but not all, situations. He viewed the game as involving relatively little strategy.[4]

In the terminology of strategic games, this kind of strategy selection chosen independently of the opponent's choices is referred to as a "dominant" strategy. Such thinking is relatively common among many coaches as well as by individuals making strategic decisions for other kinds of organizations, sometimes correctly but sometimes without a sound basis. Dominant strategies may crop up in settings where two or more opponents must choose simultaneously or even if the decisions occur sequentially, ignorance about the path chosen by the opponent means that, in effect, the decisions are simultaneous. When opponents must choose in ways that result in simultaneous choices being made, the analysis of the strategy options can proceed by using a matrix outline of the possible choices for the players and the outcomes based on the possible combinations of their choices.

A clear example of a dominant strategy crops up in baseball with regularity. A pitcher throwing a 97-mile-per-hour fastball may observe that the

Table 6.1
Simultaneous Game with Dominant Strategy

	Hitter's Anticipation	
Pitcher's Choice	Fastball	Off-Speed
Fastball	(90, 10)	(100, 0)
Off-Speed	(90, 10)	(50, 50)

Note: Payoffs = (% Outs, % Hits)

batter does not even come close to swinging quickly enough to make contact with the ball. Throwing a fastball to the batter is a dominant strategy for the pitcher regardless of the hitter's strategy. While not using the terminology of game theory, television commentators sometimes refer to the same idea when they note that when a hard-throwing pitcher is overpowering a hitter with a fastball, throwing a slower pitch such as a change-up, slider, or curve ball only provides the batter with a chance to make contact. This merely expresses the dominant strategy in slightly different words. Table 6.1 illustrates such a situation for a pitcher who chooses between his fastball and slider with the hitter guessing as to which one he will throw. The numbers in the table represent the percent of time the batter gets a hit based on the combination of the pitcher's decision and the batter's guesses. To find out if the pitcher has a dominant strategy, he considers the outcomes based on the hitter's anticipation of the pitch. If the hitter anticipates an off-speed pitch, then the pitcher is better off throwing a fastball. If the hitter anticipates a fastball, then the pitcher is still at least as well off throwing a fastball as an off-speed. The pitcher's best option is to always throw the fastball.

Another example of a dominant strategy is the common practice of throwing a fastball to a hitter when the bases are loaded and the hitter already has three balls in the count. Most pitchers throw a fastball more accurately than other pitches, and, typically, want to avoid walking the batter and forcing home a run. However, the dominance of this strategy depends on the game situation. If it is late in the game and the pitcher's team leads by several runs, the pitcher may fear giving up a grand slam home run as much or more than forcing in the runner on third with a walk.

In addition to dominant strategies, strategic games sometimes present dominated strategies—that is, strategies that should be avoided regardless of what strategy is chosen by the opponent. An obvious example in baseball occurs in the last half inning of a tie game where the home team advances the winning runner to third base with less than two out. Table 6.2 displays this choice scenario. Now, the pitcher has three options from which to choose—fastball, change-up, or slider. If the pitcher chooses fastball, the hitter does best by anticipating fastball. If the pitcher selects a change-up,

Table 6.2
Simultaneous Game with Dominant Strategy

	Hitter's Anticipation		
Pitcher's Choice	Fastball	Change-Up	Slider
Fastball	(60, 40)	(100, 0)	(90, 10)
Change-Up	(100, 0)	(70, 30)	(90, 10)
Slider	(90, 10)	(90, 10)	(90, 10)

Note: Payoffs = (% Outs, % Hits)

the hitter optimizes by choosing change-up. However, if the pitcher chooses a slider, then the hitter does just as well guessing fastball or change-up as slider, so that guessing slider is never a clear best choice no matter what the pitcher does. In other words, it is a dominated strategy for the hitter. Likewise, the pitcher can go through his best choices depending on what the hitter is guessing. If the hitter guesses fastball, the pitcher maximizes outs by throwing the change-up. If the hitter guesses change-up, then the pitcher's best option is a fastball. If the hitter is guessing slider, then any of the three pitches produces the same likelihood of an out. Just as for the hitter, slider is never the first best option for the pitcher, so it is dominated. The net result is to remove slider as an option so the table collapses to the four cells to the upper left. Now, the players reevaluate based on the reduced set of choices. In general, as decision-making contexts become more complicated, solutions for finding best strategies in simultaneous games can sometimes be found by taking step-by-step procedures and making use of the ideas of both dominated and dominant strategies. The decision maker can see if a strategy or strategies is dominated, eliminate it, and then see if a strategy is dominant among the remaining strategies.

Through selecting a dominant strategy or by eliminating dominated strategies, managers and players often find a single-best or "pure" strategy. While single-best strategies are easy to find in sports, many situations do not have a single strategy that is always best. In the vocabulary of strategic games, a mixed-strategy solution is one where it is best to mix in two or more strategies. For instance, while a pitcher may occasionally face a hitter who can be overpowered by a single pitch, such a dominant strategy is not usually the case. Instead, MLB pitchers typically find their best course of action is to mix different kinds of pitches. The mixed strategy will lead to lower batting performances by the hitters than selecting a single pitch strategy.

Table 6.3 illustrates a situation where such a mixed collection of pitches is best. It is the same as Table 6.2 except that the dominated selection of slider is removed.

If the pitcher throws only fastballs to batters and batters come to expect

Table 6.3
Simultaneous Game with Mixed Strategy

	Hitter's Anticipation	
Pitcher's Choice	Fastball	Change-Up
Fastball	(60, 40)	(100, 0)
Change-Up	(100, 0)	(30, 70)

Note: Payoffs = (% Outs, % Hits)

fastballs, the batters will average 40 percent hits. If the pitcher chooses only off-speed pitches and batters come to expect this, batters will hit 70 percent. If the hitter anticipates the wrong type of pitch, then the pitcher can always get the hitter out. It is easy enough to see that by mixing pitches, the pitcher can lower the batter's average below 40 percent. The critical decision for the pitcher is to select the best proportion of the various kinds of pitches just as a poker player needs to select the right proportion of time to bluff. Effectively mixing strategies does not usually mean a fifty-fifty split of two possible choices or splitting three choices equally in thirds. Instead, the best mix depends on the relative position of the outcomes expected.

Figure 6.2 shows how the best combination of mixed strategies is found. The vertical axis marks the hitting average of batters, and the horizontal axis marks the percent of fastballs the pitcher chooses to throw. The diagonal lines show the hitting percentage for batters if they guess only fastballs or only off-speed pitches as the pitcher increases the percentage of fastballs thrown.

For example, if the pitcher throws only fastballs but the hitters anticipate only off-speed pitches, the batting average is zero. If the pitcher throws no fastballs and the hitters anticipate only off-speed pitches, the batting average is at 70 percent. The diagonal line starting at 70 percent on the left axis and declining to zero on the right axis depicts these combinations. The graphic indicates that the pitcher lowers batting averages to their lowest point by throwing about 64 percent fastballs—the point where the two diagonal lines cross. With this proportion, hitters will bat about 25 percent. If the pitcher chooses proportions above or below this number, the hitters can raise their averages by guessing only fastball or only off-speed, depending on the direction that the pitcher deviates from the optimal percentage. The optimal ratio of fastballs to off-speed pitches will depend on the pitcher's abilities. For instance, if he throws an extraordinarily good fastball, then the line representing the percent hits when the hitter guesses fastball will shift down and to the right so that the point where it intersects the other line will be farther to the right.

Picking the right proportion of fastballs, though, covers only half of the pitcher's job. Once the appropriate proportion of the various pitches is cho-

Figure 6.2
Finding the Best Combination of Pitches

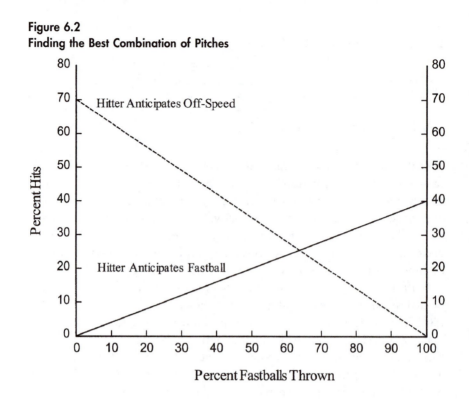

sen, then the selection of pitches leading to this proportion needs to be random. If a pitcher throws 100 pitches and the best mix is 64 percent fastballs and 36 percent off-speed pitches, the 36 off-speed pitches need to be randomly mixed in among the 64 fastballs. This need for randomizing may be obvious. Yet, pitchers and pitching coaches sometimes employ pitch combinations that do not reflect mixing at random. They often refer to saving an "out pitch" for when the batter has two strikes—usually referring to a particular kind of pitch. If this "out pitch" is a slider, though, then mixing it in more frequently when the batter has two strikes creates a pattern that hitters can exploit. Instead, a random pitch choice based on the overall proportion desired is the optimal decision.[5] It is important to note that "random" does not imply an even split between the possible pitches. Instead, it means randomizing the optimal proportions of each.

The list of examples demonstrates the importance of using a mixed strategy, finding the right proportion to mix, and randomly using the mix could go on using examples from sports or from business. Several can be found in tennis, such as the choice between hitting to the backhand or forehand on the serve or during a rally, hitting to the baseline or using a drop shot, or hitting a passing shot to the right or left of the player at the net.[6] Penalty kicks in soccer, penalty shots in hockey, play calls, snap counts, and blitzes in football also fit into this kind of mental calculus. In business settings, examples of simultaneous decisions leading to dominant, dominated, and mixed strategies are quite common ranging from labor negotiations to pricing competition, advertising and beyond. For example, in their book, *Thinking Strategically*, Avinash Dixit and Barry Nalebuff utilize the concepts to analyze matters such as magazine cover decisions for *Time* and *Newsweek*. In many situations, simultaneous games are repeated over and over so that a time element does enter and reputation building may matter, as discussed below.

INCENTIVES AND DILEMMAS: COOPERATING WHILE COMPETING

Differences of opinion exist with regard to the nature of the National Collegiate Athletic Association. From the perspective of basic economics, the NCAA operates as a cartel where cooperation places restrictions on competitive interests, attempting to maximize revenues among members by restricting payments to players among other things.[7] Others view the NCAA as a benign, if sometimes misguided, organization regulating amateur athletic contests between colleges and universities. In this view, it is a bit like a local civic organization that organizes community activities. Certainly, within the halls of the NCAA complex in Indianapolis and in its many publications, one will never hear or find words such as "cartel," "business venture," or "employee." Rather, the organization possesses its own self-invented vocabulary describing its governance of college sports. According to this vocabulary, the association provides rules and assistance to "student-athletes" and coordinates the activities of "member institutions."

Regardless of the overall view of the organization's objectives and practices or the vocabulary used to describe it, the member schools face an ongoing strategic game that presents a difficult "managerial" dilemma. On the one side, the schools desire to cooperate to achieve some kind of mutual benefit. On the other hand, the underlying reason for cooperation is so that the schools can compete with each other on the playing field. Whether to achieve more money or merely bragging rights, the coaches, players, alumni, and administrators are primarily concerned with their own school's success. If this competitive motive runs amok it can lead to illicit inducements to players, out-of-season practices, and the like. As a result of such actions, the cooperative benefits to the association as a whole will diminish if not altogether vanish. The long-term stability of the organization depends on striking a successful balance between competitive and cooperative incentives.

The compete or cooperate dilemma faced by the NCAA and its member institutions shares similarities with a dilemma from one of the most intensely studied of all games—the "prisoner's dilemma." This game derives its name from the following decision environment: two prisoners are accused of committing a robbery in which they jointly participated. They are interrogated separately, and the two strategies available are either to confess or not confess. A critical element to this game is that the players choose, more or less, simultaneously. Even if they are interrogated at different times, their lack of information on the other person's decision means they must act as if they are choosing at the same time. In terms of outcomes, both would escape with no prison time if each refuses to confess. If one confesses and one does not, the confessor receives a short sentence and the non-confessor receives a long sentence. If they both confess, then they both receive short sentences. While the best outcome for both is to not confess, the dilemma is obvious—the threat of the other prisoner cutting a deal leads both prisoners to confess and to end up with an outcome that could be improved for both if they could cooperate effectively. A multi-person variety of the same game is known as the "hostages' dilemma," explaining why it is so common for a few terrorists to hold many hostages at bay.

In business settings, such prisoner dilemmas are quite common. For instance, two rival companies may undercut each other with lower and lower prices. Both firms could increase profits through a tacit if unwritten commitment to maintaining higher prices, but because each company fears the other company will renege on this commitment, both find themselves suffering the prisoner's dilemma. Organizations who are party to cartel arrangements, such as individual nations making up OPEC, frequently find themselves in a similar situation. Agreements to limit oil production present the possibility of higher oil revenues and profits to OPEC nations. However, these agreements provide a strong incentive for secretive cheating on these quotas and producing additional barrels of oil. If enough nations cheat on the production quota, prices drop and revenues-profits drop.

In addition to noting the frequency of prisoner dilemma situations, much academic study, in terms of mathematical theory, experimentation, and observation of real-world prisoner dilemmas has been devoted to assessing ways that decision makers find their way out of the lose-lose outcome and to the best possible outcome. These studies focus on the degree and nature of the cooperation between parties necessary to achieve the improved outcomes. Early research on the subject proposed a "tit-for-tat" strategy as a means by which game players frequently found their way out of such dilemmas when the game is repeated over many periods. One book on the subject labeled these kinds of situations as *Co-opetition*.[8]

The NCAA case is especially interesting from a managerial perspective because when viewed as a cartel (or simply as an association with a cooperation-competition incentive dilemma), the NCAA has been incredibly successful by historical standards. (In fact, it has been voted the most successful monopoly in existence by the economics faculty at Harvard. The faculty use the term monopoly to include multiple firms acting as one as they do in a cartel.)[9] Most cartels fall apart or become ineffective in short order because of their inherent instability. Usually, the competitive interests of members overwhelm the cooperative schemes. The desire of each member to gain relative to the other members through finding loopholes in the agreement or outright cheating undermines the cooperative agreement, leading the cartel members back to the non-cooperative, purely competitive outcome akin to the "confess-confess" outcome of the prisoner's dilemma.

For instance, OPEC gained from cooperation on limiting oil production in the 1970s but floundered because of individual countries pursued their own gains in the years since except for a very recent revival. As a result, oil prices in inflation-adjusted terms were much lower throughout the 1990s than in the 1970s. In college athletics, the agreement that restricts benefits to athletes permits member schools to gain a greater share of the rewards from games; however, the lure to undercut this agreement, either through offering benefits not covered by the agreement or by cheating on the agreement, is strong for schools and their fans.

No doubt, the NCAA has suffered from numerous breakdowns in cooperation among the members. Many illicit gifts and loans to athletes from boosters and occasionally coaches have been widely documented. Spearheaded by a suit brought by the University of Georgia and the University of Oklahoma, the big football revenue schools won the right to negotiate their own television contracts in 1984—a blow that essentially eliminated the NCAA as a cartel in terms of the cooperative restrictions on the presentation of output but not on inputs (players). Previously, in the early 1950s, Big Ten and Pacific-ten schools had chafed against very severe limits imposed on the number of televised games. Because of the threat of losing these schools, the rest of the membership and the television committee reached a compromise permitting a larger number of telecasts. In spite of these wounds, the cartel effects of NCAA restrictions on athlete benefits have endured with schools continuing to gain the benefits of this cooperation.

How has the NCAA achieved this unusual longevity? Several factors have gone into its ability to thwart the lose-lose outcome. One is the transient nature of the people being harmed by the agreement to restrict inducements to college athletes. College players are in school for only a short time. Also, the educational backdrop behind college athletics has shielded the NCAA from antitrust suits in court regarding players. While recognizing the essentially commercial nature of college athletics, federal courts have consistently refused to grant college athletes the status of employees along with the antitrust protections that such a status would entail. (Interestingly, the NCAA was not successful in its attempt to extend pay restrictions to assistant coaches, losing a class-action suit and a big damage award.) Further, many states have made the NCAA restrictions a matter of statutory law by passing their own restrictions on payments to players and contacts with agents. All of these circumstances and events have worked to diminish the competitive incentives that often spell doom for such broad cooperative agreements.

Similar kinds of incentive dilemmas have also surfaced among professional sports leagues. For instance, in 1981 the Houston Rockets reached the NBA Finals, losing to the Boston Celtics. By 1983, though, the Rockets plummeted to the bottom of the league. Over the summer, they drafted seven-four Ralph Samson out of the University of Virginia as the first player selected in the entire draft. Even with Samson, the team did not fare better. By the last month of the 1983–84 season, the team and coach began to receive criticism as the media began to suspect that they were intentionally losing games in order to secure themselves once again the top draft selection again. Whether on purpose or by happenstance, the Rockets "attained" the worst record and selected another seven-foot college star, Hakeem Olaijawan, as the first overall pick of the 1984 draft. With their twin seven-footers in the starting lineup, the Rockets' fortunes quickly turned around as they reached the NBA Finals in Olaijawan's rookie season, again losing to the Celtics.

The Rockets had not been the first nor last team suspected of losing games intentionally in order to secure a better draft position. As a response to this backwards incentive and behavior, the NBA instituted a system by which the draft order for all of the non-playoff teams were based on lottery draws. Teams with lower records were no longer guaranteed a better draft position. This system also had its problems. The Orlando Magic gained the top spot two years in a row—the second year after just narrowly missing the playoffs. To make this less likely, the NBA adjusted the lottery system so that the worst teams would have a higher likelihood of being selected and the worst team could not fall in the draft order below a certain point. This change, though, resulted in outcomes very similar to those before the institution of the lottery system. Losing games could still pay dividends by raising the likelihood of improving the team's draft position. Other American sports also utilize the worst-picks-first draft system.

The NBA bounced back and forth in its attempts to permit lower performing teams to gain preferential draft treatment while taking away or reducing the incentive for them to lose games. The initial lottery system drastically reduced the incentive to lose games but turned out to help the "best of the worst" too much. The prelottery system and the current lottery system provide little incentive for bad teams to win. In contrast to American sports, the organizational structure of the English Football Association (soccer) and for the most part soccer leagues across the world developed in such a way as to provide a very different way of dealing with poor performing teams. The English teams are divided into a twenty team Premier League, then a First Division, and so on. At the end of a season, the three teams with the worst records in the Premier League are "relegated" to the First Division for the next season, while three teams from the First Division move up to the Premier League. Interestingly, the "relegation" system used in English soccer avoids the incentive dilemma faced by American sports leagues by establishing a set of rules in which winning is important even for teams with poor season records. The leagues relegate poorly performing teams to the lower division—an outcome all teams desire to avoid. In contrast, the usual systems in place in U.S. sports load almost all value on reaching the playoffs and winning championships, thereby creating little incentive for teams with bad records to play as well as they can once they are deep into the season.

Not only does the relegation system penalize poorly performing teams, it also creates excitement among fans whose teams are near the bottom of the league as the season nears its end. While league championships are highly valued by English soccer fans, keeping their favored team in the Premier League also stirs interest and drama. Unlike U.S. sports leagues, where cellar dwelling teams often play out the season in front of nearly empty stadiums, the teams at the bottom of the Premier League frequently maintain fan interest to or near the very end of the season. For example, at the end of the 2000 season, Bradford City staved off elimination with a victory at the end of the season. Not only was the contest played before a packed stadium, but the post-game celebration that took place in the city of Bradford rivaled any championship celebration in the United States. Likewise, at the end of the 2004 season, a long-standing English power, Leeds, fought to avoid relegation after three seasons of financial mismanagement. The fan interest in the avoidance of relegation was summed-up by a pre-teen boy who wept as the team faced imminent defeat and the finality of relegation. His bare-skinned chest read "Leeds Till I Die."

Major League Baseball, like other sports leagues, also faces the dilemma of striking a balance between competition and cooperation. The MLB case has dominated much of the discussion of these kinds of problems in recent years due to its perceived and real financial problems. The 1998 World Series matched the New York Yankees against a seemingly unlikely opponent, the San Diego Padres. Although the Padres lost the series, the opportunity to play in baseball's hallmark event marked a great achievement for the franchise, which had previously played in it only in 1984. However, losing ace pitcher, Kevin Brown, through free agency to the despised Los Angeles Dodgers during the off-season quickly soured the accomplishment. The indignity even prompted the Padres' owner to write a feature editorial in the *Wall Street Journal* in which he complained about the free agent system that allowed large-market, wealthier teams such as the Dodgers to entice and hoard talented players.

Similar complaints about the viability and competitiveness of "small market" teams arise by or on behalf of these teams in almost every season. However, the proposed contraction of two MLB franchises during the 2001–02 winter by the MLB commissioner's office expanded these kinds of complaints into a maelstrom of calls for a more cooperative financial relationship between teams. Montreal and Minnesota were the most likely targets. In the midst of the mounting controversy, the Padres' owner published a second *Wall Street Journal* editorial, "Damn Yankees," in which he alleged that MLB's structure permitted unfair dominance for teams such as the Yankees, placing many of the teams in smaller cities in financial peril.[10] Again, he prescribed a more cooperative arrangement among MLB teams with a greater degree of revenue sharing so that teams in smaller cities could be more competitive. Even beyond those with a vested interest such as the Padre's owner, much is made in the media of the downside of teams bidding players away from each other with ever-escalating salaries and the advantages held by teams in the largest markets. To limit bidding wars and the advantages of larger cities, owners—with consent from players' unions under terms of collective bargaining agreements—have adopted several cooperative mechanisms such as revenue sharing, the amateur draft, salary caps, and "luxury taxes."

One point forgotten in these kinds of analyses is that MLB is not unique. A sports league is essentially a joint ventures among rivals. Joint ventures between rivals exist outside of sports venues. Striking a correct balance between cooperation and competition carries with it important implications for customer value, and ultimately league revenues and profits, just as it does in any joint venture between business entities. On some matters, such as scheduling and rules, it is obvious that cooperation among and mutual agreement between the separate MLB teams is essential. On other matters such as on-the-field strategy, it is just as obvious the teams must behave as pure rivals, competing rather than cooperating. Many issues, though, fall in between these two extremes, requiring a delicate balancing of cooperation and competition. Too much of either cooperation or competition can create destructive and destabilizing incentives for the league. Competition among the individual teams is the very heart of what a league provides, yet too much competition can have undesirable effects. Cooperation can lead to improved financial performance but too much cooperation can stifle individual and team incentives for improvement and produce a poor product for consumers.

While some cooperation is necessary, often lost in the rhetoric about "small market teams," competitive balance, revenue-sharing, free agency, salary caps, and the associated calls for more cooperation is the fact that too much cooperation can be bad for a joint venture, even one involving sports leagues. Competition of all sorts—between teams on the field, between players for home runs, between clubs for innovative ways to market the games such as night games and broadcasts—can provide customer-building effects that are frequently overlooked in the rush by many analysts to think that more cooperation is all that is needed. These issues were first addressed back in Chapter 3, where the emphasis was on the fact that cooperation as well as competition can increase the customer base. It does not make sense that a league's rules should be so restrictive as to make, say, Kansas City, just as likely to win pennants as the New York Yankees. After all, the Yankees do have the largest fan following of any team. On the other hand, MLB teams as a unit would not benefit from the Yankees winning every championship, but as many economists have pointed out, the Yankees were much more dominant in the pre–free agency era than they have been in the post–free agency era. The Dodgers, while vilified by the Padres' owner because of their supposed monetary advantage, appeared in only one World Series from 1982 through 2001 compared with the Padres' two.

The National Football League has been held up as a model for MLB because of its revenue-sharing plans and restrictive limits on free agency that significantly reduce the off-the-field competition between teams. For the critics of Major League Baseball, the ills of the game can nearly all be laid at the feet of "too much competition." If only MLB would adopt hard salary caps or some other stringent deterrent to free agency, then MLB fortunes would improve, or so the story goes. In this view, the popularity of the NFL in recent years is almost exclusively attributed to its revenue-sharing plan.

The trouble with the degree of cooperation practiced by the NFL is that it affects owners' incentives negatively. Cooperative agreements between teams that restrict the ability to go after players or to pay a penalty for mediocrity can ultimately serve to diminish incentives for teams to excel. In a variety of NFL cities, the complaint of fans over the years has not been about their owners spending too much money, but rather, the fact that the owners of their franchise have little incentive to compete. Instead, the owners of the Bengals, for instance, can consistently place a poor team on the field but rest easy knowing that they will be as financially secure as the best teams in the league. The NFL popularity likely owes much more to the product it has to offer than to its policies limiting competition for players. As discussed in Chapter 3, football translates well to television, and leading executives from the NFL such as Pete Rozelle and Tex Schramm consciously geared the game to increase its TV appeal.

In comparing the compete-cooperate dilemma in sports leagues to joint ventures in business, a couple of points require further explanation. Sports leagues are different in that the on-the-field competition is "zero-sum." One team's victory means another team's defeat. This fact has prompted some observers, even among the ranks of economists, to see sports leagues as a place where competition between teams best serves the interest of fans and owners if restricted to non-financial, on-the-field matters. Any off-the-field, financial competition, in this view, merely means a shifting of money from one league pocket to another in an effort to win games. In contrast, businesses operating in other settings do not face this kind of zero-sum world. One company's gain does not necessarily dictate another company's loss. Absolute performance matters rather than just relative performance so that competition between firms benefits consumers.

Contrary to the view that in sports only on-the-field competition benefits customers is the fact that competition and absolute performance standards matter in sports and that cooperation and relative performance matter outside of sports. Two rival companies can gain, and in some cases help consumers to benefit also, by cooperating rather than competing. Likewise, sports teams can sometimes gain by competing rather than cooperating. Off-the-field competition between teams to develop new ways to market their products—night baseball, radio and television broadcasts, and other ways—may draw some dollars from other teams, but it also can draw new fans. Baseball teams not only compete with each other on-the-field but they also compete with other entertainment offerings. Competition between teams also provides incentive for constant improvement. This can be seen at the individual level. Developing hitters, who can hit more or longer home runs, is valued by consumers. The pursuit of excellence in the front office also matters to the quality of the product offered to consumers.

CHANGING THE NATURE OF THE GAME

A relatively recent and novel mix of cooperation and competition cropped up during the summer of 2001 when the Colorado Avalanche set out to re-sign three of their top players—forward Joe Sakic, defenseman Rob Blake, and goalie Patrick Roy. These three had been instrumental in helping the Avs capture the 2001 Stanley Cup, but all became unrestricted free agents after the season. In most sports settings, three superstar free agents would rarely be signed the same year as teams would decide to spend vigorously to try to keep one or two of them at the expense of losing one or two. Typically, the money required to sign one or two of them would make signing all three highly unlikely.

However, the Avs changed the nature of the game by negotiating not only simultaneously with all three players but negotiating cooperatively with all three as a group.[11] The team and the players knew going in that if all three stayed with the team, another Stanley Cup would be an attainable goal. The team offered the three players similar money with some differences in contract length—Roy being relatively old by sports standards received the shortest-term deal. Although each player received lucrative salaries, the team gained by being able to sign all three for less than the amount that would likely have been necessary in negotiating with all three separately. The three players gained by being able to not only stay with the team but with the full compliment of superstars from the prior championship season. The cooperative-sharing of information led to a better outcome for all participants. Obviously, this tactic would not work in every similar situation. It requires a team willing and able to spend considerable money as well as players willing to take less than full market value in order to stay put and play with a team with championship potential. Not all teams or athletes fit the bill.

Game strategy theorists refer to like tactics used by the Avs as "strategic moves." Strategic moves change some important underlying feature of the game being played. In the Avs case, they rearranged the order of negotiation from a sequential negotiation with separate players to a simultaneous negotiation, thereby altering the available choices as well as the payoffs presented to the players and the franchise. All strategic moves change something either in the order of play, the information available to players, the moves available to players, or the payoffs to players that induces a change in the outcome of a game.

Commitments in the form of promises or threats are a common means of strategically altering the nature of a game by either altering the beliefs of rivals (or partners) regarding the likelihood of a particular course of actions. In baseball, pitchers of yesteryear such as Don Drysdale, Bob Gibson, and Nolan Ryan, as well as a current pitcher such as Roger Clemens, have used their ability to throw extremely hard not just to throw the ball by batters but to change the nature of the game through implicit (and sometimes explicit) threats. Each of these pitchers has whizzed his 95-mile-per-hour fastball near or even at batters who he felt crowded the plate too much or lunged toward outside pitches too much. The threat is clear and credible—"stand too close or lunge too much and I will throw a 95-mile-per-hour fast-ball right under your chin." For the batter, the game now changes from just trying to guess the type of pitch or location of it to also worrying about inciting the anger of the pitcher. Certainly, a lot of pitchers at the major league level and below attempt to employ such threats. However, once a pitcher achieves a high level of success, then he may be able to enforce the threat without as much recourse from the league, thereby making the threat even more credible. No doubt, by the last few years of his career, Nolan Ryan had become such a baseball icon that he could knock down batters with relative impunity.

Analogous situations arise in business. A large company may respond to what it perceives as overly aggressive price-cutting by a smaller competitor by slashing price to retaliate and punish the rival or even attempt to drive it out of business. This practice may not maximize profits in the near term, but it may serve a purpose of establishing a reputation for the company that changes the decision calculus of future price cutters. Whether in sports or business, for threats or promises to be of use in altering the nature of a game, they must be credible. Whether the MLB pitchers noted above or unions who go out on strike, credibility is acquired over time through reputation through carrying out threats and promises.

PUSHING TO THE EDGE OF DISASTER

During the 1999–2000 NHL playoffs, the Philadelphia Flyers' star center, Eric Lindros, suffered a concussion from a hard but legal hit from New Jersey's Scott Stevens. This concussion came shortly after Lindros had returned to the Flyers after a concussion earlier in the season. In fact, over his career, Lindros had suffered several concussions and had become concerned about his health. He had also become frustrated with the Flyers and the physicians retained by the team. His concerns over his health and frustrations with the team led him to not report to training camp in the fall. During the course of the season, it became clear that he wanted to be traded to another team, but not just to any team. Instead, he gave the Flyers a short list of other teams with which he was willing to play.

Flyers GM Bobby Clarke, a man known for his own intransigence as both a player and executive, dug in his heels, stating that there would be no trade of Lindros. As the season progressed, rumors surfaced suggesting a likely trade with Toronto. The rumors turned into admitted talks between the two clubs but never resulted in a trade. As a result, Lindros sat out an entire season. In the end, Clarke traded him to the New York Rangers. Although all the behind the scenes maneuvering and the exact extent to which Lindros or Clarke were responsible for the meltdown never became clear, one or both sides were playing game theory hardball.[12]

Labor bargaining scenarios have often played out this way where one or both parties make strong demands and then set their feet in stone and refuse to budge even though compromise would seemingly have some benefit to both sides. On occasion, the movement to such unwavering positions may take place in a series of gradual steps. Whether gradual or all at once, this kind of behavior is known as "brinksmanship" in the terminology of strategic games. The reason for it is obvious—a desire to issue a threat that makes the opponent capitulate much more than would otherwise be obtained.

To play this kind of edgy strategy takes nerve and a willingness to live with the consequences of a breakdown in negotiation. If the rival party knows that the other party will not go through with the consequences, then the brinksmanship play will be viewed as merely a bluff and be ignored. It is this assessment of the credibility of the play that often leads to breakdowns in negotiation. Since the early 1970s, MLB and the players' union have failed to reach agreements leading to a number of work stoppages, mostly of short duration but with exceptions of 1981 and 1994. In 1981 over 50 regular season games were cancelled during the middle of the season and in 1994 nearly the same number were lost, as well as all of the playoffs and World Series. In both cases, the owners' desire to rein-in free agency led the parties to play their hand to the edge. In both cases, the players came out as more willing to live with the consequences.[13] The NHL and its players played the same push-it-to-the-limit strategy leading to a lockout prior to the 2004 season.

REPLAY

1. Identifying a few key characteristics of a situation such as the timing of decisions and the information held by yourself and the rival can by itself make a person a better strategist.

2. Just like baseball managers, effective business strategists look ahead to the range of likely outcomes and decisions and work backward when decisions involve connected sequences.

3. When a decision must be made at a point in time, looking for a strategy that is best or worst regardless of the rival's choice may help solve or, at least, pare down the problem.

4. When no single best strategy appears, strategies should be randomly mixed based on relative strengths rather than divided equally among possible strategies as bluffing in poker and pitching illustrate.

5. Making moves that change the nature of a game is not only an effective tool but may help to alleviate seemingly hopeless situations and one used by the Colorado Avalanche to keep three key, free-agent players.

6. Threats and promises must be credible to influence rivals. One should not push to the brink unless willing to live with the consequences of going over the edge.

7

Managing Innovation and Change: Branch Rickey Meets Machiavelli

Failure is not fatal, but failure to change might be.

—John Wooden, former UCLA basketball coach

One thing is clear: we don't have the option of turning away from the future. . . . No one can stop productive change in the long run because the marketplace inexorably embraces it.

—Bill Gates, Microsoft CEO

For the 1986–87 season the NCAA adopted the three-point shot set at a radius of about 19 feet from the basket. During the season, several coaches exploited the new rule at the expense of their coaching colleagues. Rick Pitino, for one, built his entire offense around the shot with his team taking many more shots per game from the 3-point range than most teams. His Providence Friars rose from relative obscurity to compete with the Big East big boys. Ultimately, the Friars advanced to the Final Four not only for only the second time in school history without any players with strong NBA potential. The UNLV Runnin' Rebels also made liberal use of the 3-point shot to advance to the Final Four in 1987. The Rebels contained several highly touted players and a coach, Jerry Tarkanian, already known for a freewheeling offensive style. His 1977 Final Four club averaged nearly 100 points per game long before the advent of the shot clock or the 3-point shot. UNLV utilized the 3-point shot extensively. Even Bob Knight, a coach known for his emphasis on defense and deliberate offensive strategy, took full advantage of the rule change. He had one of the most accurate outside shooters in college basketball in senior guard Steve Alford. That season,

Alford took over 100 3-point shots, including making 7 in the 1987 national championship game against Syracuse.

In contrast, other coaches did not adapt quickly to the new environment. Some of these, such as first year Western Kentucky University coach Murray Arnold did not like the new rule. Arnold not only voiced his opinion against the shot but only reluctantly integrated it into his offensive plans. He inherited a team that had gone to the second round of the NCAA tournament the previous season, losing to the University of Kentucky by five points. The team returned four of five starters and several talented younger players. Early in the season, the Hilltoppers excelled even against top level opposition, reaching the finals of the "Preseason NIT" and achieving a number eight ranking in a national poll. However, the finals of the NIT against UNLV foreshadowed the season for the Hilltoppers. Arnold's team led by twenty points into the second half when UNLV stormed back on a barrage of 3-point shots to win in overtime. Even though the team experienced considerable success during the season, the early season dominance eroded as they faced more teams with the willingness and ability to use the 3-pointer. In the regular season finale, a mediocre UAB team soundly defeated WKU. Even though the team won its conference tournament, their seeding fell to ninth and they had to play top seeded Syracuse in the second round on Syracuse's home floor.

Innovative ideas comprise one part of what might be broadly labeled entrepreneurship. This became a buzzword in management education during the 1990s, and its meaning can be very fuzzy. Sometimes it is merely a code word for small business management. On other occasions, it stands as a synonym for innovation. Most broadly, the term encompasses "value creation," a catchall for all the creative skills that a manager brings to the table to help the business succeed. In this chapter, the focus will be on the innovative aspects of entrepreneurship.

ADAPT OR ELSE

As Chapter 4 discussed at length, people are a key if not the key ingredient to the success of any team or organization. However, it is a mistake to view the mere presence of human beings as the only ingredient. People are important because they bring ideas and attributes that no machine can imitate. Some coaches become entranced with "mano-a-mano" victories without putting enough thought and creativity into designing or tweaking methods so as to permit their personnel to reach their highest potential. To give people a chance to succeed, they require the right tools, technology, and combinations with others—ideas lay behind all of these. As obvious as this may seem, strong forces and even very smart people within organizations obstinately resist adapting to new ways of doing things or combining resources in new ways.

In extreme contrast to this kind of foot-dragging, teeth-clenched opposition to change, great managers know that the ability to adapt and change ultimately determines survival—at least over the long haul. Superficially, teams and organizations may appear to find success without much change, but sooner or later, lack of it catches up to them. Many legendary sports figures speak to its importance. The epigram from UCLA's John Wooden, "Failure is not fatal, but failure to change might be" has been attributed to other coaches as well.[1]

The most successful hockey coach of all time, Scotty Bowman, echoed the same idea but put it even more bluntly, "I found out that if you are going to win games, you had better be ready to adapt."[2] That is a strong statement from a coach whose longevity at a championship level rivals any coach from any sport. Table 7.1 displays his achievements. He amassed nine Stanley Cups, equaling Red Auerbach for the most championships in any of the four "major" professional sports and led three other teams to the finals.

Ironically, Bowman was widely known for his no-nonsense, tight-fisted control of his teams. In spite of personnel methods that could sometimes create fear and loathing, he never became locked into any particular system to achieve success. Bowman's lack of personal relations may have cut short his stints earlier in his career, but it did not get in the way of his ability to adapt his tactics to the players he has as well as to changes in league rules and enforcement. He won those nine championships with three different clubs—Montreal (1973, 1976–79), Pittsburgh (1992), and Detroit (1997–98, 2002)—with varied strengths and weaknesses. Rather than trying to place all the players into a single mold, Bowman adapted his tactics to the talent on hand.[3] The Montreal teams featured all-round great play while the Pittsburgh team boasted one of the two best offensive players of all time in Mario Lemieux. His early Detroit teams adopted a suffocating defensive scheme known as the "left-wing lock" while his later teams in Detroit were much more offense-oriented.

Effective management at any level and in any business requires carefully crafted adjustments to the environment external and internal to the organization. Competitive pressures, technology, laws, regulations, skills of people, cultural restrictions, and other matters evolve over time. Managers wedded to particular ways of doing things rather than making well-reasoned responses to the new environment have a hard time coping. Coaches and managers are just like players in that even at the highest levels of sports, differences in abilities manifest themselves, and so it is with ability to adjust to new rules. In any kind of management situation, strate-

MANAGING INNOVATION AND CHANGE

Table 7.1
Scotty Bowman's Career Highlights

Team	Years	Highlights
St. Louis	1967-71	3 Stanley Cup Finals, 2 Divisional Titles
Montreal	1971-79	4 Stanley Cups, 5 Divisional Titles
Buffalo	1979-87	1 Semifinal, 1 Divisional Title
Pittsburgh	1991-93	1 Stanley Cup, 1 Divisional Title
Detroit	1993-2002	3 Stanley Cups, 5 Divisional Titles
Career	1967-2002	7 Stanley Cups, 11 Stanley Cup Finals, 14 Divisional Titles

gic and tactical decisions are always made in the context of environmental conditions. These conditions include preferences and incomes of consumers, the current level of know-how (technology), and rules of society including laws, regulations, and widely accepted customs. None of these environmental influences are set in stone. Often, they evolve slowly, but occasionally quantum changes crop up over short periods of time such as the 3-point rule in the NCAA.

One coach whose long run of success is attributable to his ability to stay one step ahead of the competition is Tom Landry. As an assistant coach for the New York Giants in the 1950s, Landry coordinated defensive strategies. When he took this job, defensive players typically just reacted to the movement of the ball. Landry thought that defensive players could gain an advantage by observing the patterns of behavior of offensive players. Reading of "keys" meant the defenders would observe the positioning of offensive players or the initial movement of various offensive players and use these as signals to the play's intent. By the 1960s, this "keying" on offensive players has become standard throughout the league. In 1956, he adjusted his defensive personnel and alignment to better stop the offenses of the Cleveland Browns and Chicago Bears as well as to make better use of the unique skills of one of his young players, Sam Huff. Most professional teams had to this point used five linemen on defense. In his new alignment, Landry used four linemen and placed Huff at middle linebacker along with two other "outside linebackers" with the intent of having a defense better able to respond to a run or pass. Landry's "4–3" defense is still the standard more than forty years later.

When he became head coach of the newly formed Dallas Cowboys in 1960, Landry turned his innovative ideas more to offense. If he did not pioneer the use of multiple offensive formations, he certainly popularized them as a means to complicate the challenge to the defensive of keying on a play merely by observing the pre-snap formation of the offense. He reinvented the use of the "shotgun" formation where the quarterback received the snap several yards behind the center to give the quarterback more time and better vision in obvious passing situations. He was one of the first coaches to send plays in from the sideline—a practice for which he was widely criticized by players and media alike, but a practice now universal in football. He organized game films by specific plays and by positions in order to better analyze success and failure of plays. Back on defense, he adjusted his 4–3 defensive alignment into the 4–3 "flex" in 1964 as more teams began to use multiple offensive formations. Among other things, the "flex" moved one defensive lineman back from the line of scrimmage in situations where running plays were more likely.[4] He also was one of the early coaches to use five defensive backs in obvious passing situations. Beyond the on-the-field strategies, he emphasized the evaluation of players' mental abilities and motivation in addition to their athletic abilities. Landry's success with innovations was not an accident. He called innovations "my greatest strength" and credited his background in engineering and quality control concepts with helping him recognize concepts that could be applied to football.[5] With this background, he viewed innovation as an ongoing process necessary to stay ahead of or at least keep up with the competition.

IMITATING THE INNOVATORS

Although he was elected to both the College and Pro Football Hall of Fame, won over 80 percent of his games as a college coach, led the LA–San Diego Chargers to five Western Division titles and one AFL championship, and innovated many of the elements of current offensive football strategy, Sid Gillman only briefly became a household name among average football fans. Since the 1970s, names such as Bill Walsh, Don Coryell, Joe Gibbs, John Gruden and others have become widely hailed for their innovative developments in offensive football strategy—especially in the passing game. Their ideas and adjustments to them have come to be labeled the "West Coast Offense" or "West Coast Passing Game." Usually Walsh and, to a lesser extent, Coryell are credited as the innovators with a brief reference to influences on them. Yet, Sid Gillman was already developing and deploying his radically different passing attack when Walsh and Coryell were still a long way from NFL head coaching posts. The West Coast offense for which they receive credit and used by the majority of NFL champions since the early 1980s closely reflects many much of the passing offense Gillman used. He initiated the concept of spreading the field horizontally and vertically to open up passing lanes and give quarterbacks more options to throw the ball. "He was way ahead of his time in organization, in the passing game, and offensive football," Al Davis told The Associated Press in an interview in January 2000. "In the '60s, the passing game was not yet really developed. At the advent of the AFL (in 1960), the Chargers were the flagship for all teams to follow, all teams to emulate."[6]

Beyond his influence on passing attacks and long preceding it, Gillman was an innovator in the use of film and cameras to capture the events during games and then analyze the film. Gillman's reliance on game film was attributed in large part to the fact that his family operated movie theaters in Minneapolis. In his first coaching job, at Denton University and Ohio State in 1935, he saw an advertisement for a 35-millimeter projector for $35. "We can't afford that," Mrs. Gillman recalled in an interview. "He says, 'I have to have this.' That was the beginning. He would come home. We would put up a white sheet on the wall. Sid would show me these films."

As with most any innovation, there are precursors to innovators. Sid Gillman was this kind of innovator. These people push the envelope of ideas beyond the level that most other managers and leaders are ready to consider. Even when they demonstrate success with their new ways, they generate few immediate disciples. Because of their ideas and their personalities as independent and non-conventional thinkers, they may be seen as flaky. Another half or full generation may pass before events come together in a way to support the full-scale development and adoption of ideas. By that time, the initial innovator may have faded and receive little credit for the innovations. Even histories describing sequence of events and ideas leading up to the innovation may fail to fully appreciate the early genius.

Whether in sports leagues or through industries, innovations usually disperse in the way described above. They tend to follow an "S-shaped" path as depicted in Figure 7.1. Just as with Sid Gillman, the innovation starts out slowly, at some point begins to be adopted by the majority, and then finally is adopted by the holdouts.

In the context of managerial abilities, the first part of the dispersion represents the adoption by forward-looking managers on the watch for things that can help their companies improve. The second part represents the adoption by managers, who may be more cautious, but soon respond to the competitive pressure to keep up with the leaders in the industry. The last phase of the dispersion often reflects the managers who just don't get it or are so set in their ways to bury their heads in the sand or use the innovative item sparingly and begrudgingly. In some cases, this last phase only takes place after the managers who drag their feet have been removed and replaced with new ones.

Another element of innovation illustrated by sports is that it may mean reemphasizing or remolding something that has fallen into disuse. For in-

Figure 7.1
Dispersion of the "West Coast" Offense in the NFL

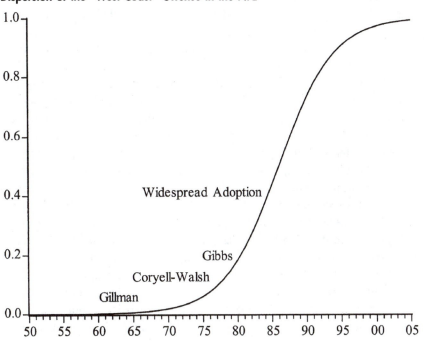

stance, Rick Pitino and some of his assistants adopted intensive shooting practice as an innovative idea. In some ways, the idea that this practice would ever have fallen out of favor as an integral part of basketball training is hard to fathom. Yet, in the emphasis on defensive schemes and other aspects of training, repetitive and extensive shooting practice had fallen out of use by a large number of college coaches by the mid 1980s. Tom Landry's use of the "shotgun" formation reflected this "innovation from the past" by taking a formation that had fallen into disuse and reintroducing it.

One of the most astounding examples of success through reemphasizing or adapting existing methods took place during the 1990 NCAA Basketball Tournament, when the Lions of Loyala Marymount made a highly publicized advance to the West Regional Finals. Their story became national news because of the death of their star player, Hank Gathers, who died from complications of a heart condition during their conference tournament. Stirred by his death and in spite of his absence, LMU marched over more highly seeded teams—New Mexico State, Michigan, and Alabama. The Michigan win was especially startling. LMU not only defeated the third-seeded, defending national champions, but humiliated them in an unprecedented 149 to 115 onslaught in which Loyola scored an eye-popping

84 points in the second half. Ultimately, the eventual national champions that year, UNLV, ended the dream run for the Lions.

Paul Westhead took over as head coach of the basketball program at Loyola Marymount University in 1985. He had previously coached the LA Lakers to a World Championship in 1980 but was fired in favor of Pat Riley over reported disputes with key players. Upon his arrival at LMU, Westhead instituted an unconventional style of play emphasizing fast-breaking offense and pressure defense. After both made or missed shots by an opponent, LMU would pass the ball upcourt rapidly, attempting to shoot very quickly upon gaining possession. When they scored, they would employ a full-court defense to attempt to influence the opponent into a quicker tempo of play. They shot a large number of 3-point shots and played pressure defense. Westhead did not invent any of these tactics, but he pushed them to extremes not seen before. For example, LMU had a goal to shoot within 3 seconds from the time when they gained possession of the ball.

Even though it led to high scoring and frenetic play, Westhead's system required discipline and sacrifice by his players. For the system to work, the LMU players had to be physically conditioned to a point exceeding the norms for college players of the era. For at least the first three years, the new system caught many supposedly more talent-laden opponents unable to cope with the pace of play. Although LMU had made only one appearance in the NCAA tournament in the prior 27 years, they earned three straight tournaments births from 1988 to 1990. In the 1988 NCAA tournament, LMU defeated a more highly seeded Wyoming team 119 to 115, before falling to traditional powerhouse North Carolina.

Whether the West Coast offense or an up-tempo playing style, these episodes indicate that one does not have to be the first person to come up with an idea to benefit from it. Utilizing ideas on which others have done experiments and endured many of the start-up costs may, in fact, be a more efficient way to profit from innovations than being at the very outset. Bill Gates and Microsoft are frequently mocked because their "Windows" mimicked rather than innovated the graphics-based interfaces now universally used. As the episodes above indicate, successful and effective adaptation is not all about being first. However, it is also not about being last. Those who often profited the most in the cases above were those who recognized the value of someone else's innovation fairly early on.

PEOPLE AS THE INNOVATION

The racial integration of baseball starting with Robinson at the outset of the 1947 season and joined by Larry Doby of the Cleveland Indians in July has been well documented as an historical episode.[7] In 1946 when Brooklyn Dodger general manager Branch Rickey surreptitiously plotted the introduction of not only the first but several blacks to join the Dodgers, the outcome of his plan was far from certain. As late as 1945, it appeared as though the chance of an African-American joining the major leagues was still far off. Owners of poorly performing teams had ignored suggestions to use black players to enhance their teams' fortunes. Philadelphia owner, Bill Veeck, had already been blocked in his attempt to bring black players to his team. Still, Rickey forged ahead and recruited Jackie Robinson along with Roy Campenella, holding his plan in such close confidence that even Campanella thought that the overtures toward him were to play with the Negro League Brooklyn Brown Dodgers rather than the National League's Brooklyn Dodgers.

Societal pressures along with Branch Rickey's motives have been mulled over extensively. Yet, whatever his broader social agenda, if he had one at all, Branch Rickey intended to utilize black players to make the Dodgers a better team. In this respect, his addition of black players to the Dodgers tapped into the innovative and entrpreneurial abilities that he had shown while serving as general manager of the St. Louis Cardinals during the 1920s and 1930s.[8] Because of the difficulty in competing for major league-level players with clubs such as the Yankees, he revolutionized the scouting and development of players by instituting tryout camps for thousands of young players. To further develop the players found to be promising, he placed them in minor league teams, starting what came be know as the "farm system"—an innovation that survives to present times, albeit in altered ownership formats. Lesser known among Rickey's contributions to the game were the use of pitching machines, specialized spring training facilities, and promotions such as ladies day and free admittance to young boys.

Innovating in the use of black ball players was not as simple as just signing someone to a contract. It demanded that Rickey overcome several obstacles in order to bring Jackie Robinson and others to the Dodgers. Rickey first had to recognize that black athletes in general and these players in particular possessed skills that make the Dodgers a better team. By itself, this was not novel—members of the black press had long touted black players as remedies for bad MLB teams. For instance, a telegram from Pittsburgh sportswriter Chester Washington to the manager of the Pirates in 1933 stated, "Know your club needs players. Have answers to your prayers right here in Pittsburgh. Josh Gibson catcher Buck Leonard first base S. Paige pitcher and Cool Papa Bell all available at reasonable figures. Would make the Pirates formidable Pennant contenders."[9] Looking back, Hall of Fame pitcher Dizzy Dean said of Satchel Paige, "[He was] the best pitcher I ever saw."[10]

Yet, agreement about the potential contribution of black players was far from universal. Rickey's assessment of blacks veered from the mainstream outlook. Whether because of lack of attention, poor evaluation, or fear of harassment, few in MLB had even hinted at the capability of black players at helping. Hall of Fame pitcher Bob Feller, for one, had played many "barnstorming" games against black teams. Moreover, he was not noted as a white player who ever begrudged the introduction of black players. Yet, he predicted that only Satchel Paige and Josh Gibson might possess major league talent. He viewed Robinson abilities with skepticism. Among major league owners and managers, only maverick Bill Veeck expressed an appreciation for what black players might add on the field.

The racial integration as an innovation story in MLB has been repeated in many other sports leagues. Atlantic Coast Conference basketball followed the same path. The growth of the University of North Carolina as a basketball powerhouse can, in part, be attributed to coach Dean Smith's willingness to be at the leading edge of the use of black athletes. While much has been made of the Texas Western's (now Texas–El Paso) NCAA championship in 1966 because of their use of five black starters against an all white Kentucky squad, NCAA Final Four history from the mid 1950s through the mid 1970s illustrates the typical path of innovation. Before the mid 1950s, segregation permitted college basketball to be dominated by all-white or nearly all-white teams. By the mid 1950s, the landscape began to change as Table 7.2 shows. The University of San Francisco won championships in 1955 and 1956 with an African American star player—future NBA legend Bill Russell. During the late 1950s and early 1960s, the Final Four saw an increasing number of teams that were not only integrated but had black players who were the keys to their success including Wilt Chamberlain at Kansas, Elgin Baylor at Seattle, Oscar Robertson at Cincinnati.

By the mid to late 1960s, the innovation was imitated more widely, and schools that extensively integrated early on soon came to dominate the Final Four. In addition to Texas Western, this list includes teams such as UCLA, North Carolina, Houston, and Michigan. During the 1960s and 1970s, many lessor known schools including Texas Western, Loyola, Jacksonville, Dayton, Western Kentucky, Memphis State, and Florida State reached their apex of basketball success during this period because of their willingness to be innovative in using black players before some of the larger schools. All of these teams reached the NCAA's Final Four over this era for the only time in school history with the exception of Memphis State, which returned in 1985.[11]

Whether looking at MLB or the NCAA, the introduction of black athletes highlights an important point. Managers tend to think innovation in terms of new tools, machines, or ways of doing something. Innovations

Table 7.2
Final Four Teams with Prominent Black Players, 1955–1965

Year	Team	Primary Black Player(s)	Result
1955-56	San Francisco	Bill Russell	Champion
1957	Kansas	Wilt Chamberlain	Runner-Up
1958	Seattle	Elgin Baylor	Runner-Up
1959	Cincinnati	Oscar Robertson	Third Place
1960	Cincinnati	Oscar Robertson	Third Place
	NYU	Tom Sanders	Fourth Place
1964	UCLA	Walt Hazard	Champion
1965	Michigan	Cazzie Russell	Runner-Up

Source: Jim Savage, The Encyclopedia of the NCAA Basketball Tournament (New York: Dell Publishing, 1990).

also include new ways of utilizing people. Another aspect of the racial integration in sports is that, as with any innovation such as the evolution of the NFL passing game noted above, the process takes time. Some existing managers are able to make the adjustment, but in other cases, the adjustment by team could only fully be realized when the old managers were replaced by new managers. In fact, the evidence shows that for both MLB and the ACC, it took the elimination or retirement of an entire generation of managers before all teams fully adopted the use of black players.

HURDLES TO INNOVATION AND IMITATION

Legendary coaches with long, long records of success such as John Wooden, Scotty Bowman, and Tom Landry have not only been disciples of innovation and change but preached its gospel. Prominent business executives have paralleled this message. Still, the roadblocks to valuable organizational chance are so frequent and widespread that the phrase "organizational inertia" has been coined as sort of law of organizations—not an ironclad law but more of a general maxim. Why is there such reluctance to innovation and change on the part of organizations and the managers within them?

In part, some coaches and managers do not see change as important. They may have seen statements such as Vince Lombardi's about football, "Football is blocking and tackling. Everything else is mythology," and observe his relatively simple strategies coupled with his success and conclude that adaptation and ideas have little to do with success. After all, even John Wooden said that basketball was a simple game. They do not see that Wooden's statement did not negate the importance of adjustment in the face of personnel or rule changes. They also do not recognize that as successful as Lombardi was, his stay at the top was short in comparison to the tenure of people like Bowman or Landry. Over a ten-year run with the Packers largely using one core group of players, the need for change and adjustment was much less than would have been the case over two or three decades. Along with buying into an overly simplistic view of effective managing, ego also can step in the way of sound judgment. Coaches and other kinds of managers can become intent on doing it "my way." Notre Dame's Frank Leahy once said, "Egotism is the anesthetic that dulls the pain of stupidity."

This does not imply that every coach with a big ego is stupid, but it does indicate that smart coaches and managers inflict harm on themselves by allowing their egos to dumb down their coaching abilities. Success frequently breeds arrogance and complacency. Additionally, success may create a risk-averse anxiety about change. As Lou Holtz put it, "When you're number one, change becomes intimidating."[12] When a team is performing poorly, change entails little if any downside risk. In contrast, making changes when a team is succeeding already raises the specter of changing the wrong thing and causing a decline in performance. Many of the innovations in MLB such as the adoption of night games illustrate this very problem. Although night baseball proved highly successful, it was by no means an easy feat. The hesitancy of the NHL to get rid of fighting and increase the size of the skating area to encourage a European style of hockey may draw from this same kind of thinking—"We're doing pretty good where we are, why risk changing?"

A coach such as Philadelphia Flyers' and former Dallas Stars' coach Ken Hitchcock stands in contrast to Scotty Bowman. Like Bowman, Hitchcock gained a reputation as a my-way-or-the-highway kind of leader who frequently butted heads with players. Also like Bowman, he obviously has coaching ability. After taking over the reins of the Stars in 1995, he built them into a contending team based on a defense-first style of play. Behind the goalkeeping gymnastics of Ed Belfour, the Stars won the Stanley Cup in 1999 and returned to the finals again in 2000. Unlike Bowman, Hitchcock did not adapt his team's tactics to the personnel on hand. During the 2000–2001 season, Belfour's play began to decline so that many of the close defensive games began to swing against them. The St. Louis Blues embarrassed the Stars, sweeping them out of the playoffs in four straight games during the second round. During the 2001 offseason, the Stars acquired three players to help produce more scoring. However, rather than adapting his system to the new talent, Hitchcock attempted to force the new players into his system and, ultimately, lost his job as the team struggled. It took a change for Hitchcock to succeed further—a change of his coaching position from the Stars to the Philadelphia Flyers where the team's personnel better fit his unflinching idea of how to play the game. The Stars rebounded from their 2001–02 season to win their division while Hitchcock took the Flyers to the Eastern Conference finals in 2004.

Maybe no better example of the failure to adapt can be found than Bob Knight as head basketball coach at Indiana University. Knight cut his coaching teeth at Army Academy at West Point during the late 1960s and early 1970s. With this experience and given his preferences, he came to Indiana in 1971 with not only a very dictatorial coaching style but with a hot temper and a brusque public manner. Even though such methods had already begun to be questioned in some circles, they played fairly well in Indiana during the 1970s. Knight's teams experienced tremendous success winning NCAA championships in 1976, 1981, and 1987, making Knight a coaching celebrity and a state icon.

Knight found out, though, that even icons, who do not adapt, can turn back into mere mortals. Over the 1990s, the performance of Knight's teams slid from exceptional to only good and, at time, average. Concurrent with these changes and preceding them, cultural views about acceptable behavior for coaches had changed dramatically since the early 1970s. On- and off-court temper tantrums by coaches, even highly successful ones, came to be viewed with much more scrutiny as well as disdain by a larger section of the population, even in mid-America. Knight had littered his career with a series of negative public incidents—a conviction in absentia in Puerto Rico for an altercation with a police officer and the on-court throwing of a chair among the most discussed. An incident involving grabbing a player around the neck and shoving him during practice placed Knight in jeopardy of his job after a videotape of the event surfaced. A subsequent event led to his dismissal by Indiana's Board. During and after these events, Knight showed defiance and complete unwillingness to adapt to the shift in external conditions that made such behavior intolerable at most leading universities.

Beyond ego-based unwillingness to see the need for change, managers fall into habits. Humans are creatures of habit. Longevity in a position begins to cut in on a manager's willingness to adapt if he or she becomes even more tied to certain ways of doing things. This fact may suggest a sort of managerial life cycle that arises. As managers age, if they become set in their ways and more tied to particular ways of doing things, they become less capable of adapting to changes in markets, technology, or rules and customs. Even highly successful coaches unable to adapt to the changes around them can put themselves at risk.

Tom Landry provides an ironic case in point of a coach who, as noted above, spent a career innovating and adapting and then fell victim to past success, and a growing entrenchment in a particular way of doing things. He came aboard as founding coach of the Dallas Cowboys in 1960 and earned a reputation as an innovator as discussed earlier in the chapter. He first gained this reputation as a defensive assistant coach for the New York Giants and carried it through his first decade or more as head coach of the Cowboys. However, Landry had made nearly all of his major adjustments by the mid 1970s. Over the next decade, other coaches such as Don Coryell at San Diego, Bill Walsh at San Francisco, and Joe Gibbs at Washington became the innovators in terms of offensive strategy and coaches such as Buddy Ryan at Chicago became the defensive innovators. By his last three or four seasons as head coach, Landry's Cowboys had become predictable and ineffective. What had been relatively novel ideas, became set in stone as the Cowboys system. Even his attempts to mix in new ideas from the "West Coast Offense" were largely thrust upon him. The team went 12 and 17 from 1986–1988 with a dismal 3–13 record in 1988, leading to Landry's removal when Jerry Jones purchased the team after that season.

As with individuals and their attachment to the status quo, organizations also become entrenched through the collective action of individuals. The slow pace of expansion has been a common one. MLB has consistently drug its feet on bringing teams to new locations. While most of the attention of the move of the Dodgers from Brooklyn to Los Angeles has fixated on the anxieties of the jilted Brooklyn fans, maybe a more relevant business question is why did it take so long for MLB to place teams on the West Coast? Even then, it only took place because the Dodgers and Giants relocated—not because MLB located new teams into these obviously lucrative markets but untapped markets. In many respects, the Pacific Coast League operated more as an alternative major league than as a minor league system in the years leading up to the Dodger and Giant move. As early as 1946, the San Francisco PCL club was making managerial moves and publicly pushing the idea of gaining MLB status. In the 1940s, the Mexican League was strong enough to serve as an alternative for some major leaguers during a labor crisis. Yet, the cities went without MLB representation until the Dodgers and Giants did not make their move until 1957, and no MLB team played regular games (other than an opening game) below the 48 states until the 2003 season.

MLB's expansions in the early 1960s and during the 1990s came about not as much because of the foresight of its managers but at the gunpoint of competition. In the 1950s, it was the talk of a rival league forming that led to the eventual placement of a second teams in the Los Angeles and New York areas and a team in Houston. In the 1990s, MLB had proclaimed that no new expansion was likely after the Marlins and Rockies. Yet, the frontburner plans of the U.S. Baseball League to go into untapped markets such as Phoenix and Tampa moved MLB's schedule ahead much more rapidly. A case in point for MLB is its move into Spanish-speaking areas. During the 2002–2003 offseason, MLB announced that the Montreal Expos would be playing some of their games in Puerto Rico. The question that should accompany this move is why had MLB not placed a team in the Caribbean, Mexico, or Latin America already when a franchise like the Expos has floundered to find a strong fan base in Montreal for so many years? Even without the Expos' struggles, these markets south of U.S. borders have been untapped even though they are hotbeds of baseball interest. Likewise, the Washington, DC market, the seventh largest television market in the United States, received attention only after the 2004 season.

The radio broadcasting of baseball games and the playing of games at night under lights are examples of the same kind of foot-dragging on changes that turned out to be wildly successful for baseball. From the 1920s up through the 1940s, both of these ideas were put forward and frequently hammered down by the objections of players, coaches, and managers. The objections to night games stalled its adoptions even though Pacific Coast League games at night drew nearly three times as many fans as day games and in spite of successful experimentation with it.[13] As late as 1945, Babe Ruth objected to night games because he thought that they would shorten players' careers.[14] MLB club owners saw broadcasts as a threat to live attendance and tried to curb its implementation in the early 1930s.[15] Finally, in 1935 MLB's Commissioner, Kennesaw Landis, gave his OK to broadcasts. However, these episodes repeated themselves when the Cubs, Braves, and Mets began sending their games over cable television "superstations" in the 1980s. Rather than seeing cable telecasts for what they were—an opportunity for MLB to expand it market relative to rivals in other forms of entertainment—MLB owners once again saw the innovation as a threat to live attendance.

These cases involving baseball highlight the fact that whenever collective action is necessary to bring change, additional obstacles to innovation crop up. These can broadly be described as "politics." The ability to implement effectively change by overcoming political obstacles and objections is one of the great skills of managing. As much as arrogance or risk aversion stymie innovation and adaptation, they do not overshadow organizational politics as a roadblock. Politics is a fact of life within organizations—not just governmental organizations. In fact, the Italian philosopher Machiavelli said, "Entrepreneurs are simply those who understand that there is little difference between obstacle and opportunity and are able to turn both to their advantage." While his writings have often been directed toward the cultivation of power, they can just as easily be interpreted as an early "how to" manual on effectively managing, including especially the management of change. Whatever the perspective to Machiavelli's writing one takes, one point is clear—political impediments to important and effective change crop up from many sources.

There is no such thing as an a-political environment, whether in sports or everyday business. Owners with a stake in protecting their "turf" conspire and lobby to keep other teams out—"rent-seeking." When a new idea requires a group decision process, the opportunity for internal politics and personal agendas to take hold increases. On most league-wide issues, the leagues require two-thirds or three-fourths majorities. If a change, such as expansion, requires the approval of two-thirds of the owners, then a minority of owners who either see direct loss or who are among the more risk averse owners can block such a move. For instance, if the owner of the Orioles views a team in Washington, DC as negatively impacting his financial situation and few other owners are by nature hesitant, then the expansion is blocked. The case of night games and broadcasting likely involves the fears and reluctance of the most cautious owners to slow down innovative ideas of those who are more daring. This is one key reason why innovations in business are often developed by smaller organizations. Innovation is normally spearheaded by the most forward looking and least risk averse owners. A single entrepreneur or small group of like-minded partners more easily take a step out into the unknown than a larger organization where more executives or committees must sign on to the change. At some point in the process, individuals who are among the more cautious in an organization are able to stall or stop the change. The role of leaders like Judge Landis becomes important in politically-driven situations. Where they are opposed to change, they can exert a great influence through manipulation of agendas or harassment of those seeking change.

On sports teams, players sometimes break into little coalitions along positional lines such as pitcher and infielders or offensive lineman and linebackers. At times, the coalitions have formed along racial lines. On other occasions, the intra-team networks are based on star versus everyone else, player age and experience, or off-the-field interests. Whatever the basis for these networks, they can become focal points for interest group activity—groups of players trying to influence team decisions to their advantage. Sometimes the group's advantage may coincide with the overall team objectives, but in many cases it may not. Similar coalitions and networks form in other kinds of organizations around functional units, pay levels, levels of management, hourly versus salaried employees, and so on. Whatever the organization, individuals and coalitions pursuing their own narrow agendas within an organization mimic the kinds of activities of government-oriented interest groups. They become information networks operating in the background, hallways, offices, and shadows. They make and enforce deals. They lobby for viewpoints; they subtly harass those who oppose them.

All managers must learn to live with a certain amount of internal politics. Players, coaches, and other kinds of employees and managers naturally draw closer to some others or have interests that are more closely aligned with others within the organization. Alliances will always tend to form on these bases. Individuals will always have some interests in pursuing their agendas that may be at odds with the health of the organization as a whole. That is the essence of the "agency problem" discussed in Chapter 2. Still, in many organizations managers do not take active steps to limit internal politics and let it and personal power plays exert far too big of a role. Managers who experience long-term success tend to implement policies that help limit the scope and negative influence of political influence on decisions.

One means to limit political maneuvering is taking actions and implementing policies that make information more transparent throughout the organization. Such policies tend to have the effect of "sunshine laws." Bill Parcells' emphasis on candor in communication is one version of such a policy. On Parcells' teams, every player not only knows where he stands but has a fairly good idea of where everyone else stands also. Another element in diminishing politics is for lead managers to make crystal clear to others that ideas matter much more than rank or ability to maneuver. Mike Krzyzewski's openness and development of input from his assistant coaches and even players plays such a role. He may not operate a complete open marketplace for ideas, but it is a long shot away from managers who develop cultures that are all based on shmooze, largesse, and political skill. People must be encouraged not only to develop and present new ideas as a kind of therapy for them, but the ideas must be taken seriously. In contrast, many coaches and managers permit cultures that do just the opposite. In many organizations, players, managers or other employees may actually endure ridicule and other penalties for honesty and new ideas. These penalties may not be put forward as such. In fact, they may be disguised as part of unrelated decisions. Nonetheless, people soon catch on to the fact that keeping your thoughts to yourself is the best policy, even if those thoughts may be very beneficial to the company.

These politics-limiting practices seen in coaching legends closely parallel those used by business leaders such a Bill Gates. In Gates' view, political maneuvering can be reduced by first making sure that everyone has the same message—a mirror of Bill Parcells. In addition, he promotes clear and direct (sometimes to the point of harsh) communication just like Parcells. Like Krzyzewski, he advocates open discussion of issues. These aspects with attempts to eliminate conflicting objectives and inter-unit rivalry define Gates' attempt to shape Microsoft's culture of innovation and adaptation.[16]

An equally important way to overcome obstacles to change is through the recruitment of creative people and put them in positions where they can help to motivate change. Just as with aversion to risk and most other attitudes, people differ with regard to their ability to envision and embrace innovation and adaptation. Positive change may, on occasion, just "happen" due to forces external and internal to an organization coming together in the right way at the right time. More often, organizational change that improves things does not just pop up in this way. Instead, it happens as a result of someone or some group making a conscious effort to adjust the way the people, policies, technology, or products of the firm. Not everything that happens, even for good, may be planned in advance. Plans may change "on the fly" as new information and knowledge is created in the very process of change. Still, significant and positive change usually requires an advocate within an organization who manages the changes, especially the political aspects. Frequently, the people who motivate change are out of the mainstream. Tom Peters coined the term "skunks" for such people who tend to promote innovation through their defiance of convention and individualistic ideas.[17]

For example, the racial integration in baseball was an exercise in innovation and entrepreneurship that social and competitive forces alone did not bring about—instead, it took the influence of these forces along with insightful and skilled management. In fact, an article by the author, Robert McCormick, and Robert Tollison in the *American Economic Review* shows that just like most other innovations, the dispersion of black players among MLB teams followed the S-shaped curve illustrated in Figure 7.2. The teams with better and more forward-looking management such as the Dodgers and Giants went first.[18] The best teams tended to use black players before the bad teams in MLB, and the full process of racial integration took about 25 years with large differences in the use of black players across teams long after Jackie Robinson took the field. The Boston Red Sox, for instance, did not field a single black player until 1959. Teams with the largest share of black players, such as the San Fransisco Giants, St. Louis Cardinals, and Los Angeles Dodgers excelled during the 1960s as many teams continued to drag their feet.

In particular, the seminal beginnings of the racial innovation with Branch Rickey displayed cunning regarding the politics, public relations, and human relations needed to make the innovation work. In fact, he went so far as to consult a sociologist regarding the qualities of the player and the supporting environment needed to make the "great experiment" a success. He condensed his list to six requisite items. First, the player had to be

Figure 7.2
Percentage of Blacks on MLB Teams, 1947–1971

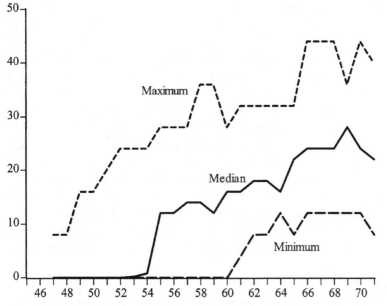

Source: Brian L. Goff, Robert E. McCormick, and Robert D. Tollison, "Racial Integration as an Innovation," *American Economic Review*, 92 (March 2002): 16–26.

"right" on the field. In one respect this point is obvious. The team needed quality players. However, in terms of the politics of introducing the first black player, one who performed poorly would damage more than just his own career. Second, the player had to be "right" off the field. Rickey realized that no matter how good the player, there would be important public relations responsibilities work that the player would have to fill well. Third, the "reaction of his own race" had to be right. By this, Rickey meant that the player could not have undue demands and expectations placed upon him by the black community. He needed to be a ballplayer—not an ambassador paraded to every conceivable event. Fourth, the reaction of the press and public needed to be "right." To a large extent, this lay beyond Rickey's control, although he could cultivate the press' attitude to some extent. Fifth, he needed the right place to season the player before pulling him to the majors. Rickey did not want the experiment ruined before it ever got off the ground. Last, the reaction of his fellow players had to be "right." This depended to some extent on Rickey and the club's manager but also on the reaction of a few key team leaders.[19]

With both sound planning and some luck, the right set of "political" circumstances fell into place. What was within Rickey's realm of influence, he

MANAGING INNOVATION AND CHANGE

meticulously managed. To ensure the right player, he spent $25,000 in scouting Jackie Robinson. He placed Robinson in Montreal so as to minimize racial issues during his minor league preparation. He also sensed that in commissioner Happy Chandler, he had an at least a facilitator if not an outright ally in brining blacks to the playing field. He also capitalized on the talents of Dodger manager Leo Durocher. While Durocher collected a reputation as both a colorful and fiery personality, he was forward-looking and very adept at handling sticky situations. For example, when a few prominent Dodgers staged a petition drive among other players to lobby to keep Robinson off the team, Durocher called a 1:00 AM meeting in which he made it clear that Robinson would help the team win pennants, and thereby, help every Dodger player. He noted that "colored" players were coming to baseball, and they had better wake up or lose out. He then ended the meeting by saying he did not want to see their petition.[20] Finally, he also mentored and assisted Robinson in dealing with the pressures associated with being the first black in an all-white sea, including handling the insults of other players and inequitable treatment from even some umpires.

Rickey's accomplishment with the Dodgers provides a template for successful innovation in most business settings. Usually, successful innovation requires more than merely inventing or discovering a technical improvement. Rather, it typically requires the successful application of technical abilities, public relations, politics, and human relations. Beyond recognizing the talent in black baseball players, Rickey had to negotiate a political and cultural minefield in order to make his innovative idea a workable reality on-the-field. In Robinson's minor league season with Montreal and during his first few years in the majors, visiting cities such as Baltimore or St. Louis created logistical problems because of the segregation policies of hotels and restaurants. Also, the spring training site in Florida posed similar problems that were more difficult because of the amount of time involved. Rickey used another innovative idea to overcome the segregation problems at spring training by purchasing an abandoned military facility near Vero Beach and creating "Dodger Town." Within this closed community, the Dodgers could sleep, eat, and train according to their own rules regarding racial integration, helping Robinson and other black Dodgers avoid the discrimination of rural Florida.

MINDLESS IMITATION

Not all successful ideas deserve imitation. Willingness to adapt, by itself, reflects only one part of the recipe for a successful manager. The other critical ingredient is the ability to adapt in productive ways. Many managers in business and in sports have torpedoed themselves, not by the lack of change, but the direction of their change or the mindless imitation of change initiated by someone else. Professional football supplies clear examples of mindless imitation versus well-conceived adaptation. Possibly the best example in recent years has been the imitation of the "West Coast Offense" mentioned earlier in connection with Sid Gillman as an innovator. This name has been given to similar kinds of sophisticated passing attacks developed primarily by Don Coryell as head coach of St. Louis in the 1970s and San Diego in the 1980s and by Bill Walsh as an assistant coach at Cincinnati in the 1970s and as head coach at San Fransisco in the 1980s. As noted above, the schemes use receivers and running backs in ways to create four or five receiving options for quarterbacks on a given play and isolate weak spots or weaknesses in specific defenders. In addition, the schemes emphasize very precise route running and timing between quarterback and receiver so that decisions are made quickly and accurately.

Without a doubt, the West Coast systems and modifications of them as used by their originators and some of their disciples have been very successful. Coryell's team twice advanced to the AFC Championship. Ex-San Diego assistant, Joe Gibbs, won three Super Bowls in Washington. Walsh's teams and those carrying on his legacy with the 49ers won five Super Bowls. Ex-San Francisco assistant, Mike Holmgren won a Super Bowl at Green Bay. In addition, the Denver Broncos used the offensive system in winning two Super Bowls. So what was the trouble? How did enlightened imitation turn into thoughtless imitation? By the late 1990s, the "West Coast Offense" had become the benchmark. Some teams drew elements from its principles, while many blatantly attempted to imitate it in every detail, hiring head coaches and assistants with extensive backgrounds in it. However, as with any particular system, success of the West Coast scheme depended heavily on its use by players with skills that closely matched the key skills required by the system. The teams who excelled using the system employed quarterbacks with exceptional skill in quickly moving from one potential receiver to another—their "progression"—and in delivering the ball with great precision and exact timing. This list includes Ken Anderson at Cincinnati, Dan Fouts at San Diego, Joe Montana at San Francisco, Troy Aikman at Dallas, Brett Favre at Green Bay, and John Elway at Denver.

Most of the teams who tried to imitate the offense did so with either mediocre quarterbacks or quarterbacks with great abilities but abilities that did not fit the system well—strong arms or quick feet but not especially accurate arms or quick decisions. Instead of evaluating and using the assets on hand to the best of their abilities, many coaches were determined to fit square pegs into round holes in the blind pursuit of imitating certain successful teams. If the pegs did not fit, then those players were discarded. As a result, many of the teams using the system faltered even though their assistant coaches came with impeccable West Coast credentials. In the hands of quarterbacks who made slower progressions from receiver to receiver or who lacked the pin-point precision demanded, the system often devolved into little more than what ex-coach and commentator John Madden has derisively called the "dump and dink" offense.

Two recent and glaring example of mindless imitation of the West Coast system occurred in Cleveland and Detroit. In Cleveland, the 49er-think emanated largely from the front office. The reborn Browns selected former 49er front office man, Carmen Policy, to be their president and CEO. He placed Dwight Clark, a former 49er player under Bill Walsh and front office executive in San Francisco, as vice president in charge of football operations. While the coach they hired, Chris Palmer, was not directly tied to the 49ers, his offensive schemes mimicked them in most respects. On offense, they selected almost exclusively young players that they could mold into the system. After a 2–14 opening year that drew little criticism, Palmer was fired after a 3–13 second year in which the team finished last in scoring, averaging only 10 points per game and scoring 3 or fewer points in six games. Clark soon followed Palmer to the unemployment line. New coach, Butch Davis, propelled the team to a solid showing in 2001 and reached the playoffs in 2002.

Because the Browns were an expansion club, the problem of tunnel vision with regard to the West Coast system is not as obvious as it has been in Detroit. The setup was nearly identical to Cleveland—the general manager, Matt Millen, played for the 49ers and he hired a head coach, Marty Mornhinwheg, who had served as offensive coordinator in San Francisco from 1997–2000 after working as an assistant under first generation 49er disciple Mike Holmgren in Green Bay. Unlike the expansion situation in Cleveland, Millen and Mornhinwheg took over a team that had finished just out of the playoffs with 9–7 and 8–8 records the two prior years and possessed several key players in their prime. In spite of this seeming solid foundation, the team plunged to a 2–14 record in Millen and Mornhinwheg's first year and the second year imitated the first with only five wins. Mornhinwheg inherited a young quarterback with four years of experience who had shown strong potential but who was not well suited to play the position, just like Joe Montana during the 49er glory days of the 1980s. The coach quickly grew frustrated with his performance and flip-flopped quarterbacks throughout the season. At the end of the 2002 season, Millen dumped Morninwheg with considerable pressure from ownership.

The Washington Redskins of the 1980s and early 1990s, along with the Denver Broncos of the late 1990s, supply interesting counterpoints to the mindless imitation. As an assistant with the San Diego Chargers in the late

1970s, Gibbs spent time at ground zero of one variant of the West Coast offense. Although one could easily see influences of the West Coast schemes with those he used with the Redskins during the 1980s, Gibbs developed many unique characteristics both around his own ideas as well as tailored around his players' talents. His offensive schemes were not merely knock-offs of those he had seen in San Diego. The same can be said of Mike Shanahan at Denver. Shanahan came out of the San Francisco–West Coast offensive coaching mill, but his offensive schemes blended in power running much more than with most teams mindlessly trying to imitate the West Coast schemes.

A similar history can be traced in professional basketball. If one looks back at successful NBA teams of the 1960s and 1970s, most teams employed two guards who traded off responsibility in bringing the ball up court and "setting up the offense." Exceptions did exist, such as Bob Cousy in the 1950s and 1960s or Nate Archibald in the 1970s. Yet, teams such as the Knicks, Lakers, post-Cousy Celtics, Bullets, and others did not run systems where only one person "ran the point." In the 1979–80 season, Earvin "Magic" Johnson entered the NBA with the Los Angeles Lakers. Johnson was a truly unique talent. Although taller than many NBA forwards at the time at six feet, eight inches, he could handle the ball and pass with an ability surpassing most smaller players. Because of these abilities, he became a prototypical "point guard." Through the rest of the 1980s and the 1990s, many NBA coaches and general managers became enamoured of the idea of having a point guard that could run an offense Magic Johnson style. The trouble was that very few if any players possessed Johnson's talents. Few could match his vision of other players and passing skills and none could match his size. Still, coaches began to put the ball in the hands of one player over and over down the court. Moreover, most of these teams did not possess the complimentary players that helped make the Lakers a great team. Magic could be a liability trying to guard smaller and quicker guards. The mix of players defensive skills among the Lakers help to offset this potential disadvantage.

Not surprisingly, the other teams that continued to excel during the 1980s and 1990s did not follow the point-guard mania. These teams included the Celtics in the 1980s with Dennis Johnson and Cedric Henderson or Danny Ainge at guard, the Pistons in the late 1980s and 1990s with Isaiah Thomas and Joe Dumars at guard, and the Bulls in the 1990s with Michael Jordan, Ron Harper, and several other players at guard. These teams continued to play systems where both guards, and sometimes forwards, carried the load much more equally in handling the ball.

Mindless imitation not only occurs in sports but has also been passed off as sound business strategy in management education circles under academic-sounding words such as "benchmarking." Benchmarking became a management buzzword during the 1990s. As with many other management buzzwords, the idea contains a kernel of good sense—identify a successful organization or set of organizations, observe key aspects of their organizational structure or decision making, and use these as a point of reference for making decisions within one's own organization. Also like many such buzzwords, the management consulting crowd picked up on the idea and quickly adulterated it into little more than a slogan that set the stage for mindless imitation. Along with the thoughtless imitation, shrewd but unprincipled managers saw the idea as a way to pick-and-choose to justify decisions already made. The trouble with benchmarking as it began to be practiced is highlighted in the sports examples described previously. Many companies and organizations instituted benchmarking schemes only to focus on one or few parts of some other organization's success and fail to see these practices as part of a bigger picture. Along with this myopia, they frequently overlooked the unique combination of resources to make the system work. In doing so, they missed the point being stressed here as so critical to the success of managers—working to integrate the decisions of management so that they work well together and utilize the resources available to their full potential.

REPLAY

1. Continual adaptation—whether by innovating or imitating—is a hallmark of great coaches. They preach it and practice it. It separates the truly great managers over the long term from the rest of the pack. Even highly successful managers who quit adapting begin to fail.

2. Effective change does not require a manager to be novel. Skillfully adopting and adapting the innovations of others, sometimes ones that have been shelved, has created many profitable opportunities in sports and business as Tom Landry showed with the "shotgun" formation.

3. The integration of Major League Baseball shows how the utilization of untapped people or bringing in new people are ways of innovating just like new technologies, products, and equipment.

4. Managers with long term records of success like Bill Parcells and Mike Krzryweski not only innovate and imitate but also create organizational cultures that reduce obstacles to innovation and imitation such as internal politics.

5. Mindless imitation is a recipe for failure. Mediocre and poor coaches frequently adopt this kind of monkey see, monkey do model. Carefully observing and analyzing the successful practices of other people and organizations can spur thinking about adaptation, but applications must be made with regard to the assets and limitations on hand.

8

Managing versus Meddling: Andy North Learned Not to Be Too Perfect

Rick, you're too controlling. Sit down. Relax.

—Boston Celtic fan to Celtic coach Rick Pitino

Most of what we call management consists of making it difficult for people to get their work done.

—Peter Drucker, management expert

The evening of April 3, 1983 did not unfold as expected for the University of Houston basketball team. In the Regional Finals and National Semifinals of the 1983 NCAA tournament, the Cougars had dispensed of highly regarded Villanova and Louisville with spectacular dunking and shot blocking performances. Most observers and likely the team itself expected a relatively easy victory over North Carolina State University in the National Final along with more tape for the highlight reels of the self-proclaimed brothers of "Phi Slamma Jamma." Surprisingly, North Carolina State had led for much of the game and limited Phi Slamma Jamma to a single dunk by Hakeem Olajewon. In spite of the disappointment, Houston pulled ahead by a margin of five points with about seven minutes remaining in the game.

Then, Houston head coach Guy Lewis made a monumental decision. He instructed his team to hold the ball and run time off the clock before attempting any shots. The Cougars quickly lost the momentum they had fought so hard to gain. Moving away from their typical relaxed, up-tempo style, their offense sputtered, they missed some key free throws. NCSU forward Lorenzo Charles put in an errant last second shot to make champions out of NCSU and a celebrity of coach Jim Valvano. Valvano received praise for his coaching down the stretch, but in fact, his strategy of fouling to get the ball back was both obvious and necessary. Instead, the outcome more likely turned on Guy Lewis' controversial management decision to slow the game down.

Why did a coach who had gained a reputation as one who "let his players play" decide to deviate from this strategy? Reporters put this question to Lewis, who defended it in terms of the foul trouble on his team, but the move received considerable debate among commentators. Beyond the specifics of basketball coaching, Guy Lewis likely succumbed to one of the greatest plagues of management—being drawn into thinking that doing something is preferable to doing nothing.

WHEN TO MANAGE

Golf and basketball are not very similar as sports, but in trying to make decisions to lead to the best possible outcomes, golfers and coaches like Guy Lewis face similar situations. For example, prior to the 2001 U.S. Open, an ESPN anchor asked golf analyst and former U.S. Open winner Andy North what, if anything, he had learned from his recent years of observing other golfers play as an analyst much more than playing himself. North responded by saying he "learned not to try to be too perfect." During the course of the tournament, a reporter asked Mark Brooks, who would ultimately lose to Retief Goosen in a playoff, what he had learned from winning his first "major" at the 1996 PGA Championship. He answered, "Everybody is going to hit some bad shots out there," which simply phrases Andy North's response a little differently.

At first glance the responses by North and Brooks might seem odd. After all, perfection is the goal. The kernel of their answers, however, teaches one of the most important lessons for any player, coach, or business manager—making adjustments may not improve performance, and may, in fact, diminish it. Put a little differently, a manager (or self-manager in a golfer's case) of any kind must learn where a manager's input adds value and where it subtracts value. This seems simple, but the desire to improve performance coupled with the opportunity and ability to make adjustments available to managers frequently makes tinkering nearly irresistible. Even successful managers can become overly infatuated with their management expertise, thinking that additional manipulation equals improvement. In fact, successful managers may be even more prone to developing this attitude because of their past success.

Among the various ideas credited to management advisor and innovator Edward Deming, this basic principle probably tops the list as most critical for managers to grasp. No matter where one looks, production and performances of all kinds exhibit variation. Athletics provides prime examples. In golf, shots stray to the right, left, short, and long of the target. In basketball, nearly identical "alley-oop" passes may lead to widely different results—a momentum building dunk in one situation or a costly turnover on a different occasion. The same running play in football that gains twenty yards one time fails to advance pass the line of scrimmage another time.

Coaches or players may rant and rage over the less desirable outcomes. To manage effectively over the long haul, though, a manager must firmly grasp the parts of the variation in outcomes that are indeed "manageable," and the parts that are endemic to the structure of the system or game. Whether in NCAA Championship basketball games, U.S. Open golf tournaments, or operating a manufacturing plant, knowing the difference between what can be "fixed" with a tweak or two verses the things that cannot is an indispensable tool for a manager. It defines the difference between effective managing and merely meddling. At best, meddling does nothing. At worst, it spells disaster.

Many coaches, players, and managers of all kinds could learn a valuable lesson from the thermostat in their home or apartment. This simple-to-use device teaches the basic difference between managing and meddling. Most thermostats are designed to activate and deactivate the heating and cooling system in a house within a range. If the thermostat is set at 73 degrees with the AC switched on automatic, then the system may switch on the cooling unit and fan when the temperature reaches 74.2 degrees and switch off when the temperature reaches 71.8 degrees. Using the logic of many coaches and managers, if the observed temperature is at 74 degrees, then something needs to be done, so the thermostat is turned down, say to 72 degrees. However, if the thermostat is operating normally, this will eventually lead not only to a lower than desired temperature, but one that is lower than the range of temperatures from just setting the thermostat at 73 degrees and leaving it there. This meddling scenario of thermostat adjustment contrasts to a situation where the thermostat is genuinely out of kilter. If the homeowner notices a repeated pattern when the temperature runs hot or cold, for instance at night, then an adjustment makes sense and can improve performance. Or the homeowner may accept the desired temperature range as the norm for the thermostat, but think that a different thermostat engineered to tighter specifications would be helpful. Both of these cases represent effective management as opposed to the meddling case above.

The problem is that managers and players have trouble in separating these two. Major league baseball hitters and analysts become concerned about the player with a career .300 average "mired in a 6 for 32 slump."

No doubt the 6 for 32 stretch (a 0.187 clip) is far below the .300 average, but by the same reasoning, a 10 for 25 stretch (a .400 average) is "too hot" although this terminology is seldom used. In 500 at bats during a major league season, hitters that, on average, get 3 hits in 10 at bats are very likely to experience subsets where the average is well below and well above .300. Extra batting practice, although commonly employed to cure such slumps, likely makes little difference. The outcomes are normal given variations in reaction time, swing path, pitchers and pitches, sizes of ballparks, sizes of foul territory, and so on. It would be much more astounding to see a career 300 hitter go through a season getting about three hits in every set of ten at-bats than not. In his book, Joe Torre relates a story relevant to this point concerning third baseman Scott Brosius. The Yankees traded for Brosius in spite of a substantial decline in his hitting statistics the prior year with the Oakland Athletics. As Torre put it, "He [Brosius] tries too hard to fix things . . . You always hear how it is important to make adjustments in baseball. But a player can make so many adjustments that he loses sight of what he was doing right from the start."[1]

Golf, by the very nature of the game, tends to develop golfers into obsessive "tinkerers." There are dozens of small changes directly at the control of a golfer that can influence the flight or roll of a golf ball from how firmly the club is gripped, to the type of grip, to how much the left hand is rotated on top or under the club, to where the ball is placed in relation to the right or left foot, to the plane on which the club is taken back from the ball, to how straight the left arm is kept during the swing, to how far back the club is taken during the backswing. The list of things available for manipulation goes on and on. The multitude of adjustments possible coupled with the desire to play better, however, can cause golfers, even at the professional level, to fall victim to the same disease that gripped Guy Lewis toward the end of the 1983 NCAA basketball championship game— "meddleitis"—manipulating processes and events simply because the urge "to do something" is so strong.

Putting tests on the percentage of putts made by a gravity-based machine conducted by an engineer-turned-author illustrate the point.[2] The machine could be adjusted for distance and rolled the ball with considerably less variation than a human would who was using a putter. He conducted tests on a pool table, on greens before foot traffic disturbed them for the day and after foot traffic altered the green, and on putts of different lengths including straight and breaking putts. After calibrating and optimizing the machine, the engineer could experiment with putts of different lengths to determine the percentages made under ideal green conditions as well as conditions that are less than ideal as the condition of the green deteriorates through use during a day. These percentages represent the absolute maximum overtime that anyone might expect to make. For instance, if only 10 percent of 30-foot points drop using the specialized putting device, it is unrealistic for a golfer to try to make adjustments to his game after failing to sink any 30-footers during a round.

Rather than tinkering around the edges with variation that is built-in, a golfer who is determined to improve his game must commit to the time, effort, and frustration necessary to alter major components of his swing. An example of this is the game's best player—Tiger Woods. Woods entered the professional ranks with unequaled amateur credentials including three U.S. Amateur victories. He shocked the golfing world with a runaway victory at the Master's. Still, he sensed that he would not be able to achieve his goal of surpassing Jack Nicklaus' major victories simply be tweaking the edges of his game. His distance control on his iron play lacked consistency as did his direction of his tee shots. With coach Butch Harmon, the player who was arguably as good as anybody in the game set out to bring major adjustments to his game. The payoff was not instantaneous. When it came, Woods vaulted to a position head and shoulders above the rest of the field, racking up majors and even winning four in a row—a sequential Grand Slam.

Woods' efforts were analogous to designing and building a new thermostat capable of more accurate temperature control. These efforts though may take weeks, months, or even years to fully work through. However, over the course of a single tournament or several tournaments, much less a single round, making "fine-tuning" adjustments may only increase the number of errant shots or the size of the errors. Rather than tinkering and adjusting endlessly, most players would do well by making decisions that clearly improve outcomes—leaving a certain club in the bag, trying to hit more conservative shots, and the like—than attempting countless small adjustments. In addition, a stray shot here or there should not be cause to change course or make adjustments unless such shots indicate an obvious pattern that the player knows how to correct—not experimenting in correcting.

Jack Nicklaus noted that when playing U.S. Open courses where straight driving was a key, he would look in his bag on the tee box, start with the longest hitting club, and proceed down until he found a club he felt very confident he could hit in the fairway. Rather than adjusting this and that, he took his game, at least in the short term, as it was and made appropriate decisions. Golfers of lesser stature than Nicklaus could likely learn a lesson from him. One wonders how many players would be better off on the PGA tour if they fired their "swing coaches" except for offseason periods where they have decided to reengineer their swings or during periods of exceptionally bad play.

John Wooden, whose teams won 10 NCAA championships in 12 years, might have grasped this distinction between the manageable and unmanageable as well as any coach. Former UCLA standout and TV sports commentator Bill Walton noted that a great thing about Wooden was that "he allowed us great freedom on the court." Without any more information, many managers, especially in sports, would take a statement like Walton's to imply that Wooden exerted little influence on his players. Yet, in contrast, Wooden was noted as a coach firmly in charge by his former players and assistant coaches. Even by 1960s standards, he was known as strict and demanding. The things that he viewed as within his ability to control, he did. He was dedicated to developing player and team skills in the setting where he had the most opportunity to "engineer" his teams—in practice. In fact, while he viewed himself as a very good practice coach, he thought he was only an average coach during the game, but that this did not matter too much.[3] One of his favorite maxims was "failing to prepare is preparing to fail."

Wooden's approach to management differed greatly from many, especially in basketball. He never stalked along the sideline as a maniacal figure attempting to dictate the moves of his players down to their every step, every pass, every shot or debate with the referees about every call. He did not scream at his players on the sidelines of games or during practice. Wooden understood that implementing and controlling key elements of his team's performance did not imply micro-managing every action they took. To Wooden, the freedom he gave his players on the court did not diminish his input and control as a manager or compromise the team's performance. Instead, he enhanced their performance by not limiting their creative abilities on the court too much. This kind of approach to management has often been a rare commodity in business just as in sports. However, it has had its outspoken advocates. Jack Welch, CEO of General Electric put it plainly, "I dislike the tenets that have come to be associated with 'managing'—controlling, stifling people, keeping them in the dark, wasting their time on trivia and reports. Breathing down their neck."[4]

In spite of the success of people like Torre, Wooden, or Jack Welch, the idea of "manager" as active controller is deeply embedded in the psyche of many. Managers in business as well as sports see "managing" as all about controlling something and tweaking something. It takes a person of great self-control to imitate the managerial self-discipline of a John Wooden. A person must control the urge to over-manage, to try to make adjustments beyond his or her control. Moreover, in all kinds of sports settings, much like in politics or management in general, coaches prefer the appearance of "doing something" to the perception of doing little or nothing.

Coaches such as Houston's Guy Lewis, Nolan Richardson (formerly of the University of Arkansas), and Jerry Tarkanian of Fresno State, for three examples, have often been derisively viewed as coaches who enrolled quality athletes and then "just rolled the ball out there." These kinds of criticisms likely originate from their lack of meddling as much as from anything. These three coaches shared fourteen trips to the NCAA tournament's "Final Eight" and eleven trips to the NCAA Final Four—accomplishments not equaled by very many groups of three coaches regardless of players skill. In fact, Guy Lewis hardly ever receives mention or listing among the great college coaches even though his 26 tournament wins place him among the elite of college coaching. Whether Lewis, Richardson, or Tarkanian excelled in every aspect as coaches or not, the kinds of attributes evidenced by their teams—excellent passing and ball movement, well-coordinated defensive efforts, exceptional conditioning and effort—resulted from coaching and preparation and not just because the players showed up on the court. Even Bob Knight, who won three national championships at Indiana University, for all of his bluster did not engage in exaggerated attempts to manipulate every decision of his players during games. Instead, he worked in practice on teaching his players to develop thinking and observational skills of their own. To be honest, some coaches who have a bent for meddling and hyper-management have been successful. Yet, their success has come about in spite of these traits rather than because of them. Their success owes itself to other critical aspects of management practiced by the John Woodens—attention to player and team development, attention to opponents strengths and weaknesses—and not to the over-the-top attempts to directly control everything going on during a game or in the players' personal lives.

MLB hitters, PGA golfers, college basketball players, employees, and machines and equipment develop real problems that require fixing. The lesson here does not teach abstinence from actively trying to fix or avoid these problems. Rather, the critical managerial skill emphasized here is in distinguishing normal variation from abnormal variation. This management (or self-management) skill is in short supply. In the era of slow-motion video and swing coaches, most hitters and golfers are inclined to read in problems where none exist just as are many business managers whose MBA training or desire to please higher-ups drive them to want to "do something."

WHAT TO MANAGE?

During the lull between the 1988 and 1989 football season, Arkansas oilman and former University of Arkansas football player Jerry Jones purchased the most popular franchise in the NFL, the Dallas Cowboys. Jones immediately stamped his imprint on "America's Team" by replacing legendary head coach, Tom Landry, with his former college teammate and coach of the University of Miami, Jimmy Johnson. He also axed renowned general manager Tex Schramm, highly regarded player personnel director Gil Brandt, and most of the other "front office" personnel. Whether based on fact or hype, the Cowboys had gained a reputation as a model sports organization.

Even though the Cowboys suffered through a dismal season in during the last year of the Landry-Schramm regime, the none-too-delicate sacking of Schramm and especially Landry shocked the Cowboys' fans and media. When the team's performance sank even lower during Jones' first year in the 1989 season, 15 losses and 1 win, he became a whipping boy for frustrated fans and writers. Who did this *nouveau riche* hillbilly think he was firing a legendary coach, bringing his college buddy who knew nothing of the NFL, and essentially taking over the role of general manager as well as owner? Didn't he know that owners are not GMs in the NFL? Not only did Jones' methods differ from the Cowboy traditions, but the apparent proof of their failure lay in the pudding.

Two Super Bowl victories for the Cowboys in the early 1990s quelled the outrage. Then Jones feuded with Jimmy Johnson, who departed in a startling sequence of events during the 1994 offseason. As the team moved through a series of coaches hand-picked by Jones—first another college acquaintance and coach Barry Switzer, then respected NFL offensive coach Chan Gailey, and finally Cowboy defensive coach Dave Campo—it became obvious that Jones' influence in the organization was ever expanding. To his duties of overseeing the business side of operations as well as acquiring and compensating players, he now directly influenced which players would play and even what style of offense would be run. Although the team picked up another Super Bowl trophy under Switzer in 1997, the performances deteriorated. By 1999, the team lost as many as games as it won. During the 2000–2002 seasons, the Cowboys were able to maintain a status only slightly above the worst teams in the league. Toward the end of the 2002 season, the reality of losing humbled Jones to the point where he approached and landed Bill Parcells as coach. While all the details of their personal conversations are not know, it is certain that a strong-willed and successful coach like Parcells did not accept the job without clearing the air regarding his decision making role with team.

The Jerry Jones saga and the unfortunate (for Houston Cougar fans) decisions of Guy Lewis share subtle similarities. They both deal with the breadth and detail of managerial control. In Guy Lewis' case the issue centered on when to intervene actively to attempt to manipulate outcomes. In the Jerry Jones case, the issue centered on a how broadly a manger should try to manage within an organization. Had the media and fans been right all along? Did Jerry Jones overstep his bounds way back in 1989 and just luck out, or had he done a reasonable job as owner/GM until the broohaha with Johnson? Can an owner be a GM? How much influence should a GM have over on-the-field decisions? Beyond the specifics of Jerry Jones and the Cowboys or even sports teams, the question of just how much power should reside in one person's hands is important for all kinds of organizations. What is the reasonable scope of decision making authority?

Even where all might agree that greater specialization of management functions is beneficial, the size of the business and marketplace can serve as a limiting factor. In the developmental years of many sports leagues, it would be common for a coach to serve as the de facto general manager, at least for all player related decisions, simply because there was not enough revenue being generated to support separate functions. Vince Lombardi served as GM during his entire tenure as head coach with the Packers. This combination of functions did not come about as a result of long discussions or planning about organizational roles. Instead, when Lombardi joined the Packers in 1958, the team could hardly afford separate functions. After a decade of success, Lombardi stepped down as coach but maintained the GM role.

In the words of the famous eighteenth-century economist and philosopher Adam Smith, the degree of specialization is limited by the size of a market.[5] An owner-entrepreneur of a small retail grocery store, of necessity, may well have to provide the financial capital as well as function as the operations manager, purchasing agent, clerk, and a custodian. As a business grows in size and scope, the financial necessity of wearing so many hats diminishes as the necessity of delegating decision making responsibilities increases.

As markets grow and provide greater revenues to producers for those markets, the question of how to slice up managerial roles becomes pertinent. Studies of managers have identified many different roles. An extensive and widely cited study by John Kotter indicated that effective managers tend to be agenda setters, advocates for these agendas (as opposed to detached goal setters), and builders of extensive interpersonal networks for acquiring information and implementing policies.[6] However, in many enterprises, a top level manager may play many roles—entrepreneur-strategist, operations supervisor, human resource manager, conflict resolver, organizer, dealmaker, and so on. Just how deeply an owner or general manager chooses to become involved in various functions at a business is not set in stone. Clearly, time places constraints on how widely one person can distribute his time as does knowledge. Beyond time, the issue hinges on the relative abilities of a manager and how those abilities add value to a firm when roles are combined versus separated and the speed with which decisions need to be made. For example, Bill Gates and other top managers at Microsoft initially funneled nearly all decisions through themselves. As the pace of change in the computer industry became faster, this top-heavy allocation of decisions created a bottleneck that Microsoft eventually scrapped.

While the Jerry Jones saga may, at first glance, appear as a textbook example of a manager casting his net far too widely, his tenure with the Cowboys illustrates both that over specialization of management functions sometimes becomes entrenched by mere convention and that too much consolidation of decision making authority is not a good thing. One important axiom among economists applies here—there is an optimal amount of just about everything including empowerment and consolidation. The basic principle guiding the distribution or consolidation of decisions within an organization, even sports organizations, is that decisions should be distributed to the people or units who hold the best combination of information and incentives for getting decisions right. Sometimes this means empowering additional decision makers—sometimes this means kicking decisions up the line and consolidating them.

No doubt, Jerry Jones displayed a lack of public relations savvy and people skills in the way he handled the takeover of the Cowboys and the ouster of Landry. In spite of this, Jones did expose a bloated front office situation in Dallas. The former GM, Tex Schramm, had pulled off some promotional coups in his time, taking the team from expansion oblivion to becoming "America's Team" that so many either loved or loved to hate. He had also succeeded in setting up an excellent scouting system. On the other hand, he had also been given a blank check by the Cowboys' principal owner Clint Murchison. Although wildly successful and popular, the Cowboys success and popularity had not translated into dollars for Murchison. Schramm had run the organization much like a not-for-profit entity, pouring nearly every cent back into some expense or another. Jones, determined to win but also determined to make money from winning, cleaned up this mess and reinstituted the idea that the team existed to help the owner make money by reducing what he viewed as unnecessary expenses in the front office. This meant combining many of the roles of the "business side" of the operations with the "football side."

The most controversial move in this regard that Jones made was to consolidate the role of GM, or at least some aspects of the job, into his own office. Jones would make player acquisition decisions with input from head coach Jimmy Johnson and negotiate player contracts. The idea of an owner making "football" decisions drew scoffs and howls from many fans and media. While non-traditional, the idea was not as outlandish as many made it out to be. In viewing it through the perspective of putting the decisions in the hands of someone with the information and incentive to get the decisions right, Jones' reasoning makes sense. If the proof is in his performance, he performed the job admirably, at least for several years.

The owner-as-GM problem troubled many people who argued that Jones was a mere commoner. In the terms used here, he lacked the specific knowledge needed to make sound football decisions. However, Jones had played the game at the college level. Further, in evaluating players, most GMs in any sport accomplish their task from years of observations in exactly the same spot as Jones—the seat of their pants. As with many guilds and professions, those in the jobs sometimes oversell the degree of specialized knowledge necessary to do the job. Where the Jones–Cowboys story began to go fall apart was not when Jones took over as GM, but when the rift developed between himself and Jimmy Johnson. Potentially, the biggest problem with Jones or any owner consolidating parts of the GM function in their own office is the temptation to reach farther and consolidate more of the power within the organization. Moreover, the owner possesses the inherent ability to define his own functions, eliminating constraints on his role. It is this temptation that overwhelmed Jones.

Jimmy Johnson's ego and will matched Jones's. Although Jones owned the team and could, in principle, do what he wanted, the presence of Johnson placed effective limits on Jones. As long as Johnson stayed as coach, Jones' input into on-the-field coaching decisions was very limited. At the same time, Johnson exerted considerable influence over the players acquired so that Jones and Johnson more or less split GM duties between them. Once Johnson exited, Jones brought in coaches that held much weaker power bases within the organization. No longer faced with effective constraints on his power, Jones expanded his scope of decision making, dominating player acquisition decisions as well as imposing himself into on-the-field coaching decisions. Some writers and analysts have suggested that this destroys a team because many players begin to look past the coach as the primary decision maker for on-the-field issues. While this may be true, Jones' actions likely had negative effects in other ways. For one, while he was as good as many GMs around the league in assessing players' skills and negotiating with them, Jones did not hold the kind of specialized knowledge necessary to make coaching decisions. Instructing the coach on which players to use or which offensive style to employ not only undercut the coach's authority but intruded into areas where Jones held little expertise.

Second, and maybe as important, Jones' power grab within the organization made the head-coaching job much less attractive to many job candidates. To some extent, by the time Jones hired Chan Gailey and certainly by the time he fired him and hired Dave Campo two years later, Jones had spoiled the pool of job applicant by his own actions. What "brand name" coach wanted to work for an owner who knew no limits to his intrusions? The answer was none. Gailey's departure created an opening in one of the most highly visible coaching positions in all of sports, and yet, none of the "big names" in coaching seemed interested. Five years earlier, Jones could have likely picked from among several of the most prominent coaches in professional or college football. After courting and talking to a few highly touted names, Jones settled for promoting his own defensive coordinator. Only after enduring several losing seasons did Jones bite the bullet and acquire Bill Parcells, a coach who walked in with the kind of power base (and then some) with which Jimmy Johnson held when he took over as coach.[7] After the years of struggle, Parcells lifted the team from a 5–11 record to a 10–6 playoff team in his first season.

The adventures of Jerry Jones and the Cowboys, though, are just one in a series of cases within sports organizations where the issue of consolidation or distribution of decisions has cropped up in recent years. This issue of "full control" of the sports-side of team operations has become a common bargaining chip for coaches in high demand. Bill Parcells acquired it with the New York Jets. Mike Holmgren, after two trips to the Super Bowl and one championship ring with the Green Bay Packers, chose to leave and become head coach of the struggling Seattle Seahawks. Reportedly, one of the enticing aspects of the Seattle job for Holmgren is that he would be the GM as well as head coach. Other coaches who gained this level of authority included Dan Reeves with the Atlanta Falcons, Pat Riley with the Miami Heat, Don Nelson with the Dallas Mavericks, Bill Belichick with the New England Patriots, and Tom Coughlin with the Jacksonville Jaguars, and a few others.

Interestingly, many of the same writers who so strongly question the expansion of an owner's decision making authority were slow to question the expansion of a head coach's decision authority with a much less critical eye. After all, as the thinking goes, should not a coach have complete control over the players he must use? One metaphor used is "if a coach is going to have to cook the meal, shouldn't he get to pick the ingredients?" Yet, just as with an owner expanding his sphere of influence, consolidating more power in the hands of a head coach raises serious issues. The data related to whether consolidating decisions works to benefit teams is mixed. During the Dallas Cowboys' long run of success from the mid 1960s to the early 1980s, the splitting of coaching and GM functions became the "model" for sports teams. Coaches such as Bill Parcells experienced success while playing both roles, others have met mixed success or floundered. The case of Rick Pitino provides interesting details.

In April of 1997 Rick Pitino made the decision to leave his post as head coach at the University of Kentucky to take what he described as the one job that could entice him to leave—the head coaching slot for the Boston Celtics of the NBA. Pitino had become the unofficial king of the Bluegrass State after rebuilding the Wildcats into a national powerhouse. In addition to the Kentucky job, he had proven his coaching prowess by taking the Providence Friars to the NCAA tournament in 1987 and by improving the New York Knicks during a brief stay there. Although he coveted the Celtic coaching job, the issue of breadth of his managerial control was a key part of his decision. Pitino negotiated a deal that gave him the title of President of Basketball Operations, granting him effective control over roster decisions along with his coaching duties. The reasoning behind the consolidation of basketball operations in Pitino's hands followed the typical lines. He would not be burdened by the players cast on him by a GM. Players would know that they answered to Pitino alone, thereby helping him avoid any undermining of his authority by a GM. He would have a free hand to hire support personnel, assistants, and scouts to his liking without interference.

The reality of Pitino's subsequent tenure raised serious questions about the consolidation of roles not unlike the expansion of Jerry Jones's power with the Cowboys during the mid to late 1990s. Pitino first moved to clear his roster of veteran players either by trading them or by making little or no effort to resign free agents. This would supposedly "free" him to sign younger players that would be easily molded into his system. In his first draft with the Celtics, he selected former University of Kentucky star Antoine Walker early in the first round. The next year he drafted Ron Mercer out of Kentucky. In total, he had as many as four former Kentucky players on his roster. In a surprising move, Pitino shelled out significant dollars to obtain 7-foot Travis Knight, a player with one year of college experience thought to have potential but not highly regarded as a pro prospect. Then, as Walker's rookie contract neared its expiration, Pitino made the signing of Walker to a long term deal his number one priority. In the salary cap era, this was tantamount to tabbing Walker as his "franchise player" on which future championships would rise or fall. Yet, Walker's performances on the court, while at times strong, were inconsistent. Moreover, he did not have the personal characteristics and maturity to be a team leader. His off-season conditioning was questioned, and he and Pitino bickered.

During Pitino's first season, the team won 36 (of 82) games as opposed to only 15 in the prior season. After this initial improvement, the engine began to sputter and break down during the second season. The team fell back to only 19 wins as the internal issues on the team grew. The third season ended with 35 wins but a terrible run over the last two months left the Celtics out of the playoffs again. Pitino's fourth season began poorly and by January 2001, he had resigned. By the end of the 2002–2003 season, Pitino's successor, Jim O'Brien, not only had guided the team to 49 wins but with essentially the same set of players the team advanced to the Eastern Conference Finals.

Pitino's downfall could be laid at different sources. Some analysts questioned his coaching strategy others his general managing skills. Clearly, he had troubles with player-coach relations at times. On the other hand, the running joke circulating in Boston was that Rick Pitino's worst enemy as coach was Rick Pitino the GM. Whatever the relative weaknesses in one or the other job, the Boston episode illustrates the difficulty of attempts to play both roles. In many ways, Pitino tried to operate as coach–GM much as he did in his college coaching position. However, because of differences in the "regulatory environment" between college and professional basketball, the difficulty of combining these tasks differs greatly. A college coach may possess complete control over player "acquisition" and removal. However, NCAA rules permit a maximum of four years of playing eligibility. While players are still critical to success, they turn over with great frequency, making a mistake less costly over the long run. Restriction on rewards to players means that salary considerations and limits imposed by salary caps do not enter the picture. Plus, college coaches can be more autocratic. College players can only transfer to another team after sitting out for a year. The players are younger and poorer, making them less inclined to challenge an autocratic coach's authority.

Pat Riley has lived out a reality not completely unlike Pitino's. Riley took over the helm of the Los Angeles Lakers near the beginning of the 1981 season. The team had won 7 of 11 games that season, 66 percent of its games in the 1980–81 season, and league championship during the 1979–80 season under coach Paul Westhead. Rumors circulated that star player Magic Johnson was unhappy with some of Westhead's use of players so Westhead was fired and Riley promoted from Assistant Coach. Riley guided a star-studded team including greats such as Johnson and Kareem Abdul-Jabbar to seven appearances in the NBA finals from 1982–1990 and five titles. He left the Lakers after the 1990 season and joined the New York Knicks starting the 1991–92 season. He took over a team that had won 39 games the prior year (but 45 and 52 the two prior to that) and won between 51 and 60 and made the finals once before he left after the 1995 season. In New York as in Los Angeles, he stepped into a team that already possessed very gifted players.

Riley then took over both the GM and head coaching jobs for the Miami Heat starting with the 1995–96 season. As with the Knicks, he bumped a near 50 percent winning team up to 60 percent from 1996 through 2000, making the Eastern Conference finals in 1997. However, in 1998, 1999, and 2001 the team lost in the first round of the playoffs and in the second round in 2000. In 2001 the Charlotte Hornets swept the three games in humiliating fashion. By the 2001–2002 season a combination of injuries and poor personnel decisions led to a losing season—one that had been abysmal for the first half. The 2002–2003 season started just as poorly, leading to speculation about Riley's future as both GM and head coach. In part, Riley's interaction with players had grown negative to the point of likely causing many free agents to avoid the team.

In fact, the tide has apparently turned against the idea of coach–GM combination. Just prior to the 2003–2004 season, Riley stepped out of the head coaching part of his job. Mike Holmgren, after failing to reach the playoffs during his tenure with the Seahawks gave up his position as general manager with the team. Before his dismissal as head coach late in the 2003 season, Dan Reeves had already relinquished his position as general manager. Interestingly, after letting Reeves go, the Falcons owner made the comment that in his search for a new head coach, he was interested in hiring "a coach and not a king"—a direct slap in the face of the coach as sole decision maker model that had been on the upswing during the 1990s.[8]

At the professional level, splitting the GM and coaching duties introduces important checks on each function. By the nature of the job, a coach is going to have run-ins with players from time to time. A coach who doubles as GM may be tempted to make personnel changes too swiftly in light of such troubles. Where these duties are split, the coach may be forced to try to work out the situation. On the other side, the coach may benefit from isolation from the salary negotiations that arise between a player or his agent and the General Manager. In addition, while coaches clearly should have significant input into the selection of players, coaching is a full-time job during the season, permitting little time for evaluation of other players. Rolled together, all of these points reemphasize the gains that can be achieved through specialization, at least up to a point. They do not indicate that no one could ever be successful in combining functions. There are examples of coaches who have done both jobs relatively well. Yet, these may best be viewed as the exceptions rather than the rule.

The lesson here for business managers in general is that the decision over what to manage is vital. A small operation requires the owner-manager to wear many hats. On occasion, in a desire to avoid some of the unpleasant operational and personnel duties, owner-managers are too quick to dump these responsibilities on others, incurring costs that are too high for the business or leaving them in the hands of individuals who lack the owner-manager's motivation or expertise. In a twist of the same problem, some owner-managers in these settings may even avoid learning as much as they should about day-to-day operations under a mistaken belief that getting involved in operational details will steer them away from the more important financial and marketing matters. In such settings, a good manager must be involved in the oversight of all functions of a business—production, marketing, financial. Naturally, areas where the supporting workforce is stronger in expertise and motivation may require less attention, but the owner–manager who sees himself as only the entrepreneur, only the chief financial officer, or only the production manager is setting the stage for failure. While problems do crop up for managers of small businesses in terms of where to circumscribe their responsibilities, the biggest issue is frequently time. Everything needs to be done and the owner–manager has simply to devote the time to do it. It's not surprising that successful owners of small business often have little time for other interest, especially during the formative years of the business and that owners who do have time often find themselves without a business in relatively short order.

More complex issues arise as to what to manage as a business grows to a level that will financially support subordinate managers.[9] As with sports managers, a person may have multiple skills that permit forays into different functional areas of the business. A few people, like a Bill Parcells, are able to bite off a large piece and make it work. As sports managers illustrate, though, it is frequently the case that people who would be good at doing multiple jobs are not very successful at trying to juggle them at the same time. They may keep all the balls in the air for a while, but the complexity of the tasks lead them down a path where one ball drops after another, and they find themselves in trouble. The Rick Pitino story illustrates the problems that can arise. Rather than doing a smaller set of functions very well and working with another competent person doing a complimentary job, a manager tries to handle too many functions and fails.

Ego may play a part. Successful managers sometimes gain a feeling of invulnerability. Due to the same motive, working with someone within an organization who is a peer or even a boss may strike someone as threatening or undesirable. Many managers in and out of sports often grow into "controlaholics" whether by their underlying personality or the conditioning on the job. Even the manager without a big ego may fall into the trap of taking on too many responsibilities. In part, a desire to make sure that two or three jobs are done right may encourage a manager to tackle too much. A coach who has experienced the consequences of poor general management or who has had a bad working relationship with a GM may be led into thinking that broadening his own responsibilities is clearly a better way.

In business as in sports settings, the complexity of this issue arises because it is not, or should not, be cast in all-or-nothing terms. A coach should be involved in personnel decisions and practices just as any manager would want to be involved in the hiring process. Frequently, roles and responsibilities get attached to people based on simplistic titles. For instance, an "offensive coordinator" may have primary responsibility for designing and calling plays as well as making on-the-field personnel decisions. Does having an offensive coordinator mean that a head coach should not be involved in the designing of offensive strategy or situational tactics during games? Seemingly, any head coach would want to be involved in such matters even if leaving much of the responsibility to the assistant. The same would be true of defensive coaching. It is a bit odd to see head coaches who become involved solely with the offensive or defensive side of the ball. Likewise, it would make sense to have offensive and defensive coaches interact to some extent to explore weaknesses and strengths in their own clubs as well as in the opponents. Surprisingly, many head coaches become involved solely on one side of the ball and many teams do not encourage and facilitate interaction between their offensive and defensive coaches.

The same situation sometimes arises in business, where a CEO may concentrate almost entirely on financial matters or almost solely on marketing strategy. Likewise, many companies develop cultures where business units become more like rivals than partners. The Vice President for marketing and the Vice President for operations may spend hardly any time interacting and if they do, the interactions resemble competitive rather than cooperative behavior. Finding the right balance between involvement in and delegating decisions is an ongoing balancing act. David D'Alessandro, CEO of John Hancock Financial Services, noted that he had seen a boss who "spent half his day fielding reports from employees about whom they had spoken to . . . he perpetuated the myth that only he could do things right." In contrast, he had also observed managers who "delegate responsibilities to so many different subordinates that no one is in charge."[10] No single algorithm exists for determining the degree of involvement and delegation. It differs across industries and companies as well as over time. The overriding principles boil down to two things: 1) who within the firm is best positioned to collect, possess, or process the information necessary for sound decisions, and 2) does this person have the motivation, either internally or externally, for using the information correctly?

DO MANAGERS WEAR OUT?

Anyone who has ever followed sports casually knows that the performance of professional athletes follows a cycle. Among those with extensive careers, performance typically improves for the first few years, and then a plateau is reached that may be sustained for a long time with some ups and downs. Finally their productivity diminishes unless they retire relatively early. The length of each stage depends on the particular sport and athlete. Certainly, some players may even have a late-career renaissance or upswing such as Barry Bonds in hitting home runs. Still, the improvement-plateau-decline cycle can be seen over and over.[11]

Beyond the questions posed above as to how far managers should extend their reach within an organization or how much they should actively try to manage outcomes, a key question about managerial duties is whether their performance tends to follow a cycle much like that of players. While seldom discussed, the same kind of cycle may also appear in the careers of many sports managers. Like players, some managers make an immediate splash, but in many cases where sports managers played out long careers, there is improvement, a plateau, and if they hang on long enough, an eventual decline. These swings can be seen in the careers of baseball managers such as Earl Weaver, Sparky Anderson, and Dick Williams or football coaches such as Tom Landry, Chuck Noll, and Joe Paterno.

In trying to go beyond anecdote, difficulties arise in measuring systematic tendencies for such life-cycles among managers. For example, college basketball and football have had their share of long-running, successful coaches. However, most college coaches work their way up from lesser known schools to "big-time" programs. For example, Bob Knight and Mike Krzyzewski both started at Army before moving on to coach Indiana and Duke. Such career jumps make record comparisons a bit like comparing apples and oranges. Another problem is that the relative contribution of managers and general managers to team performance differs across sports, generally inversely correlated to the degree of team interaction. Also, coaches land head-coaching positions at different ages and bring with them more or less assistant coaching experience. Like players such as Sandy Koufax, some managers retire relatively early while "still on top." All of these issues make the estimation of the variations in managerial performance problematic.

While no perfect data exists, Figure 8.1 presents an exploratory view into the career performance cycles for thirteen NFL coaches. All of the coaches included in the sample coached for over 15 years, received considerable acclaim as coaches, and have retired. The data presented in the figure reflect comparisons computed first for each coach based on his career winning percentage and then summarized over the 13 coaches in the sample for the first three years and the last three years of their careers. The median winning percentage relative to career average is shown along with the maximum and minimums. For example, based on first year performance, the median performance for the 13 coaches was 9 percent below career winning percentage, while the maximum individual was 30 percent above ca-

Figure 8.1
Early and Late Career Performance for Longtime NFL Coaches
(Performance as Percent of Career Average)

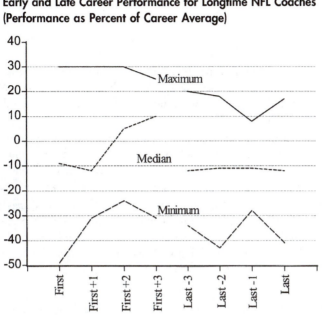

Notes: Coaches included all have 17 or more seasons of experience (Brown, Ewbank, Gillman, Grant, Halas, Knox, Lambeau, Landry, Levy, Noll, Owen, Shula, Stram). Median, maximum, and minimum values for each year are computed relative to the other coaches in the sample.

Source: www.profootball-reference.com

reer average (Chuck Knox) and the minimum individual was 49 percent below career average (Chuck Noll). Tom Landry's first year performance (−60 percent) was not used in the graph because he coached a first year expansion club. Overall, the results in Figure 8.1 lend some credence to the idea that long-running coaches have a cycle to their careers. While some stepped right in and performed well immediately, at the median, performance improved over the first three years and jumped above long-term career averages. The last three years show the opposite effect. At the median, the coaches fell more than 10 percent below the overall career averages.

In business enterprises these problems manifest themselves in different ways. In some jobs requiring demanding physical labor, workers may indeed mimic athletes in that their skills and abilities just diminish with age. In other situations, workers skills or knowledge may depreciate not so much due to age itself but just due to changes in technologies, markets, and so on. Companies may sometimes develop policies to deal with these issues such as retraining workers. Or, in other cases, people may be reassigned or transferred.

REPLAY

1. All production settings, from filling soda bottles to golfing, experience normal ups in downs in performance. These are "built-in" to the system. No amount of tinkering, yelling, or hand wringing will reduce these swings and will likely make things worse.

2. Where swings in performance are normal, the only means to improve is to carefully rethink the whole mix people, machines, and systems and how they fit together. Such change involve significant time and cost. Tiger Woods' jump from golfer with great potential to great golfer reflects just this kind of commitment.

3. Decisions within an organization or team should be parsed out based on combinations of abilities, information, limitations, and incentives. Sometimes this means centralizing decisions more—sometimes it means decentralizing them more as the swings in combining GM and coaching functions help illustrate.

9

Managing and Leading: Parcells to Gibbs and In-Between

Leaders are like eagles . . . they don't flock. You'll find them one at a time.

—Knute Rockne, former Notre Dame football coach

Kids don't learn leadership from a class—you learn leadership and organization in games.

—John Madden, former Oakland Raiders coach

Among the coaches and sports executives mentioned in the preceding chapters, some suffered through poor records, some amassed solid results, and a few posted legendary careers. The first eight chapters wove stories about these sports figures around a framework drawn from either well-established principles or ideas closely related to these foundations. In this chapter, the focus is on the personal attributes and characters of some of the more successful sports managers. By it nature, this kind of examination requires a different approach. Rather than relying on an established framework to provide reference points, the principles about leadership are pieced together by looking at common attributes among the legends of sports. The question at the forefront is, what are some of the leadership intangibles that are mutually shared among great sports leaders?

The study of leadership goes way back. The biographies of great leaders throughout history have dominated the field. For obvious reasons, many have chosen statesmen or military leaders such as George Washington, Abraham Lincoln, Dwight Eisenhower, or George Patton. In recent years, the professional experiences and viewpoints of business executives and entrepreneurs such as Lee Iacocca, Jack Welch, Bill Gates, Tom Peters, or

Warren Buffet have become the subject of interest. Whereas in bygone years, the books about sports figures tended to chronicle their coaching careers from more of a historical or biographical perspective, now many of the books about sports figures fit into the "leadership" niche. As much as anything, the coaches-turned-consultants and philosophers sell their experience and knowledge about leadership. Whether based on extensive biographies, nuggets of proverbial wisdom, or snappy sound-bites, the beliefs, actions, and viewpoints of successful sports figures have taken on near cultic dimensions. More recently, the study of leadership has emerged as a field of academic study in universities with entire programs devoted to it. Whether this is really a valuable enterprise or fad-of-the-generation is yet to be determined.

The study of leadership contains many inherent difficulties and frequently spirals into little more than nonsense peddled by management consultants who are long on style and short on substance. Because of these difficulties and abuses, this discussion does not even attempt to provide a "how to" manual on effective leadership. No such manual exists, as the epigram from John Madden implies, and the sources that claim to offer such sweeping advice are little more than fraudulent vehicles whose main purpose is to enrich their authors. Instead, the intent here is to provide those in leadership positions or aspiring to leadership food for thought about what may distinguish poor leaders from average ones, and average ones from great ones. Also, it is intended to provide individuals or groups whose job it is to hire leaders—whether a manager, a corporate board, a university committee, or other—ideas about leadership to ponder.

WHAT IS LEADERSHIP?

Whether in business or sports, two key questions are: 1) what is leadership, and 2) how is it separate from management? The ever-expanding diversity of leadership definitions make answering these questions difficult. There are about as many different ideas and sound bytes about effective leadership as there are opinions about politics or beauty. Among mainstream business consultants and writers, the diversity definitions can be dizzying. One tack taken in defining leadership attempts to boil the explanations down to a simple, resounding maxim. For instance, John Maxwell says, "Leadership is influence—nothing more, nothing less," while Peter Drucker observes, "A leader is someone who has followers."[1]

Other writers and observers flesh out leadership principles or responsibilities in more detail or provide more of clinical, textbook-like definitions. Examples include, "Leadership is characterized as the ability of an individual or entity to establish a direction and develop a vision of the future by implementing strategies for producing the results needed to achieve the vision."[2] The two tasks at the heart of the popular notion of leadership are "goal setting and motivating."[3]

Still, in other cases, the thoughts of great thinkers from antiquity are used. An oft-quoted and more thorough definition brought forward from ancient times is offered in *The Art of War*: "Leadership is a matter of intelligence, trustworthiness, humaneness, courage, and sternness . . . Reliance on intelligence alone results in rebelliousness. Exercise of humaneness alone results in weakness. Fixation on trust results in folly. Dependence on the strength of courage results in violence. Excessive sternness in command results in cruelty. When one has all five virtues together, each appropriate to its function, then one can be a military leader."[4]

Sports figures have also chimed in on the problem of defining leadership. Here is a smattering of their efforts: "Leadership is getting someone to do what they don't want to do, to achieve what they want to achieve."[5] "They have to be salesmen and have to get their players, particularly their leaders [among the players], to believe in what they are trying to accomplish on the basketball floor."[6]

Whatever particular definition is chosen, they all tend to emphasize what basic dictionary definitions emphasize—leading involves interacting with and enabling other people. If this is leadership at a general level, what then separates management and leadership? Dictionaries give overlapping definitions of the two terms so that a broad construction of management makes them more or less synonymous. The dean of management consultants, Peter Drucker, separates leadership from management in a way that has been frequently referenced by other writers and students: "Management is doing things right; leadership is doing the right things." This same way of thinking is echoed in the very title to Part I of a book about Jack Welch and his "GE Way"—"Act like a leader—not a manager."[7]

The distinction drawn by Drucker and Welch has become commonplace in business education and consulting. They derive the difference in the terms by narrowing the meaning of management. Broken down, the term "management" is commonly used to define a more restricted set of responsibilities and expectations than the term "leadership." Leadership encompasses the widest scope of tasks including setting or changing the direction for an organization in terms of its goals, culture, and structure as well as providing the parameters within which those following the leader operate and facilitating their work. In contrast, management often is used to refer to accomplishing a predefined set of tasks or supervising pre-set system to ensure its smooth operation. In this world, the leader defines the policies to be pursued along with general guidelines for pursuing them and the manager fills in the operational details. In this vein, Welch explains leadership in terms of words such as "facilitating change" and "motivating" while managing is about "supervising."

HOW TO STUDY LEADERSHIP

Even if a Drucker-like definition of leadership is accepted, the next question is how does one study it? Good leaders are a lot like good teachers—we may recognize one but be hard-pressed to clearly explain what it is that makes them good. This problem has and continues to plague leadership as a field of study.

When looking over the biographical studies and opinions about leadership, whether among business or sports figures, it is a considerable challenge to separate the qualities that actually make some people successful leaders versus the qualities that they themselves or others perceive make them successful. Just as with company policies and strategies, some individuals may be the proverbial blind squirrel that finds the acorn—they succeed in spite of certain personal characteristics rather than because of them. Yet, because they are successful, their followers and admirers bestow importance on a particular set of characteristics, and then others seek to imitate these qualities. In other cases, the entrepreneur or coach may, indeed, posses leadership characteristics that help bring about the success but observers and disciples identify the wrong set of attributes contributing to their results. Often, the personal attributes that happen to stick out most prominently attract the lion's share of attention, but they are not necessarily responsible for the lion's share of the person's success as a leader.

Coaches such as Vince Lombardi and Bill Parcells illustrate this tendency to elevate the most obvious traits to the status of important. For both, their acerbic tongues have been among their most most obvious and frequently documented personality traits. As noted earlier, Parcells even credits his biting criticisms with being at the very heart of his ability to build successful teams. Yet, both Lombardi's and Parcells's leadership tenures may have been just as successful without the extreme verbal assaults. The verbal assaults may have merely been baggage along for the ride. Their records as football coaches owe more to their shared ability to judge talent and commitment among players, their ability to place players in situations where they can excel, or other qualities.

Just as leadership studies may fixate on highly visible but possibly superfluous traits such as a sharp tongue, they can also focus too much on the development of warm fuzzy feelings in a work environment. While an Oprah-like culture may be appealing to people, it may or may not have much to do with success. As Drucker puts it, "Effective leadership is not about making speeches or being liked." The general point comes back to

the difficulty of determining cause and effect by simple observation discussed in the very first chapter. Separating genuinely important principles
from the faux-important not only presents problems for the study of management policies and strategies but also the study of leadership qualities.
However, the analysis of policies and strategies by researchers in economics, finance, statistics, and related areas does contain significant scientific
qualities. In contrast, the study of "leadership" and "entrepreneurship" often
amounts to little more than musings drawn from personal experiences and
biographies of leaders.

Did Vince Lombardi produce championship teams in Green Bay because
of or in spite of his intimidating style? Were Joe Gibbs' sleepovers in his
office at Redskins headquarters an integral part of his teams winning ways
or merely a security blanket to calm his anxieties? Given the lack of hard
data that exists in the study of leadership, there may be no definitive way
to answer these and similar questions. At the very minimum, though, it is
critical to keep these kinds of questions in mind when examining the personal characteristics of leaders in an attempt to organize a list of "how to
be a good leader." As with the study of management strategies and policies, it is also critical to keep in mind principles that are definitive in nature as a framework within which to study leadership. If the anecdotal
observation of leaders seems to tell us something that is at odds with one
of these well-grounded principles, then we should seriously question
whether that personal attribute is genuinely important.

Beyond identifying successful leadership qualities, difficulties arise in attempting to transfer these qualities across individuals. Leadership skills are
not just policies or tactics that can be studied and imitated. Rather, these
qualities, by their very nature, tend to be personal and idiosyncratic. The
ability to find the right balance between promoting creativity and setting
specific direction cannot be canned and just passed along. Recognizing and
installing the right set of helpers in leadership roles requires discretion not
easily imitated. No amount of study will demarcate precisely the times
when plain-spoken criticism versus gently worded encouragement is required. To the extent that personal "charisma" matters, one does not obtain charisma merely by observing people with it and then aping their
actions. If not inborn, these qualities are acquired through life experiences
that are not just unique in some of their specifics but are experienced in a
sequence that may be just as important as the experiences themselves. For
these reasons and many others, the acquisition of leadership abilities is similar to the painting analogy drawn in Chapter 1. With study and practice,
almost any person can improve, but there are also likely innate qualities
that lead some people to be better than others for any given level of study
and effort.

These stumbling blocks to defining leadership and identifying the traits that make for successful leaders has led some to conclude leadership is defined by results. In the end, results are the proof of the pudding. The leadership-is-in-the-results view is advocated by many leaders and "experts" including Drucker. The only trouble is that such a view identifies success only after the fact. It offers no guidance or direction to those who would like to draw from the experiences of others to improve their own leadership skills. With the preceding caveats and difficulties in mind, the rest of this chapter attempts to sort out some of the qualities that have made for successful leaders in sports teams.

LEADERSHIP PREREQUISITES

In the literature about leadership and among highly successful sports figures, several common attributes are frequently mentioned. While it would be foolhardy to dispute the importance of these traits, some of these qualify more as prerequisites for effective leadership rather than the factors that discriminate decent leaders from excellent leaders. No doubt, effective leadership demands these characteristics. Few if any coaches or general managers find any degree of success without possessing them. However, the attributes are also shared by a wide variety of coaches and managers who never experience enormous success. As a result, possessing these qualities is not sufficient for dividing mediocre leaders from great ones. Nonetheless, someone aspiring to be a leader or who is being considered for leadership without these qualities probably needs to redirect their aspirations.

One personal characteristic common to most every sports leader who has found even modest success is an enthusiasm for what they do. Vince Lombardi and Tom Landry could not have been more different personalities in many obvious ways, but they both held a passion for football. In Lombardi's case, this passion exhibited itself in much more obvious ways than it would for someone more introverted like a Tom Landry, but they both shared a near single-minded focus on making their teams better. John Wooden and Bob Knight may represent as wide of a contrast in personality as one might find, yet like Landry and Lombardi, they both pursued excellence in basketball teams with a fire in their bellies.

The importance of enthusiasm and passion for leaders transcends sports. It is certainly as important in business ventures as it is in sports. Investment entrepreneur Charles Schwab noted, "A man can succeed at almost anything for which he has unlimited enthusiasm." In many cases, only those passionate about leading may withstand the storms and overcome the roadblocks to becoming a leader—the nature of the journey demands it. For example, the nature of assistant coaching positions weeds out most individuals without a passion for the game. From the high school level through the college ranks, coaches put in huge chunks of time, especially during the season. An assistant high school football coach may spend 7:30 to 2:30 Monday through Friday in a classroom, participate in football practice or other coaching duties from 2:30 to 8:00 Monday through Thursday, spend all Friday night at a game, and then spend many hours on the weekend preparing plans to face the next opponent. Seventy- to eighty-hour-per-week workloads are common during the season. At the professional and college ranks, such time obligations are also common during the season.

Another commonly cited attribute among leaders that best fits into this "prerequisite" category is that they are "doers." John Wooden said, "Everybody has a suggestion. Not everybody has a decision. Perhaps that's why there are so few leaders, or at least good ones." Decisive action is a hallmark of coaches. They develop the ability to think on-the-go and to commit to a course of action. Joe Namath explained the importance of decisiveness for leadership very well when he said, "To be a leader, you have to make people want to follow you, and nobody wants to follow someone who doesn't know where he is going."[8] In sports as in business, leaders must develop plans and make decisions when time to make decisions is precious—sometimes excruciatingly sparse. A player goes down to injury and a coach must make the appropriate adjustments on the fly during the game or in a day or two leading up to a game. A general manager and coach may have only minutes to make up their mind about the draft selections that will determine their team's course for many years. The examples could go on and on. People that find satisfaction only in the intellectual contemplation of hypothetical choices or those who can never get off the fence when a decision seems 50–50 do not inspire confidence in others. They may bend with anxiety under the ongoing pressures that leaders face. One of John Madden's favorite quips during broadcasts, "It doesn't matter if the horses are blind, just load the wagon," humorously expresses the requirement for decisive doing that is incumbent upon leaders.

While enthusiasm and active, decisive decision making are common features among successful leaders, neither one goes very far in discriminating legendary coaches and sports executives from those who fail abysmally. Most coaches exhibit "Type A" personalities just to survive in coaching for any length of time. As noted above, the time commitment alone tends to weed out people who are lazy or who have little enthusiasm for what they do. The development path from assistant to head coach also tends to develop decisiveness as a common trait among coaches whether or not they really make good leaders. For these reasons both qualities are more accurately labeled as prerequisite for leading than as the critical traits that distinguish bad from good from great leaders. It is this difference between good and great leaders that is of special interest here.[9]

LEADER AS THINKER?

From only a casual acquaintance with the coach and his methods, Vince Lombardi would hardly stand out as an example of the "thinking man's" coach. He didn't rely on complicated or tricky schemes. Instead, he preached and promoted physical preparation, repetition, precise execution, and effort. He thought coaches that could only draw up plays were "a dime a dozen," insisting that the more important quality of a coach was to motivate players to their highest performance level. His aggressive and even intimidating tactics captured much of the attention of the coaching profession as well as the public during his tenure and immediately thereafter.

Because of his emphasis and personal style, one might think Lombardi hardly illustrates the importance of mental ability and effort to leadership. Nonetheless, Vince Lombardi serves as a prime example of a coach who went far beyond the possession of passion and a loud mouth to one who combined passion with intellect—a combination of attributes that has separated other great coaches from average and poor ones. Lombardi's loud and forceful personality and lack of innovative schemes drowned out the perception of his intellectual side that has only been more clearly depicted in anecdotes and biographies well after his career ended. These paint a clear picture of him as a manager who meticulously mapped out his plans. Whether one agrees with all his methods or not, he pursued clearly-thought-out methods. This is not to say that all his decisions were driven by cool, detached reflection. He was not an introverted monk. Instead, he was an immensely passionate man according to all close to him. Still, as noted in more detail in an earlier chapter, when he arrived as coach and general manager of the Packers in 1959, he did not just launch into slogans and tirades. Instead, he devoted himself to an orderly, meticulous, and comprehensive evaluation of his players based on past Packer films in order to determine how to best use the players on hand.

Other great coaches who seem to stand out more for their passion, dogged pursuit of perfection, and bluster more than their intellect also fit the model of thinker–coaches when their methods are viewed with greater scrutiny. Bill Parcells' blaring and sometimes demeaning sound bytes steer attention away from his pensive characteristics. Whether his own perceptions about his success are correct or not, the very fact that he was willing to write an article for the *Harvard Business Review* about building teams suggests an ability at introspection and self-awareness not always appreciated or commonly found among coaches. Even a coach on the fringe of acceptable behavior, such as Bob Knight, accomplished great achievements with his teams because of his ability to out-think opposing coaches and transfer these thoughts to players rather than because of berating his players. Arguably, Knight's best quality as a coach is his ability to identify the strengths of the opponent and make game to game adjustments to offset these strengths.[10]

As in the rest of contemporary culture, sports commentators throw around the label of "genius" haphazardly and cheaply. Set against the discovery of fundamental equations of physics, the development of computer algorithms, or the solving gigantic engineering problems such as tunneling under the English Channel or digging through mountains or jungles in Panama, decision making by sports coaches and executives hardly qualifies as displays of genius in any respect. Even in everyday business settings, a CEO or Vice President overseeing the operations of 100,000 employees involving hundreds of locations and intricate supply and distribution networks dwarfs the decisions faced by sports managers overseeing thirty or forty players in games where the boundaries are well-defined in advance. Even as far as games go, the sequential strategy options that a Major League Baseball manager goes through pale in comparison with a chess master. In this kind of broad context, managers in sports are not among the great thinkers in society.

Yet, within the confines of their own industry, great coaches and executives in sports are the thinkers at least relative to others in their field. This does not mean that every coach is a master strategist or leading-edge innovator. It does imply that whatever aspects of strategy or tactics they leaned more heavily upon, they gave genuine thought to what they were doing. They did not fall back on merely spur-of-the-moment, seat-of-the-pants thinking or imitate-my-mentor, follow-the-pack thinking. Rather, they excel at defining some of the key problems to be solved and using considerable mental effort to solve those problems.

John Wooden typified the coach as thinker. On the one hand, Wooden saw basketball as a relatively simple game. He did not try to over-complicate the game for himself, his assistants, or his players. He boiled down his basic strategy as "[We] get in condition, learn fundamentals, and play together."[11] Yet the simplicity of his basic strategy masked a great deal of thought that he gave as to how to best train his players and implement his strategy. He purposefully and methodically developed his conditioning drills and practices to develop and perfect his fastbreak strategy with the intent of "outrunning the other team" during the second half.[12] His philosophy concerning turnovers cut against the prevailing wisdom in that he saw turnovers as the natural consequence of playing with initiative and forcing the action. He gave considerable thought to the kinds of players he wanted, "players of spirit just short of temperamental," as well as to how to best deal with individual players' needs on and off the court.[13] He was not just flying by the seat-of-his-pants or trying to step directly in the shoes of another coach that he may have held in respect.

This list of great coaches who could be used as examples here goes on and on. Because he devoted much of his mental energies to innovation, Tom Landry stands out as an obvious example. Joe Gibbs and Bill Walsh, two highly successful football coaches from the 1980s, brought many of the same qualities of contemplation and thought. Among Major League baseball managers, Earl Weaver and Sparky Anderson were two Hall of Fame managers whose careers overlapped. Although the two men differed in many personality traits, both studied their own decisions in detail. Among more recent MLB managers, Joe Torre and Tony LaRussa have experienced as much success as any pair over the last twenty years. Again, their personalties differ and their points of emphasis are not identical, but they both place considerable importance on the mental aspects of the game. In college basketball, Mike Krzyzewski stands out not only because of the winning dynasty he built at Duke, but in many ways he not only typifies the thinking coach, but probably stands at a near extreme as a "philosopher–coach" in much the same way as John Wooden a generation before him.

Another way that the importance of thinking among leaders surfaces is in the emphasis that coaches place on "preparation." Coaches of widely varying styles but with tremendous records of success sound like clones of each other when it comes to preparation. Joe Paterno, the winningest coach in college football history, said, "The will to win is important, but the will to prepare is vital." Many of coaching legends have made similar statements. Most often in sports, the physical side of preparation is emphasized because of the hours spent in on-the-field and on-the-court practicing. Yet, an emphasis on preparation presupposes thinking about how it is you are going to prepare. Bear Bryant's phrasing of the maxim highlights this angle. He held to three main rules for coaching—number three was "Have a plan for everything." Even with regard to the physical drills and exercises, a coach must sort out which of these will really help the team. Great leader-coaches do that—others just fill out a practice schedule based on mimicking ones they have seen before. As a specific example, Eddie Sutton, is noted for specialized instruction to players on to how to guard a bigger player or a quicker player.

The lesson here for mangers in business or leaders of all kinds is critically important. Leaders like Wooden, Landry, Weaver, Krzyzewski, Lombardi, and the others are "intellectuals" in the sense that they use their intellect. No single characteristic may be more common among great coaches than their analytical abilities and efforts. It may be conjecture, but it is based on widespread observation. The ability to think about problems is the main attribute separating the great coaches from the good, average, and poor ones any more than their ability and consistent commitment to using their brain power—not in some ivory-tower, esoteric way, but in concrete, analytical ways. They could think about problems at a very concrete level as well as stepping back from a problem or dilemma a bit to gain a broader perspective. "Vision" may be one of the prerequisites for successful leadership, but it cannot succeed without thoughtful decisions to make those visions a reality. Plenty of leaders have great "visions" and clearly defined "objectives." Almost any coach alive has the same "vision"—to make their team into a perennial winner of the World Series, the Super Bowl, the Stanley Cup, or the like. Tom Landry put it this way, "Setting a goal is not the main thing. It is deciding how you will go about achieving it and staying with that plan."

Confusions have arisen about the connection between thinking and leading. For one, studies by behavioralists such as Mintzberg have indicated that most business leaders are not thinkers—instead, they tend to be "doers." This observation, while likely correct, is misleading. In the specific cases of sports coaches and managers, to the person, they are doers—whether their records are among the worst in history or among the best. As noted above, being a "doer" is most likely a prerequisite for being a leader of any value at all or, in most cases, even becoming a leader. People that are "nondoers" rarely aspire to be leaders, and if they do, they are rarely chosen or accepted. The other misleading aspect of the observation is that it does not discriminate between bad leaders and good ones. As just noted, a large percentage of the coaches who are "doers" happen to be coaches with very poor records. In contrast, the legendary sports leaders are also doers but fit into the classification as thinkers.

A second confusion regarding thinking and leading frequently emerges. Developing into an effective leader requires more than just mental effort. It demands an open-minded quality that may not come naturally. As John Madden puts it, "Coaches have to watch for what they don't want to see and listen to what they don't want to hear." Whether bouncing ideas off of others or just within the walls of their own mind, they consider ideas. They were and are people given to introspection, at least regarding their teams if not their own personalities. They put valuable people around them and give them genuine opportunities to provide input that is often used as opposed to superficial input that serves no purpose other than to try to make subordinates feel as if they are having input.

Thinking-based leadership also stands out against a mindless fixation on the path chosen by another leader or organization. All of the great coach–leaders carved out their own mold. In part, their paths grew out of their differing and strong personalities, but it emerged from thinking about the issues in front of them in face of the context of those decisions—their team's assets, liabilities, technological limits, rules, and so on. They did not just pick up some book of a successful coach or leader and say, "Here's my guidebook—let me follow it to the letter." On the other hand, they drew from their experiences with other coaches and players and paid attention to the tactics of mentors and peers without trying to become clones of them.

This "intellectual" aspect of leadership stands in out in opposition to the "give-me-just-the-bottom line" mentality that some managers in sports and business seem to think makes for effective leadership. Every problem to be solved or issue to be discussed cannot be boiled down to three bullets, a snappy, one-page executive summary, or a two-minute briefing. The rough outline of an issue may be summarized in those ways, but some decisions regarding the operation of a sports team or any organization require deeper understanding and contemplation by decision makers. No doubt, through luck and ignorance of others, many people have risen to the leadership of various organizations by a "thought-free" process relying on well-tailored suits, smooth talks, and few management buzzwords borrowed from the latest management guru. However, these leaders are outstanding only in their own estimation who survive only because limited information and luck permits their weaknesses to be overlooked. The leaders with genuinely long-lasting contributions to an organization possess the ability to bring thoughtful and significant ideas to leadership matters.

LEADER AS A LEADER OF LEADERS?

Earlier in this chapter, a quote from Los Angeles Lakers coach Phil Jackson noted the importance of getting the players, "particularly their leaders," to believe in the things the coach is trying to accomplish. Embedded in Jackson's statement is the recognition that the coach is not the only leader on the team. He may be the "lead leader," but the views of the leaders among the players themselves matter also. It would be overstating the case to indicate that all legendary sports leaders have recognized the critical importance of leaders below them. In fact, later in the chapter, this is one of the shortcomings noted in Tom Landry. Yet, this seems to be the exception rather than the rule. Duke's Mike Krzyzewski goes out of his way to note the importance of developing leaders among his players. As he says, "I want players to talk in the huddle because they might notice something that I cannot see from the sidelines." Allowing player-leaders to make adjustments on-the-fly is crucial in his outlook.[14] The NHL's Scotty Bowman, although widely recognized as a coach in firm control of his teams, is also widely recognized as utilizing the leadership of veteran players on his teams such as the Detroit Red Wings' Steve Yzerman.

In all but the smallest of organizations where one person can or must handle many functions, fostering and developing leadership among subordinates would seem axiomatic. As Krzyzewski's comments make clear, no single person possesses all the information relevant for making leadership decisions. Beyond information limitations, no single leader can be at all places at the same time. The proximity of players to each other on the court or the playing field permits them to make adjustments that the coach cannot make. In addition, sometimes players are best suited to take the lead and deal with some kinds of personnel matters better than the coach or general managers. In initiating and implementing change, the buy-in and promotion of ideas by respected players can make the difference between success and failure as Phil Jackson notes.

Not only is this an important quality of many legendary sports leaders, but like the leader-as-thinker point, it separates great leaders from mediocre ones. Many leaders in sports and business limit their effectiveness because they do not appreciate the importance of subordinate leaders. It becomes a power play. They feel a loss of power and control by granting meaningful decision authority to subordinates, and, therefore, they downplay leadership of others. They may give lip service to empowerment of others or set up supposed leadership posts for subordinates, but at the end of the day, they completely dominate all decisions. They may pick the team captains, but the team captain role may be nothing more than an honorary title for the person who calls the coin flip before the game—and the coach may even tell the player whether to pick heads or tails!

LEADER AS VISIONARY OR TECHNICIAN?

In the literature dealing with leadership in business, it has lately been in vogue to stress the leader's role as that of visionary and deemphasize technical expertise. In fact, a whole generation of leaders in the 1990s was practically reared on books and seminars touting the leader as the vision-setter or goal-setter and demeaning leaders who pursued operational issues very much.

An examination of sports leaders uncovers intriguing cases. For one thing, in sports requiring a lot of coordination among team members such as football, all coach-leaders attained their leadership role first by displaying strong "technical" skills—directing offensive or defensive strategies. In sports such as baseball or basketball, coaches may not have served as coordinators of entire units but oversaw development of particular skills or personnel such as pitchers or hitters, shooting or defensive skills. As assistant coaches turn into head coaches, their duties broaden to include selection of players, interaction with media, and other matters in addition to overseeing the development of strategy, tactics, and use of players. Some coaches choose to maintain their roles as the prime coordinator of certain "operational" aspects. For example, many football coaches choose to be the offensive or defensive coordinator for their teams. In other cases, the coaches appoint assistants over these operational areas and offer supervisory control over the whole operation. On occasion, they switch. During the 2002 season, Jim Fossel, head coach of the New York Giants took direct supervision of offensive strategy after his team had struggled.

One point to be highlighted here is that there have been varying degrees of operational involvement by coaches who achieved high levels of success. Tom Landry, although a defensive specialist as an assistant coach, oversaw the offense while in Dallas. Bill Walsh also was intimately involved in the offensive strategy. Vince Lombardi, coaching before coaches sent plays in during the game, did little in the way of operational moves during games. The bottom line is that there is no hard and fast rule that dictates exactly how much involvement a successful leader should have with operational details. The "right" amount depends on the person's skills, the skills of those on the team around him, and the organizational problems at hand.

Operational expertise is very important even where the coach may choose to let subordinates make many of these decisions. This technical knowledge and ability inspires respect among followers and tends to help keep the leader in touch with realistic expectations from those doing the work. In almost any organizational setting, nothing undermines leadership more quickly than a lack of respect that grows out of a sense that the leader is out-of-touch or outright ignorant of operational limits and capabilities. A coach who has worked closely with players as an assistant and gained their respect for fairness and for ability to make effective decisions is likely to inspire confidence and respect when given the reins of overall leadership.

In business as in sports, few things eat away at respect between leaders and employees more than a feeling that the leader has no idea what the employee is doing or has "pie-in-the-sky" expectations of what is possible. At SAS Institute, known for its great leader-employee relations, one of the co-founders and executive vice president is still involved in writing software code on occasion. As one observer put it, "Managers who understand the work that they oversee can make sure that details don't slide. At SAS . . . managers understand what their groups do—so unrealistically optimistic promises about time-tables and completion dates are relatively rare."[15] The focus in the 1990s on the leader-as-visionary sometimes trivialized and even mocked managers who possessed an intimate knowledge of operational aspects. Sports examples, along with those like SAS, illustrate that leadership, even effective vision setting, benefits from the buy-in that comes when those charged with fulfilling the leader's visions have a sense that the leader is on the right track, sets obtainable goals, and understands what is going on "in the trenches."

LEADER AS INSPIRING PERSONALITY?

Maybe no element of leadership generates more attention or confusion than the ability of a leader to inspire others. Whatever the precise term one might use for this characteristic, it attracts a lot of attention among leader-wannabes and observers. However, several questions surface regarding the ability to inspire. Fundamentally, what really dictates the ability to inspire others?

For many, the ability to inspire others derives mostly from personal "presence." As NFL Films producer and president, Steve Sabol, once remarked about Vince Lombardi's leadership that, "It was all the voice."[16] Maybe this is an overstatement of the reality—a Lombardi with a Tom Landry voice would have still been Lombardi in most of the important ways. Still, Sabol notes a common perception related to great coaches— their ability to command attention and respect through some aspect of their personal presence, style, or charisma.

Although this kind of observation is common, a broad overview of highly successful coaches would hardly support its importance. People such as Vince Lombardi, Bill Parcells, Bob Knight, and other like them have proven highly successful with their loud and brazen personal styles and gift (or curse) for speaking. In contrast, legendary coaches such as John Wooden and Joe Gibbs projected a much more mild-mannered and even-tempered approach of a mid-western factory manager or strong but soft-spoken preacher. Phil Jackson quotes Oriental philosophers while Parcells and Knight quote George Patton. John Madden threw his arms and hands in every direction, wearing his passion on his sleeve, while Tom Landry, Bill Walsh, and Joe Gibbs often came across more like detached engineers working with a large and complicated piece of machinery. Overall, the great coaches have succeeded with some being outspoken and some softspoken, some short-tempered and some patient, some detached and some overtly passionate, some philosophical and down-to-earth, quick-witted and some humorless. With such diversity, it's hard to determine that the ability to inspire others derives mainly from presence or style.

In viewing presence, the mistake is frequently made of viewing some obvious stylistic feature of a coach and noting the respect that it engenders even when the feature may be maddening such as Parcells' sharp tongue. In most cases, though, the respect is given to the person because of the success achieved and the focus upon and respect for the personality feature only follows along as an effect rather than a cause. Would Woody Hayes have been a highly successful coach at Ohio State had he been in better control of his temper? The answer seems to be certainly, yes. The former players who speak with admiration for him do so in spite of this personality flaw. In some cases, even as extreme as Hayes', players and admirers come to chuckle about personality flaws of admired leaders and may even remember the outbursts in an endearing way much like some fraternity members think back upon hazing.

Saying that personal presence or charisma of a leader is not a generally important quality does not imply that presence and charisma never matter. While inspirational pre-game or halftime speeches likely matter little on a week to week basis—even many coaches admit their limits—Knute Rockne's famous "win one for the Gipper" oration may have been a decisive factor on that given day. In sports and business management, leaders can swing to both ends of the spectrum with regard to presence. On the one hand, some may tend to discount it almost completely, viewing style and presence as little more than an extraneous nuisance. To them, they can effectively lead through direct communication to their staff and through impersonal edicts whether transmitted in person or indirectly through memos or staff members. On the other hand, in observing legendary leaders who possessed charismatic personal qualities, some managers have placed all of their stock in trying to imitate a certain style in leadership. Rather than leading, they are like actors playing parts. Even a leader as noteworthy as General George Patton may have suffered from this "leader as actor" syndrome. In Patton's case, though, he had substantive leadership skills to go with the persona. The problem arises when a leader of lesser ability begins to "play to the camera" and become far too image-conscious.

Rather than some element of personality, the ability to inspire others likely comes from the ability to instill confidence and respect. Two things contribute to this. First, a leader who demonstrates competency in his decision making ability secures buy-in from those being led. Joe Gibbs may not have had a great presence, but his decisions made very clear to his players (after a rough start) that he knew what he was doing. This is likely one reason why coaches who have succeeded in past positions are able to repeat their success in new places. A Bill Parcells who has twice won the Super Bowl with the Giants, took the New England Patriots to the Super Bowl, and elevated the New York Jets to the playoffs, steps into his Dallas Cowboys job with immediate buy-in from players.

A second way to inspire players to follow is by showing a genuine interest in them. Because players or employees are unique individuals with their own agendas, most people respond to leaders who appear to have a genuine interest in them. Coaching legends such as Grambling's Eddie Robinson and UCLA's John Wooden preached this message at length. Even as volatile as Woody Hayes could be or as bombastic as Vince Lombardi could be, most of their players that were able to withstand the abuse came to see them as coaches who had a passion both for winning and for the players' welfare. In contrast, many coaches imitated Lombardi's or Hayes's abusive techniques without ever planting the seed of trust and confidence.

NOBODY'S PERFECT

Sports leaders, just as all leaders, have feet of clay. They all carry flaws. For their staunchest devotees, pointing out the weaknesses legendary figures such as a Bear Bryant or a Woody Hayes amounts to damnable heresy. Considering these less-than-desirable traits may be just as important as evaluating their strengths. Noting and discussing the weaknesses of great leaders is both comforting and educational. It is comforting in that it makes clear that to be a successful leader, even one of legendary proportions, does not demand perfection. Attempts by admirers to turn Bear Bryant or Vince Lombardi or any leader in politics, the military, or business into an icon with no imperfections invites trouble. It not only distorts the truth but sets up an unrealistic standard for those who would try to become great leaders themselves. As the quote from golfer and sports analyst, Andy North, explained in Chapter 8, "I figured out not to try to be too perfect." His point about managing his golf game applies just as easily to leading in general. One can become obsessive and destructive to self and others by pursuing an unachievable standard of faultless leadership. Bryant, Lombardi, Rockne, Wilkinson, Wooden, Krzyzewski, Anderson, Bowman, and others became great leaders while continuing to suffer from the limitations of all mortals.

Beyond the comfort of seeing great leaders as human, examining their frailties also provides educational opportunities. It is easy enough to identify weaknesses of leaders who fail and lessons can be learned from them. However, looking at the shortcomings of great leaders also provides key lessons for those who have a genuine interest in becoming better leaders themselves. Poor leaders garner few disciples; they build no cult-like followings. Great leaders tend to amass sizable followings sometimes with religious zeal. Learning from the missteps these successful leaders may be as important as learning about their strengths. The reasoning is simple. The Vince Lombardis, Woody Hayes, or Scotty Bowmans of the world may be able to overshadow their flaws because of their immense strengths, unique employment environment, past achievements, or just luck. Disciples who blindly attempt to imitate these leaders' styles may end up adopting the weaknesses of the master without enjoying the strengths or circumstances needed that helped the master overcome or mitigate the weaknesses. It is essentially the same problem discussed in Chapter 7 regarding the practice of "benchmarking"—attempting to mimic the practices of the successful.

Even among wildly successful coaches and managers, it is not hard to pick out things that had they behaved differently most likely would have improved success. Tom Landry is an excellent starting point. Landry's success, both in terms of the heights it reached along with its longevity, is enviable. Landry brought important leadership strengths such as innovative thinking, meticulous planning, and objective and extensive evaluation of the mental and physical skills of players. In spite of these attributes and his enviable record, Landry's shortcomings as a leader almost certainly cost him championships.

In particular, he failed to fully appreciate the importance of team leaders and the human side of the game he coached. In quarterbacks Don Meredith during the 1960s and Roger Staubach during the 1970s, Landry possessed the kind of player–leaders that other players rally behind. Both players were talented athletes—Staubach probably more so—and both were endowed with intangible qualities important for the leadership roles that the quarterback position entails. Yet, Landry under-valued these qualities, especially in the case of Meredith. Don Meredith has never fully explained his reasons for leaving the game at such an early age, limiting his remarks to "It wasn't fun anymore." The accounts written by others and hints dropped by Meredith point toward Landry's tight-fisted control and view of players, even his quarterbacks, as little more than pieces in a machine. Meredith walked away from the game in his prime, disenchanted. His move is more surprising in that Meredith was not a petulant player requiring stroking and coddling from a coach. Instead, what he needed as much as anything from Landry was the recognition and acceptance of Meredith's importance as an on-the-field leader of the team. Landry's unwillingness to see or at least fully appreciate the importance of Meredith's leadership ability and his need for respect and trust drove Meredith away from the game at the time when the team could challenge the Packers' dominance and seemed poised to be able to pass them. Instead, the Cowboys that had pulled equal with the Packers by 1967 took backward steps in the next two seasons. Landry himself mildly admitted his error with Meredith in this regard in his own book.

Landry's experience with Staubach was not as volatile, but even in this case, Landry only slowly came to appreciate the combination of physical skills and the intangible leadership qualities in him. Although Staubach had joined the team in 1969, Landry alternated him with Craig Morton as late as the 1972 season. In spite of the Cowboys' successful run during the 1970s, Landry never seemed to fully appreciate the importance of a player like Staubach. Instead, Landry's fixation on strategy dominated his thinking. Even when Staubach might have played another season or two, Landry seemed more than content with the prospect of filling his backup, Danny White, into the role. Again, it seemed as if Landry viewed it as the exchange of one part of a machine for another. The irony in Landry's lack of appreciation of the importance of the intangible, on-the-field leadership abilities of Meredith and Staubach is that Landry had placed such importance on evaluating the mental abilities of players that the Cowboys scouted and not just their physical skills.

These specific shortcomings of even a great coach such as Tom Landry highlight the fact that leaders need to recognize and value the leadership of those around them. Usually, in an organization of any size at all, there will be leaders at various levels important for accomplishing various tasks. It is easy for a top leader to overvalue his or her contribution to the success of the organization relative to these subordinate leaders just as Landry undervalued Meredith and, to a lesser extent, Staubach. In fact, Landry's intentional distancing himself from his players so as to make more dispassionate player decisions only raised the importance and value of player–leaders like these two.

Legendary hockey coach, Scotty Bowman, and baseball manager Dick Williams present different examples from Landry of great coaches with clear weaknesses. Although they led teams in different sports, they shared many attributes in common. Both attained the highest levels of success with a variety of teams. Bowman guided the Montreal Canadiens and Detroit Red Wings to eight titles and also built very competitive, playoff-caliber clubs in St. Louis and Buffalo. Williams took the Boston Red Sox (1967), Oakland Athletics (1972, 1973) and San Diego Padres (1984) to the World Series and even succeeded in turning the Montreal Expos into a playoff contender.

One persistent question in both of their cases is why did coaches of such obvious talent and success make so many coaching stops? Typically, coaches with their records direct one or two clubs for an entire career. As skillful as they were in decision making, both Bowman and Williams lacked some of the "people skills" that help produce longevity in a particular location. Their defenders might claim that they were "their own men" and refused to cowtow to owners, general managers, or players, resulting in their abbreviated tenures in places. No doubt, they were fiercely independent thinkers, but the same can be said of other coaches who did not become coaching gypsies. There is a line between independence and insolence—between motivation and destruction. Even talented leaders must work with others—owners, supervisors, peers, subordinates. Like other leaders throughout history and across different fields, sometimes talented leaders begin to view themselves as islands to themselves. In the case of Bowman and Williams, the same hockey or baseball knowledge and the same decisions would have led to the same success without the caustic personalities that created unnecessary friction, as long as the team performed well.

This is a good place to address the question of "character" and its importance to leaders. One can hardly pick up any lengthy discussion of leadership without the topic of "character" or a synonymous term surfacing. Leaders in all kinds of fields harp on its importance. For example, General Norman Schwarzkopf said, "Leadership is a potent combination of strategy and character. But if you must be without one, be without the strategy." Coaches love to preach to their players about the importance of "character" and "discipline" to their players—playing hard no matter what the score, playing unselfishly, devoting onself to improvement, and so on. Still, coaches, even legendary coaches, are frequently not exactly examples of high moral character.

Yet, what does character mean? If it means hardworking, then most coaches are of high character. If it means sticking to a certain set of values, then many would also qualify. However, will any values do as long as you stick by them closely? Members of the Mafia uphold a certain "code of honor" but are hardly standards of virtue. Many coaches have been unwilling to live by standards of unselfishness and integrity that they so often preach. The study of "character" is practically impossible without getting into moral issues and views that go far beyond the scope of this book. In a more narrow consideration of great coaches and problems they have run into because of character flaws, examples such as Dick Williams or Bob Knight are instructive. They are obviously skilled but at times lack a key feature of character, such as self-control or self-discipline, and this character flaw hampered them. Other great coaches have also suffered due to similar weaknesses.

The questionable aspects of Vince Lombardi's methods and personality have also been widely documented and discussed. It is difficult to diminish the accomplishments of a coach whose teams dominated for an entire decade. Still, while his Packer teams enjoyed a tremendous run, his tenure as head coach was relatively brief. The championships won under his leadership coincided with one core group of players. As noted above, while much has been made of his insistence on flawless execution and physical preparation, maybe his most underappreciated tool was his ability to assess talent. Like many coaches, though, his passions for the game ran so strong, and at time with little restraint from good sense, that they had negative consequences. Before being hired as head coach by the Packers, Lombardi had been distraught over his inability to land a head coaching job. Lombardi and others have speculated as to the reasons why, but his temperamental outbursts even as an assistant coach may have cost him an earlier head coaching position.

Maybe the clearest case of lack of control of temperament and its cost is that of Bob Knight. Likely, only his skillful acquisition and utilization of players in winning three national championships during the 1970s and 1980s permitted him to stay in his position as long as he did. He went through many scrapes due to his lack of self-control that would have sunk almost any coach with a lesser record—an altercation with a Puerto Rican police officer, a trash can on an LSU fan's head, a wrestling match with an athletic director, a chair thrown across the playing floor, a potted-plant thrown and striking an athletic department secretary, accosting (pushing, striking, or other, depending on one's perspective) a player in practice, and the like. The national championships and the public accolades they brought insulated him from stricter or swifter discipline, but probably also permitted him to become bolder in thinking his behavior was beyond scrutiny, or at least, control of even his university bosses. A run of less successful teams combined with continued outbursts such as the physical abuse of a player finally brought his employment at Indiana to an end.

Coaches such as Bowman, Williams, Knight, and Lombardi illustrate the point that self-discipline is indeed a virtue among leaders. Frequently, leaders are in a position to avoid some of the consequences that might befall people without celebrity status, but this does not mean that lack of self-discipline is beneficial to either one's team or one's self. Bowman and Williams wore out their welcome in several locations. Lombardi probably delayed his rise to a head coaching position. Knight probably lost out on talented players who came to see his antics as too extreme. Ultimately he lost his job. Bowman, Williams, Lombardi or Knight might defend their actions as just being extensions of "who they are," but control of self is a virtue that does not end with childhood. All four of these coaches certainly demanded self-discipline on the part of their players but sometimes exercised a different value system for themselves. No doubt, these coaches excelled as leaders because of offsetting strengths and in spite of this weakness, but the flaws imposed costs in spite of their great skills. People of lesser skill would likely suffer even greater consequences.

REPLAY

1. The most obvious personal characteristics of coaches and managers usually invite imitation. Disciples, observers, and the leaders themselves may frequently

overestimate the importance of some skills and underestimate the importance of others.

2. Enthusiasm and a decisive, "doer" mindset are nearly universal among successful sports leaders. However, they are also nearly universal among those who fail as sports leaders.

3. Legendary sports leaders are thinkers—not just "give-me-the-bottom-line" leaders. Even coaches known for their straight-ahead and simple styles such as Vince Lombardi are usually under-appreciated for mental efforts.

4. Demonstrated competency and interest in those being led inspire people to follow much more so than particular personality styles, as the wide divergence between a Bill Parcells and Joe Gibbs illustrates.

Notes

1. SPORTS AND BUSINESS: IS SPORT BUSINESS OR IS BUSINESS SPORT?

1. Jerry Kramer, *Farewell to Football* (New York: World Publishing, 1969): 198–99.

2. Bill Parcells, "The Tough Work of Turning Around a Team," *Harvard Business Review* (November 2000): 180–81.

3. Robert Heller, *Tom Peters* (London: Dorling Kindersley, 2000): 27.

4. See, for instance, Henry Mintzberg, "The Manager's Job: Folklore and Fact," *Harvard Business Review* (July–August 1975): 49–61.

5. David Besanko, David Dranove, and Mark Shanley, *Economics of Strategy* (New York: Wiley, 1996) make this point in their Preface.

6. John Micklethwait and Adrian Woolridge, *Witch Doctors: Making Sense of Management Gurus* (New York: Times Books, 1996) detail many of these episodes.

7. Chapter 1 of Besanko, Dranove, and Shanley, *Economics of Strategy*, contains more details on these points.

8. Bill Parcells, "The Tough Work of Turning Around a Team," 180.

9. The author has taught a special topics MBA course on complex problem solving that summarizes material in this field. See www.wku.edu/~brian.goff/homepage.htm.

10. Further discussion of the sports as economics laboratory is provided in Lawrence Kahn, "The Sports Business as a Labor Market Laboratory," *Journal of Economic Perspectives* (Summer 2000): 75–94, and Goff and Tollison, *Sportometrics*, Chapter 1.

2. MANAGING FUNDAMENTALS: BENCHING A HALL OF FAME PITCHER

1. Many of these have been collected from Rickey's own writings. See *Branch Rickey's Little Blue Book* (New York: Macmillan, 1995). Chapter 3 deals extensively with his view of baseball's "fundamentals."

2. See David Maraniss, *When Pride Still Mattered: A Life of Vince Lombardi* (New York: Simon and Schuster, 1999): 376.

3. Maraniss, *When Pride Still Mattered*, 377.

4. James Brickley, Clifford Smith, and Jerold Zimmerman, *Managerial Economics and Organizational Architecture* (Chicago: Irwin, 1997). Chapter 2 provides an excellent discussion on individual motivation in managerial and organizational contexts.

5. A detailed discussion of the choice of Ruth as a hitter versus pitcher appears in Edward Scahill, "Did Babe Ruth Have a Comparative Advantage as a Pitcher?" *Journal of Economic Education*, 21 (Fall 1990): 402–10.

6. Jim Savage, *The Encyclopedia of the NCAA Basketball Tournament* (New York: Dell Publishing, 1990): 709–10.

7. Joe Torre and Henry Dreher, *Joe Torre's Ground Rules for Winners* (New York: Hyperion, 1999): 129.

8. See Brickley, Smith, and Zimmerman, *Managerial Economics*, Chapter 1 and Preface.

9. See Allen Barra, "Seattle's Defying Reason," *Wall Street Journal*, July 27, 2001, for further discussion of how Seattle thrived after losing star players.

10. The example here is from David Lionhardt, "Caution is Costly," at www.nytimes.com, July 30, 2003. The article includes additional examples.

11. See Frederick Mosteller, "Lessons from Sports Statistics," *The American Statistician*, 51 (November 1997): 305–10, for a good introduction to a variety of distributions from sports including baseball, football, and golf.

12. The evidence is presented in Brian L. Goff, William F. Shughart, and Robert D. Tollison, "Batter Up! Moral Hazard and the Effects of the Designated Hitter Rule on Hit Batsmen," *Economic Inquiry*, 35 (July 1997): 555–61.

13. Economist Richard Thaler has written on this and related topics where economics and psychology meet. See Richard Thaler, *Quasi-Rational Economics* (New York: Russell Sage Foundation, 1991).

3. MANAGING MARKETS: NASCAR AND SOUTHWEST AIRLINES?

1. Several sources have documented NASCAR's growth. See, for example, "NASCAR's Rise as Our New Pastime," available at www.medialifemagazine.com. Also, an examination of NASCAR's compensation structure is provided in Peter von Allmen, "Is the Reward Structure in NASCAR Efficient?" *Journal of Sports Economics*, 2 (February 2000): 62–79.

2. James Quirk and Rodney Fort, *Paydirt* (Princeton, NJ: Princeton University Press, 1992), provide an extensive discussion of many of the basic economic issues related to sports leagues and their financial situation. Gerald Scully, *The Business of Major League Baseball* (Chicago: University of Chicago Press, 1989) focuses directly on baseball.

3. The points, implicit in basic economics, are explicitly expressed in Shlomo Maital, *Executive Economics: Ten Essential Tools for Managers* (New York: Free Press, 1994). Maital is an economist in MIT's Sloan School of Management.

4. These data are from www.thatsracin.com.

5. See Brian Goff, *Spoiled Rotten: Affluence, Anxiety, and Social Decay in America* (Boulder, CO: Westview Press, 1999) for quantitative and anecdotal analysis of the economic growth across all income classes through the eighties and nineties.

6. A brief chronology of Southwest's history is available at www.iflyswa.com. The financial data is from biz.yahoo.com.

7. See Robert Heller, *Bill Gates* (London, Dorling Kindersley, 2000): 44 for a more detailed discussion of Microsoft and the marketplace.

8. In fact, nearly all serious statistical studies of competitive balance indicate that it has remained unchanged or increased during the era of free agency. See Rodney Fort and James Quirk, *Pay Dirt*, Princeton, NJ: Princeton University Press, 1992; Craig Depken, "Free Agency and the Competitiveness of Major League Baseball," *Review of Industrial Organization* 14 (1999): 205–17; and Brad Humphreys, "Alternative Measures of Competitive Balance in Sports Leagues," *Journal of Sports Economics* 3 (July 2002): 133–48.

9. Veeck's perspective on free agency and other matters are detailed in Bill Veeck, *The Hustler's Handbook* (Durham, NC: Baseball America Classic Books, 1996).

10. See Michael Leeds and Peter von Allmen, *The Economics of Sports* (Boston: Addison-Wesley, 2002): 184.

11. See Simon Rottemberg, "The Baseball Players' Labor Market," *Journal of Political Economy*, 64 (1956): 242–58.

12. Estimates of the dollar value of "star quality" for a number of players is provided in Charles J. Mullin and Lucia F. Dunn, "Using Baseball Card Prices to Measure Star Quality and Monopsony," *Economic Inquiry* 40 (October 2002): 620–32.

13. For commentary on this issue, see Mark Kreidler, "Posterity Suffers in NFL Parity," December 3, 2002, at espn.go.com/nfl/kreidler_mark/1470714.html.

14. See Red Auerbach and Ken Dooley, *MBA: Management By Auerbach* (New York: Wellington Press, 1991).

15. The NCAA contract was signed for 11 years in 1999. The NBA contract was signed in 2002. These figures are from money.cnn.com and www.usatoday.com.

4. MANAGING PEOPLE: THE MEN BEHIND DEAN SMITH AND BOBBY KNIGHT

1. Robert Slater, *Jack Welch and the GE Way* (New York: McGraw-Hill, 1999): 96.

2. See Shlomo Maital, *Executive Economics: Ten Essential Tools For Managers* (New York: Free Press, 1994), Chapter 5.

3. David Maraniss, *When Pride Still Mattered* (New York: Simon & Schuster, 1999): 209–11, provides these and other details on Lombardi's early days with the Packers.

4. See Darryl Howerton, "The Blazers Monopoly," *Sport*, 91 (April 2000): 36.

5. John Wooden and Jack Tobin, *They Call Me Coach* (Chicago: Contemporary Books, 1988): 220.

6. See George Anders, "After Hitting It Big on Web, Mr. Cuban is Scoring in the NBA," *Wall Street Journal*, April 22, 2003.

7. Marty Burns, "Starting at the Top," available from sports.yahoo.com/nba/news/cnnsi, March 14, 2003.

8. See Bill James, *The Bill James Guide to Baseball Managers* (New York: Scribner, 1997): 242.

9. See Mike Krzyzewski and Greg Doyel, *Building the Duke Dynasty* (Lenexa, KS: Addax Publishing): 37.

10. Wooden, *They Call Me Coach*, 141.

11. See Lou Holtz, *Winning Every Day: The Game Plan for Success* (New York: HarperBusiness, 1998), especially Chapter 5 for Holtz's views on adapting.

12. James, *Guide to Baseball Managers*, 212.

13. In spite of these successes, Hartley was fired during the 2002–03 season as his highly talented team sputtered during the first half of the season.

14. See J. MacMullan, "Slogging Through His Own Mess," *Sports Illustrated* 92 (March 13, 2000): 98.

15. See I. Thomsen, "My Way or the Highway," *Sports Illustrated*, 93 (December 11, 2000): 58.

16. Labor economics provides an extensive literature on this subject. An example specifically related to sports are Ronald G. Ehrenberg and Robert Smith, "Do Tournaments Have Incentive Effects?" *Journal of Political Economy*, 98 (December 1990): 1307–24. Many other examples could be cited.

17. Maraniss, *When Pride Still Mattered*, 376.

18. Maraniss, *When Pride Still Mattered*, 377.

19. Holtz, *Winning Everyday*, 98–99 and 127–28.

20. Maraniss, *When Pride Still Mattered*, 327.

21. Jim Savage, *The Encyclopedia of the NCAA Basketball Tournament* (New York: Dell Publishing, 1990): 709.

22. Wooden, *They Call Me Coach*, 141.

23. These quotes are from Bill Parcells, "The Tough Work of Turning Around a Team," *Harvard Business Review* 78 (November 2000): 180–81.

24. See Mike Krzyzewski and Donald Phillips, *Leading with the Heart, Coach K's Successful Strategies for Basketball, Business, and Life* (New York: Warner Books, 2000): 68.

25. See Joe Torre and Henry Dreher, *Joe Torre's Ground Rules for Winners: 12 Keys to Managing Team Players, Tough Bosses, Setbacks, and Success* (New York: Hyperion, 1999): 37.

26. Wooden, *They Call Me Coach*, 235.

27. For a more detailed perspective on Jackson and his methods, see Sam Smith, *The Jordan Rules* (New York: Simon & Schuster, 1992); M. Rowland, "Guru," *Los Angeles Times Magazine*, 45, January 2000, 60–67; and C. J. Farley, "The Philosopher Coach," *Time*, March 20, 2000, 61–62.

28. S. L. Price, "Lords of Discipline," *Sports Illustrated*, 95 (October 22, 2001): 78–82.

29. Details are provided in Keith Dunnavant, *Coach: The Life of Paul Bear Bryant* (New York: Simon & Schuster, 1996): 99.

30. From a *Florida Times-Union* online story August 28, 2002 at www.jacksonville.com/tu-online/stories.

31. See John Madden and Dave Anderson, *One Knee Equals Two Feet* (New York: Jove Publications, 1987): 195.

32. Krzyzewski, *Leading with the Heart*, 36.

5. MANAGING INFORMATION: MIKE KRZYZEWSKI AS CIO

1. See Paul Zimmerman, "Armed for the Playoffs," *Sports Illustrated*, 55 (December 21, 191): 18.

2. See Tom Landry and Gregg Lewis, *Landry* (Grand Rapids: Zondervan, 1990): 151–52, for more detail.

3. Leonard Koppat, *The Man in the Dugout* (New York: Crown Publishers, 1993), relates more detail about the use of information by baseball managers including LaRussa (357) and Williams (322).

4. See Max H. Bazerman, *Judgment in Managerial Decision Making* (New York: Wiley, 2001) for further discussion. Also, a *Wall Street Journal* editorial draws this analogy to the Enron episode. See Holman Jenkins, "How Could They Have Done It," *Wall Street Journal*, August 28, 2002.

5. Mike Krzyzewski and Donald Phillips, *Leading with the Heart: Coach K's Successful Strategies for Basketball, Business, and Life* (New York: Warner Books, 2000): 68.

6. Krzyzewski, *Leading with the Heart*, 73.

7. See James A. Brickley, Clifford W. Smith, and Jerold L. Zimmerman, *Managerial Economics and Organizational Architecture* (Chicago: Irwin, 1997), Chapter 12 for a more complete discussion of this principle.

8. See Robert Slater, *Jack Welch and the GE Way* (New York: McGraw-Hill, 1999): 96.

9. Joe Torre and Henry Dreher, *Joe Torre's Ground Rules For Winners: 12 Keys to Managing Team Players, Tough Bosses, Setbacks and Success* (New York: Hyperion, 1999): 74.

10. One of the author's colleagues at Western Kentucky University, Richard Cantrell, provided this information from his firsthand experience at Southern Illinois University.

11. See M. Silver, "Miracle Worker," *Sports Illustrated* (January 17, 2000): 35.

12. Krzyzewski, *Leading with the Heart*, 85.

13. Krzyzewski, *Leading with the Heart*, 94.

14. John Wooden with Jack Tobin, *They Call Me Coach* (Chicago: Contemporary Books, 1988): 113.

15. Wooden, *They Call Me Coach*, 107.

16. See www.wku.edu/~brian.goff/Homepage.htm for an overview of failure analysis applied in organizational settings.

17. Red Auerbach and Ken Dooley, *MBA: Management By Auerbach* (New York: Wellington Press, 1991): 189.

18. From www.yahoo.sports.com September 11, 2002.

19. Auerbach, *MBA: Management by Auerbach*, 189.

20. From Bruce Brown, *1001 Motivational Messages and Quotes for Athletes and Coaches* (Monterey, CA: Coaches Choice, 2001).

21. Harold Sackrowitz, "Refining the Point(s)—After-Touchdown Decision," *Chance*, 13 (Summer 2000): 29–34, provides an informative overview of some of the statistical issues that compound the difficulty of finding the optimal decision.

22. John Madden and Dave Anderson, *One Knee Equals Two Feet* (New York: Jove Publications, 1987): 55.

23. See J. McCallum, *Sports Illustrated*, 92 (April 10, 2000): 47.

24. Dispelling or at least shooting big holes in such streak explanations has become quite common among a set of cognitive psychologists starting with Daniel Kahneman. For a readable example, see Donald G. Morrison and David C. Schmittlein, "It Takes a Hot Goalie to Raise the Stanley Cup," *Chance*, 11 (Winter 1998): 3–7.

25. The classic exposition of this is given by Burton Malkiel, *A Random Walk Down Wall Street* (New York: W.W. Norton, 2003). Malkiel, who has spent time in the Ivy League and on Wall Street has mischievously tricked many a Wall Street "chartist" with graphs that seemingly depict hot and cold streaks for a stock but are nothing more than a series of random ups and downs.

26. See Michael Porter, *Competitive Strategy* (New York: Free Press, 1980) and Michael Porter, *Competitive Advantage* (New York: Free Press, 1985). A critique is offered in John Mickelthwait and Adrian Woolridge, *Witch Doctors: Making Sense of the Management Gurus* (New York: Times Books, 1996), Chapter 7.

6. MANAGING GAMES WITHIN GAMES: DO BASEBALL MANAGERS HAVE BEAUTIFUL MINDS?

1. Sylvia Nasar, *A Beautiful Mind: A Biography of John Forbes Nash, Jr., Winner of the Nobel Prize in Economics, 1994* (New York: Simon & Schuster, 1998).

2. See Avinash Dixit and Susan Skeath, *Games of Strategy* (New York: W. W. Norton, 1999): 65–70 for a more thorough discussion of the contests between Kasparov and "Big Blue."

3. Avinash Dixit and Barry Nalebuff, *Thinking Strategically* (New York: W. W. Norton, 1991). Chapter 10 provides a detailed example of this kind of thinking in America's Cup racing.

4. See John Wooden and Jack Tobin, *They Call Me Coach* (Chicago: Contemporary Books, 1988).

5. The use of an "out pitch" may be a desirable tool, if the relative combinations change once a hitter obtains two strikes. It may be that with two strikes, a dominant strategy may arise.

6. Dixit and Nalebuff, *Thinking Strategically*, 172–83, discuss the tennis serve example.

7. This perspective on the NCAA is presented at length by the author and colleagues in Arthur A. Fleisher, Brian L. Goff, and Robert D. Tollison, *The NCAA: A Study in Cartel Behavior* (Chicago: University of Chicago Press, 1992).

8. See Adam Brandenburger and Barry Nalebuff, *Co-opetition* (New York: Doubleday, 1996).

9. The most recent vote is reviewed by Robert Barro, "The Best Little Monopoly in America," *Business Week* (December 9, 2002): 22.

10. John Moores, "Damn Yankees," *Wall Street Journal*, May 14, 2002.

11. More detail on this unique bargaining strategy is provided in a *Rocky Mountain News* story by Jim Benton, "3 into 1 is Answer for Avs," www.rockymountainnews.com, July 10, 2001.

12. An informative article on Clarke as Flyer General Manager is "Flyer Fans Paying Price for Clarke's Glory Days," USAToday.com, May 1, 2002.

13. Michael Leeds and Peter von Allmen, *The Economics of Sports* (Boston: Addison-Wesley, 2002). Chapter 8 provides an extensive overview of labor negotiations in sports.

7. MANAGING INNOVATION AND CHANGE: BRANCH RICKEY MEETS MACHIAVELLI

1. John Wooden and Jack Tobin, *They Call Me Coach* (Chicago: Contemporary Books, 1988): 119.

2. From "Quotations on Coaching and Leadership," www.wow4u.com/coaching/.

3. See Douglas Hunter, *Scotty Bowman: A Life in Hockey* (Toronto: Penguin Books, 1999), for an extensive look at Bowman's career and methods.

4. Many of these innovations are discussed in Tom Landry and Gregg Lewis, *Tom Landry* (Grand Rapids, MI: Zondervan, 1990): 154–58.

5. See Landry, *Tom Landry*, 154.

6. Many of the details of Gillman's contributions exist either as oral history or encyclopedic information. These quotes related here are gleaned from "Hall of Fame Coach Sid Gillman dead at 91," www.nfl.com, June 24, 2003, and John Nadel, "Hall of Fame Coach Sid Gillman Dies," mac-sports.ocsn.com, June 24, 2003.

7. The most widely cited history is Jules Tygiel, *Baseball's Great Experiment* (New York: Oxford University Press, 1983).

8. Racial integration as an innovation is discussed in Brian L. Goff, Robert E. McCormick, and Robert D. Tollison, "Racial Integration as an Innovation: Empirical Evidence from Sports Leagues," *American Economic Review* 92 (March 2002): 16–26.

9. From Geoffrey C. Ward and Ken Burns, *Baseball: An Illustrated History* (New York: Knopf, 1994): 247.

10. Tygiel, *Great Experiment*, 27.

11. See Jim Savage, *The Encyclopedia of the NCAA Basketball Tournament* (New York: Dell Publishing, 1990).

12. Lou Holtz, *Winning Every Day: The Game Plan for Success* (New York: HarperBusiness, 1998): 79.

13. *New York Times*, August 10, 1930 and September 7, 1930.

14. *New York Times*, July 10, 1945.

15. *New York Times*, December 8, 1931 and October 20, 1932.

16. See Robert Heller, *Bill Gates* (London: Dorling Kindersley, 2000).

17. See Robert Heller, *Tom Peters* (London: Dorling Kindersley, 2000).

18. See Goff, McCormick, and Tollison, "Racial Integration," 16–26.

19. See David Halberstam and Stout, eds., *The Best American Sports Writing* (Boston: Houghton-Mifflin, 1995): 223 for the reprint of the original 1955 *Sports Illustrated* article.

20. See Roger Kahn, *The Era 1947–1957* (New York: Ticknor and Fields, 1993): 36.

8. MANAGING VERSUS MEDDLING: ANDY NORTH LEARNED NOT TO BE TOO PERFECT

1. Joe Torre and Henry Dreher, *Ground Rules for Winners* (New York: Hyperion, 1999): 129.

2. See Dave Pelz, *Putt Like the Pros: Dave Pelz's Scientific Way to Improve Your Stroke* (New York: HarperCollins, 1989).

3. John Wooden and Jack Tobin, *They Call Me Coach* (Chicago: Contemporary Books, 1988).

4. Robert Slater, *Jack Welch and the GE Way* (New York: McGraw-Hill, 1999): 27–28.

5. Adam Smith, *Wealth of Nations* (New York: Bantam Books, 2003): 4.

6. John Kotter, *The General Managers* (New York: Free Press, 1982): 60–72.

7. David Besanko, David Dranove, and Mark Shanley, *The Economics of Strategy* (New York: Wiley, 1996). Chapter 18 provides a discussion of many of these varied roles of managers, and in particular, the manager as power holder. Also see Jean-Jaques Taylor, "A Working Relationship for Jones, Parcells, at www.dallas morningnews.com, July 25, 2003, for more discussion of the power-sharing of Jones and Parcells versus that of Jones and the previous head coaches.

8. See *Atlanta Journal Constitution*, December 18, 2003.

9. See James Brickley, Clifford Smith, and Jerold Zimmerman, *Managerial Economics and Organizational Architecture* (Chicago: Irwin, 1997), Chapter 10 for an extensive discussion of the economic influences behind the complexity of job allocation and bundling.

10. From Carol Hymowitz, "The Confident Boss Doesn't Micromanage or Delegate Too Much," *Wall Street Journal*, March 11, 2003.

11. Gerald Scully, *The Business of Major League Baseball* (Chicago: University of Chicago Press, 1988) provides statistical evidence regarding such tendencies.

9. MANAGING AND LEADING: PARCELLS TO GIBBS AND IN-BETWEEN

1. See John Maxwell, *The 21 Irrefutable Laws of Leadership* (Nashville: Thomas Neslon, 1998). Drucker quote is from Frances Hesselbein, Marshall Goldsmith, and Richard Beckhard, eds., *The Leader of the Future* (New York: Jossey Bass, 1996).

2. From John P. Kotter, *Leading Change* (Cambridge: Harvard Business School Press, 1996).

3. From John Gardner, *On Leadership* (New York: Free Press, 1990).

4. Sun Tzu, *The Art of War* (Mineola, NY: Dover Publications, 2002).

5. From Tom Landry (with Gregg Lewis), *Tom Landry* (Grand Rapids, MI: Zondervan, 1990).

6. Phil Jackson, *Sacred Hoops* (New York: Hyperion, 1996).

7. Robert Slater, *Jack Welch and the GE Way* (New York: McGraw Hill, 1999).

8. Peggy Anderson, *Great Quotes from Great Sports Leaders* (Franklin Lakes, NJ: Career Press, 1994): 68.

9. See Jim Collins, *Good to Great: Why Some Companies Make the Leap and Others Don't* (New York: HarperBusiness, 2001), for another perspective on the differences between good and great leaders.

10. John Feinstein offers a detailed accounting of this skill in John Feinstein, *Season on the Brink* (New York: Macmillan, 1986).

11. Jim Savage, *The Encyclopedia of the NCAA Basketball Tournament* (New York: Dell Publishing, 1990): 708.

12. Savage, *NCAA Basketball Tournament*, 708.

13. John Wooden and Jack Tobin, *They Call Me Coach* (Chicago: Contemporary Books, 1988): 113.

14. See Mike Krzyzewski and Donald T. Phillips, *Leading with the Heart: Coach K's Successful Strategies for Basketball, Business, and Life* (New York: Warner Books, 2000): 73.

15. From Charles Fishman, "Sanity Inc," www.fastcompany.com, 21 (January 1999).

16. See David Maraniss, *When Pride Still Mattered* (New York: Simon and Schuster, 1999): 372.

Selected Bibliography

Anders, George. "After Hitting It Big on Web, Mr. Cuban Is Scoring in the NBA." *Wall Street Journal* (April 22, 2003).

Auerbach, Red, and Ken Dooley. *MBA: Management by Auerbach*. New York: Wellington Press, 1991.

Barra, Allen. "Seattle's Defying Reason." *Wall Street Journal* (July 27, 2001).

Barro, Robert. "The Best Little Monopoly in America." *Business Week* (December 9, 2002): 22.

Bazerman, Max H. *Judgment in Managerial Decision Making*. New York: Wiley, 2001.

Besanko, David, David Dranove, and Mark Shanley. *Economics of Strategy*. New York: Wiley, 1996.

Brandenburger, Adam, and Barry Nalebuff. *Co-opetition*. New York: Doubleday, 1996.

Brickley, James A., Clifford W. Smith, and Jerold Zimmerman. *Managerial Economics and Organizational Architecture*. Chicago: Irwin, 1997.

Collins, Jim. *Good to Great: Why Some Companies Make the Leap and Others Don't*. New York: HarperBusiness, 2001.

Depken, Craig. "Free Agency and the Competitiveness of Major League Baseball." *Review of Industrial Organization* 14 (1999): 205–17.

Dixit, Avinash, and Barry Nalebuff. *Thinking Strategically*. New York: W. W. Norton, 1991.

Dixit, Avinash, and Susan Skeath. *Games of Strategy*. New York: W. W. Norton, 1999.

Dunnavant, Keith. *Coach: The Life of Paul Bear Bryant*. New York: Simon & Schuster, 1996.

Ehrenberg, Ronald G., and Robert Smith. "Do Tournaments Have Incentive Effects?" *Journal of Political Economy* 98 (December 1990): 1307–24.

Farley, C. J. "The Philosopher Coach." *Time* (March 20, 2000): 61–62.

Feinstein, John. *Season on the Brink*. New York: Macmillan, 1986.

Fleisher, Arthur A., Brian L. Goff, and Robert D. Tollison. *The NCAA: A Study in Cartel Behavior*. Chicago: University of Chicago Press, 1992.

Gardner, John. *On Leadership*. New York: Free Press, 1990.

Goff, Brian. *Spoiled Rotten: Affluence, Anxiety, and Social Decay in America*. Boulder, CO: Westview Press, 1999.

Goff, Brian L., Robert E. McCormick, and Robert D. Tollison. "Racial Integration as an Innovation: Empirical Evidence from Sports Leagues." *American Economic Review* 92 (March 2002): 16–26.

Goff, Brian L., William F. Shughart, and Robert D. Tollison. "Batter Up! Moral Hazard and the Effects of the Designated Hitter Rule on Hit Batsmen." *Economic Inquiry* 35 (July 1997): 555–61.

Goff, Brian L., and Robert D. Tollison, eds. "Sports as Economics." In Goff and Tollison, eds., *Sportometrics*. College Station, TX: Texas A&M University Press, 1991.

Heller, Robert. *Bill Gates*. London: Dorling Kindersley, 2000.

———. *Tom Peters*. London: Dorling Kindersley, 2000.

Hesselbein, Frances, Marshall Goldsmith, and Richard Beckhard, eds. *The Leader of the Future*. New York: Jossey Bass, 1996.

Holland, Gerald. "Mr. Rickey and the Game." In David Halberstam and Glenn Stout, eds. *The Best American Sports Writings of the Century*. Boston: Houghton-Mifflin, 1995.

Holtz, Lou. *Winning Every Day: The Game Plan for Success*. New York: Harper-Business, 1998.

Howerton, Darryl. "The Blazers Monopoly." *Sport* 91 (April 2000): 36.

Humphreys, Brad. "Alternative Measures of Competitive Balance in Sports Leagues." *Journal of Sports Economics* 3 (July 2002): 133–48.

Hymowitz, Carol. "The Confident Boss Doesn't Micromanage or Delegate Too Much." *Wall Street Journal* (March 11, 2003).

Jackson, Phil. *Sacred Hoops*. New York: Hyperion, 1996.

James, Bill. *The Bill James Guide to Baseball Managers*. New York: Scribner, 1997.

Jenkins, Holman. "How Could They Have Done It?" *Wall Street Journal* (August 28, 2002).

Kahn, Lawrence. "The Sports Business as a Labor Market Laboratory." *Journal of Economic Perspectives* (Summer 2000): 75–94.

Kahn, Roger. *The Era 1947–1957*. New York: Ticknor and Fields, 1993.

Koppat, Leonard. *The Man in the Dugout*. New York: Crown Publishers, 1993.

Kotter, John. *The General Managers*. New York: Free Press, 1982.

———. *Leading Change*. Cambridge: Harvard Business School Press, 1996.

Kramer, Jerry. *Farewell to Football*. New York: World Publishing, 1969.

Kreidler, Mark. "Posterity Suffers in NFL Parity," at espn.go.com/nfl/kreidler_mark/1470714.htm (December 3, 2002).

Krzyzewski, Mike, and Greg Doyel. *Building the Duke Dynasty*. Lenexa, KS: Addax Publishing, 1999.

Krzyzewski, Mike, and Donald Phillips. *Leading with the Heart, Coach K's Suc-*

cessful Strategies for Basketball, Business, and Life. New York: Warner Books, 2000.

Landry, Tom, and Gregg Lewis. *Landry*. Grand Rapids: Zondervan, 1990.

Leeds, Michael, and Peter von Allmen. *The Economics of Sports*. Boston: Addison-Wesley, 2002.

Lionhardt, David. "Caution Is Costly, Scholars Say." *The New York Times on the Web*, www.nytimes.com (July 30, 2003).

Lucas, Robert E. "1991 Fisher-Schultz Lecture" (Econometrics Society European Meetings, September 1991).

MacMullan, J. "Slogging Through His Own Mess." *Sports Illustrated* 92 (March 13, 2000): 98.

Madden, John, and Dave Anderson. *One Knee Equals Two Feet*. New York: Jove Publications, 1987.

Maital, Shlomo. *Executive Economics: Ten Essential Tools for Managers*. New York: Free Press, 1994.

Malkiel, Burton. *A Random Walk Down Wall Street*. New York: W. W. Norton, 2003.

Maraniss, David. *When Pride Still Mattered: A Life of Vince Lombardi*. New York: Simon & Schuster, 1999.

Maxwell, John. *The 21 Irrefutable Laws of Leadership*. Nashville: Thomas Nelson, 1998.

Micklethwait, John, and Adrian Woolridge. *Witch Doctors: Making Sense of Management Gurus*. New York: Times Books, 1996.

Mintzberg, Henry. "The Manager's Job: Folklore and Fact." *Harvard Business Review* (July–August 1975): 49–61.

Moores, John. "Damn Yankees." *Wall Street Journal* (May 14, 2002).

Morrison, Donald G., and David C. Schmittlein. "It Takes a Hot Goalie to Raise the Stanley Cup." *Chance* 11 (Winter 1998): 3–7.

Mosteller, Frederick. "Lessons from Sports Statistics." *The American Statistician* 51 (November 1997): 305–10.

Mullin, Charles J., and Lucia F. Dunn. "Using Baseball Card Prices to Measure Star Quality and Monopsony." *Economic Inquiry* 40 (October 2002): 620–32.

Nasar, Sylvia. *A Beautiful Mind: A Biography of John Forbes Nash, Jr., Winner of the Nobel Prize in Economics, 1994*. New York: Simon & Schuster, 1998.

Parcells, Bill. "The Tough Work of Turning Around a Team." *Harvard Business Review* 78 (November 2000): 180–81.

Pelz, Dave. *Putt Like the Pros: Dave Pelz's Scientific Way to Improve Your Stroke*. New York: HarperCollins, 1989.

Porter, Michael. *Competitive Advantage*. New York: Free Press, 1985.

———. *Competitive Strategy*. New York: Free Press, 1980.

Price, S. L. "Lords of Discipline." *Sports Illustrated* 95 (October 22, 2001): 78–82.

Quirk, James, and Rodney Fort. *Paydirt*. Princeton, NJ: Princeton University Press, 1992.

Rickey, Branch. *Branch Rickey's Little Blue Book*. New York: Macmillan, 1995.

Rottemberg, Simon. "The Baseball Players' Labor Market." *Journal of Political Economy* 64 (1956): 242–58.

Rowland, M. "Guru." *Los Angeles Times Magazine* 45 (January 2000): 60–67.

Sackrowitz, Harold. "Refining the Point(s)—After-Touchdown Decision." *Chance* 13 (Summer 2000): 29–34.

Savage, Jim. *The Encyclopedia of the NCAA Basketball Tournament.* New York: Dell Publishing, 1990.

Scahill, Edward. "Did Babe Ruth Have a Comparative Advantage as a Pitcher?" *Journal of Economic Education* 21 (Fall 1990): 402–10.

Scully, Gerald. *The Business of Major League Baseball.* Chicago: University of Chicago Press, 1989.

Shapiro, Carl, and Hal R. Varian. *Information Rules: A Strategic Guide to the Network Economy.* Boston: Harvard Business School Press, 1999.

Slater, Robert. *Jack Welch and the GE Way.* New York: McGraw-Hill, 1999.

Smith, Adam. *Wealth of Nations.* New York: Bantam Books, 2003.

Smith, Sam. *The Jordan Rules.* New York: Simon & Schuster, 1992.

Taleb, Nassim M. *Fooled by Randomness.* New York: Texera, 2002.

Thaler, Richard. *Quasi-Rational Economics.* New York: Russell Sage Foundation, 1991.

Thomsen, I. "My Way or the Highway." *Sports Illustrated* 93 (December 11, 2000): 58.

Torre, Joe, and Henry Dreher. *Ground Rules for Winners.* New York: Hyperion, 1999.

———. *Joe Torre's Ground Rules for Winners: 12 Keys to Managing Team Players, Tough Bosses, Setbacks, and Success.* New York: Hyperion, 1999.

Tygiel, Jules. *Baseball's Great Experiment.* New York: Oxford University Press, 1983.

Veeck, Bill. *The Hustler's Handbook.* Durham, NC: Baseball America Classic Books, 1996.

von Allmen, Peter. "Is the Reward Structure in NASCAR Efficient?" *Journal of Sports Economics* 2 (February 2000): 62–79.

Ward, Geoffrey C., and Ken Burns. *Baseball: An Illustrated History.* New York: Knopf, 1994.

Wooden, John, and Jack Tobin. *They Call Me Coach.* Chicago: Contemporary Books, 1988.

Zimmerman, Paul. "Armed for the Playoffs." *Sports Illustrated* 55 (December 21, 1981): 18.

Index

About the Author

BRIAN GOFF is Distinguished University Professor, Department of Economics, Ford College of Business, Western Kentucky University, where he has served on the faculty since 1986 and teaches undergraduate, master's, and MBA courses. He is the coauthor of several books, including *Spoiled Rotten* and *The National Collegiate Athletic Association*, and dozens of articles on economic and public policy in such publications as *American Economic Review*, *Economic Inquiry*, *Public Choice*, and *Social Science Quarterly*.

CPSIA information can be obtained
at www.ICGtesting.com
Printed in the USA
BVHW040919110819
555254BV00053B/204/P